THE LOW-CHOLESTEROL COOKBOOK

Over 170 easy and delicious recipes for the health conscious

**RECIPES:
ANGELIKA ILIES, DORIS MULIAR, EDITA POSPISIL
RECIPE PHOTOGRAPHS:
MICHAEL BRAUNER**

KEY PORTER BOOKS

Library and Archives Canada Cataloguing in Publication

Muliar, Doris

   The low-cholesterol cookbook / Doris Muliar, Edita Pospisil, Angelika Ilies.

Includes index.

ISBN 1-55263-709-3

   1. Low-cholesterol diet—Recipes. I. Pospisil, Edita II. Ilies, Angelika III. Title.

RM237.75.M84 2006   641.5'63847   C2005-906113-8

The publisher gratefully acknowledges the support of the Canada Council for the Arts and the Ontario Arts Council for its publishing program. We acknowledge the support of the Government of Ontario through the Ontario Media Development Corporation's Ontario Book Initiative.

We acknowledge the financial support of the Government of Canada through the Book Publishing Industry Development Program (BPIDP) for our publishing activities.

Key Porter Books Limited
Six Adelaide Street East, Tenth Floor
Toronto, Ontario
Canada M5C 1H6

www.keyporter.com

Electronic formatting: Jean Peters

Printed and bound in Hong Kong

06 07 08 09 6 5 4 3 2 1

Publisher's Note: The contents of this book are not intended to be used as a substitution for consultation with your physician. All matters pertaining to your health should be directed to a health care professional.

Content

Lowering Cholesterol

Everyone would like to live a long and healthy life free of disease—a desire clearly reflected in the many surveys generally conducted at the start of a new year, for example. The most frequent response is that good health is the most important thing in life, which makes sense. If even minor ailments can have a significant negative impact on our well-being, what would happen in the event of a serious illness?

Indications that something isn't right are usually evident long before illness actually strikes. And the fact is, it's possible to counter-act this trend before it's too late.

This is especially true for cardio-vascular disease.

A whole range of serious condi-tions falls under this heading, including heart attack, stroke and circulatory disorders. Half of us will die from some form of cardio-vascular disease. But we can now delay or even prevent cardiovascu-lar disease so we can live long and disease-free lives.

How is this possible? Because we know that specific risk factors are responsible for this disease. Referred to as lipometabolic disor-ders, these risk factors can be summed up simply as high blood cholesterol, high blood pressure, diabetes, significant excess weight and smoking. Clearly, the risk is greatest when several risk factors are present at the same time. But it also means that it's possible to lower the risk by reducing or pre-venting the effects of the risk factors.

The risk factors are easy to rec-ognize: Smoking is self-evident; a scale provides information on a person's weight; blood pressure and the presence of sugar in urine are both easy to measure. However, a blood test is required to deter-mine the level of lipometabolism.

By the time we are 20, every one of us should know our cholesterol level and, more important, what exactly cholesterol is. Too much LDL cholesterol in the blood promotes the development of cardiovascular disease, while HDL cholesterol works against it. The higher the HDL cholesterol level and the lower the LDL cholesterol level, the lower the risk of cardio-vascular disease.

The greatest risk factors for a heart attack are high LDL and low HDL cholesterol levels; for a stroke, it's high blood pressure. For anyone who wants to prevent a heart attack, the most important thing to do—though hardly the only thing to do—is to keep the amount of LDL cholesterol as low as possible and the amount of HDL cholesterol as high as possible. Changes in a person's biochemistry also affect LDL and HDL levels. But a poor diet, alone or combined with biochemical changes, can lead to a rise in LDL cholesterol. A significantly higher LDL cholesterol level—more than 190 milligrams per deciliter (mg/dL) or 4.9 millimoles per liter (mmol/L) —is usually due to a combination of biochemical changes and poor diet.

So it always makes sense to lower LDL cholesterol through dietary changes, especially if medication is required to achieve a lower LDL level. As a result, milder medica-tions or lower doses that are much easier to tolerate can then be pre-scribed. And this is especially important because these medica-tions have to be taken for life and the fewer, the better.

There's another reason for checking LDL cholesterol levels sooner rather than later: A person experiencing chest pain is suffering from a 70% narrowing of the coro-nary arteries. Besides, we know today that most heart attacks occur even though there's no distinct narrowing of the coronary arteries. In most cases, there were no prior chest pains. Therefore, when it comes to avoiding a heart attack, early prevention is the key.

This book will show that you don't need to radically change or restrict your diet to reduce LDL cholesterol. Rather, you need to modify your diet by combining individual nutritional elements in an appropriate way. We're talking change, not revolution. And there's still time. By starting slowly and exploring the possibilities, you'll soon be on your way to success.

Good luck!
Dr. Werner Richter

Cholesterol: Essential or Harmful?

Cholesterol is an essential element. It's an important component of the cell wall, it plays a key role in the way nerve tissues function, and it provides the source material for sex hormones. In the skin, cholesterol helps produce vitamin D, which is essential for strong bones since it controls the amount of calcium that is stored. More important, quantitatively speaking, is the liver's conversion of cholesterol into bile acids that help extract fat and cholesterol from food in the intestine.

Body cells produce large quantities of cholesterol and can cover daily requirements independently of any cholesterol supplied by what we eat. And cholesterol is extracted from animal-based but not plant-based foods.

High cholesterol and its consequences

A high concentration of blood cholesterol over an extended time raises the risk of the arteries becoming clogged, a condition called atherosclerosis. Cholesterol is deposited on the artery walls, which become narrower, seriously restricting or halting the flow of blood. The body's tissues—which depend on these arteries for their blood supply—become seriously damaged as blood flow is disrupted over a long period. The ultimate risk is a heart attack, which means that tissue, as well as entire organs, will die.

The blood vessels at greatest risk of these kinds of deposits are the ones that supply blood to the heart—the coronary arteries. The ensuing illness is referred to as coronary artery disease. There's seldom any pain associated with this kind of damage. In most instances, atherosclerosis develops unnoticed and its worst effects, heart attack and stroke, are often completely unexpected. Cholesterol is insidious. You don't feel it or see it. Even if the coronary arteries are 70% blocked, there is often no pain when resting. Only when stress is placed on the body or blood pressure do slight pains in the chest area start—a case of so-called angina pectoris.

Risk factors for lipometabolic disorders

The risk factors for cardiovascular disease are closely related to dietary habits and lifestyle.

High cholesterol remains the most dangerous risk factor for coronary artery disease and the possibility of a heart attack. In the case of narrowing of the arteries in the brain and the possibility of a stroke, high blood pressure continues to be the most important risk factor. On the other hand, smoking is the most significant risk factor threatening the arteries in the legs. A combination of all the risk factors poses the greatest risk for all organs.

Many studies have shown that diet plays a major role in the development of coronary artery disease. Consuming too many calories and too much fat—a pattern altogether too common in the West—creates a dangerous situation in which the risk factors of excess weight, lipometabolic disorders, diabetes and high blood pressure can arise.

A lack of vitamins and fiber, too little physical exercise, stress, alcohol and nicotine also contribute to a higher heart attack rate.

Pain first occurs when the artery is more than 70% blocked and the supply of oxygen and nutrients to the tissues fed by the artery is no longer sufficient. The feeling of tightness in the chest is a typical sign of angina pectoris. For most people, however, a heart attack is unexpected: More than two-thirds of all heart attacks occur when the arteries have been reduced less than 50%. Another 20% occur when the arteries are 50% to 75% blocked, and one in every six heart attacks occurs in the most extreme cases of clogged arteries. So prevention is key.

Reducing cholesterol levels

A fat-modified diet is essential to any treatment of high cholesterol. "Fat-modified" doesn't mean avoiding all foods that contain fat, but you should review your diet to identify any obvious and hidden sources of fat from animal-based food sources and reduce the amount if necessary.

➤ Choose vegetable-based fats, as these even boost lipometabolism.

➤ Instead of eating calorie-rich foods, choose whole-grain products, vegetables, potatoes and fresh fruit more often to curb your appetite.

➤ Drink alcoholic beverages only occasionally, and never more than one or two drinks.

➤ Control your weight because excess weight is a risk factor for atherosclerosis. Long-term weight loss can improve cholesterol levels.

➤ Exercise regularly. Physical activity can improve blood cholesterol values. The best types of activities are endurance sports such as jogging, cycling or swimming.

Where to Go for Advice

American Heart Association
National Center
7272 Greenville Avenue
Dallas, TX 75231
1-800-242-8721
www.americanheart.org

American College of Cardiology
Heart House
9111 Old Georgetown Road
Bethesda, MD 20814-1699
1-800-253-4636, ext. 694, or
301-897-5400
www.acc.org

Heart and Stroke Foundation of Canada
222 Queen Street, Suite 1402
Ottawa, ON K1P 5V9
613-569-4361
ww2.heartandstroke.ca

British Heart Foundation
14 Fitzhardinge Street
London W1H 6DH UK
020 7935 0185
Heart Information Line
08450 70 80 70
www.bhf.org.uk

British Cardiac Society
9 Fitzroy Square
London W1T 5HW UK
+44 (0) 20 7383 3887
www.bcs.com

European Atherosclerosis Society
Altonagatan 7, SE 211 38
Malmö Sweden
+46 40 240 750
www.eas-society.org

European Society of Cardiology
The European Heart House
2035 Route des Colles
B.P. 179–Les Templiers
FR-06903 Sophia Antipolis
France
+33.4.92.94.76.00
www.escardio.org

Knowing your cholesterol level

Measuring cholesterol is one component of the preventive medical checkup. Beginning at age 35, you should have your cholesterol checked every two years. But it might be wise to have a test even sooner, especially if there are indications that cardiovascular disease already exists in your family—if a family member has had a heart attack or a stroke, for example. If this is the case, ask your doctor if it also makes sense to test your children's cholesterol.

Cardiovascular Disease

Approximately 40% of all patients don't survive their first heart attack. For this reason, everyone needs to understand the gravity of the risk factors that can lead to a heart attack in his or her own particular case.

Cardiovascular disease is the biggest cause of illness and death in North America and Europe. A reduction in the amount of oxygen reaching the heart muscle is the principal cause of angina pectoris, and this is almost always attributable to untreated atherosclerosis of the coronary arteries. When no

From a third to a half of all deaths in the Western industrialized nations can be traced back to cardiovascular disease. In 2001, for example, it accounted for about 34% of the deaths in Canada. Of those deaths from circulatory system diseases, 55% were due to ischaemic heart diseases, which include conditions in which the heart muscle is damaged or works inefficiently because of an insufficient blood supply. Another 21% were from cerebrovascular diseases, the vast majority caused by what is commonly known as a stroke. In the United States, cardiovascular disease accounted for nearly 38% of all deaths in 2000. In England, the figure was 39% for 2003. The statistics for Europe are even worse—nearly 49% of all deaths in 2004. Clearly, we only get as old as our arteries. But in many instances, early prevention can help to delay or even avert these situations.

precautions are taken, heart disease continues to escalate over the years. It's a gradual process that rarely, or only in the late stages, causes any pain. More than 80% of sufferers unexpectedly have a heart attack, while others experience limited heart function due to the slow deterioration of heart muscle tissue and the increasingly strained efforts of the heart muscle itself.

Who's at greatest risk?

Practically anyone who leads a stressful life or maintains an unhealthy lifestyle can be struck by cardiovascular disease. Lack of physical activity, lack of sleep, stress, a poor diet and overeating are all examples of this kind of lifestyle. These conditions offer fertile ground for many of the risk factors responsible for the numerous types of cardiovascular disease.

Recognized risk factors include lipometabolic disorders, high blood pressure, smoking, diabetes and significant excess weight. However, the risk is also great in families where someone has already experienced a heart attack early in life (before age 60 in men, before 70 in women). As the number of risk factors increases, so too does the probability of a heart attack. Even if blood cholesterol has been significantly lowered, thereby greatly reducing the risk of heart attack, all risk factors have to be monitored and controlled to prevent such an event.

Atherosclerosis

Atherosclerosis or arteriosclerosis—also widely referred to as hardening of the arteries—is one

of commonest causes of cardiovascular disease. Atherosclerosis arises through a chronic narrowing of the coronary arteries, leading to a heart attack. In its most advanced stage, it can lead to a severe drop in the amount of oxygen reaching the heart muscle. If the artery remains untreated, and narrowing continues until 70% of the coronary artery is blocked, blood flow will be severely restricted. The tissue fed by the arteries no longer receives enough oxygen and nutrients—and all it takes for a serious circulatory problem to develop is for just one area not to get enough oxygen. The complete blockage of an artery as a result of too many platelets being deposited on the artery wall can lead to a heart attack.

Healthy arteries from the inside out

Like all blood vessels, the wall of a coronary artery that supplies oxygen and nutrients to the heart muscle consists of three layers. Each plays an indispensable role.

1. The inner lining, called the endothelium, is responsible, among other things, for ensuring that no blood clots form and that no disease-inducing particles reach the artery wall. It acts as a kind of protective layer.
2. The middle layer, composed of muscle cells—the so-called smooth muscle cells—regulates the widening or narrowing of the arteries. It plays a major role in ensuring circulation meets the demands made on the body.

The Stages of Atherosclerosis

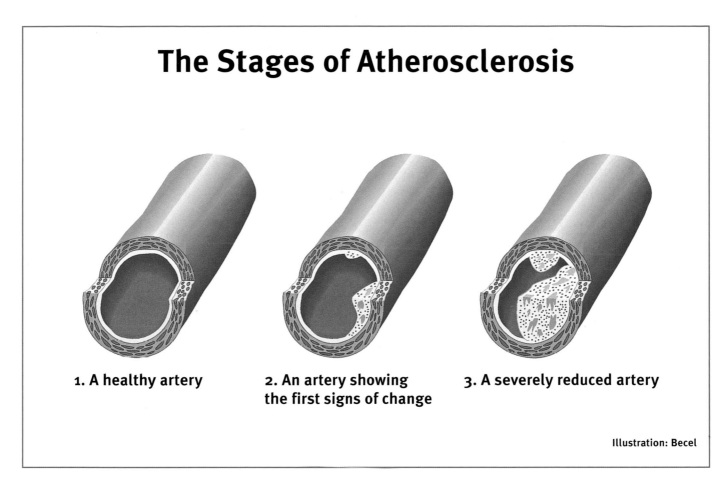

1. A healthy artery

2. An artery showing the first signs of change

3. A severely reduced artery

Illustration: Becel

3. The outer layer consists of connecting and supporting tissue and is covered in the tiniest blood vessels. These supply oxygen and nutrients to the artery walls.

How arteries become clogged

The inner lining of the artery wall in particular plays an important protective role. It's exposed to everything carried by the blood—including aggressive substances. These can severely damage the endothelium and cause inflammation, which makes the arteries even more permeable and more vulnerable.

Lipometabolic disorders that go hand in hand with high cholesterol limit the functioning of the endothelium. Changes that lead to diseased artery walls are triggered by an increase in the amount of cholesterol deposited on the damaged inner lining of the artery. Cholesterol is then absorbed into cells and in between tissue fibers.

This situation eventually results in an increase in the number of smooth muscle cells and connective tissue fibers. These harmful growths cause the damaged artery wall to bulge, thereby reducing its size. The absorbed cholesterol is prevented from entering the bloodstream by connective tissue fibers and the endothelium. The thin layer of connective tissue could yield and the inner lining of the artery break down. Where a breach in the artery wall occurs, a blood clot forms that will either reduce or completely block the coronary artery, depending on its size—a situation that can result in reduced blood flow or even a heart attack.

Atherosclerosis needs cholesterol to develop. The growth of the connective tissue fibers and smooth muscle cells in the walls of the coronary arteries is of considerable importance for this disease. Lipometabolic disorders that accompany high cholesterol, as well as high blood pressure or smoking, permanently disrupt the protective function of the endothelium, thereby clearing the way for atherosclerosis to develop.

Targeted prevention

By middle age, some people have already become subject to cardiovascular disease. If the risk factors are identified early and targeted treatment begun in childhood, it's possible to combat atherosclerosis in a timely manner. And a particularly effective way to prevent it is by maintaining a healthy lifestyle and diet.

The whole family can benefit from a change in diet. The most important thing is to consume fewer animal-based foods that are high in fat. As long as excess weight isn't an issue, there's no need to eat a calorie-reduced diet. Eating a variety of foods low in animal fats is the key.

Excess Cholesterol

As we've already seen, cholesterol is a vital nutrient, essential for many tasks and functions in the human body (see page 6). So why can cholesterol also pose a danger to the cardiovascular system?

HDL and LDL: Lipoproteins

To understand the connection between cholesterol, atherosclerosis and heart attacks, we need to say a few words about the different blood fats and how they're metabolized.

Since fat and cholesterol are not water soluble, it isn't easy for the blood to carry them away. To overcome this disadvantage, they're wrapped in a shell made of protein. These spherical-shaped complexes composed of protein and fat are called lipoproteins (from the Greek *lipos,* or fat) and vary according to their density. When it comes to high cholesterol, the two most important representatives of this family need to be recognized: Low-density lipoprotein (LDL) supplies both fat and protein to body cells, while high-density lipoprotein (HDL) bonds to unneeded cholesterol and transports it back to the liver.

To simplify our understanding of these opposite tasks, LDL is commonly referred to as "bad" cholesterol and HDL as "good" cholesterol.

The role of LDL: To supply cholesterol

If your doctor diagnoses a high cholesterol level that is critical to your health, this means a high concentration of LDL cholesterol. LDL contains the largest amount of cholesterol in the blood. It carries cholesterol to the various organs in our bodies, where special absorption points—receptors—transfer the cholesterol to the body cells. If there's too much LDL swimming in your bloodstream, or if the number of receptors is insufficient or there are no more receptors, then the LDL accumulates in your blood. Macrophages (phagocytes), which represent a kind of police force that protects the body from anything that might damage its health, are responsible for eliminating the accumulated LDL. They absorb the LDL and store it until the macrophages themselves become embedded in the artery wall, saturated with cholesterol and no longer able to regulate LDL absorption.

This is a dangerous situation because the saturated macrophages can actually trigger the atherosclerosis process. With time, little bulges appear, narrowing the artery and endangering the flow of blood. Should a blood clot lodge itself in this narrowing, the artery would be completely blocked, resulting in a heart attack.

LDL concentration in the blood

Harmful excess amounts of blood LDL can be the result of an inherited disorder of the metabolism. People who suffer from familial hypercholesterolemia, for example, have fewer LDL receptors on body cells. Poor diet also plays an important role in how LDL is metabolized.

The amount of LDL circulating in the blood depends, on the one hand, on the amount that has accumulated and, on the other, on how much is being absorbed into the body cells. This last function is dependent on the number of LDL receptors. If these special receptors are overloaded, the cells won't absorb any more LDL—a situation that can occur at concentrations of approximately 200 mg/dL (5.2 mmol/L).

The role of HDL: To eliminate cholesterol

HDL is produced in the intestines and liver, as well as through the decomposition of other lipoproteins in the blood. It can also attach itself to the macrophages and reabsorb the cholesterol originally carried by the LDL. The HDL transports the cholesterol back to the liver, where it is metabolized into bile acid and eliminated through the intestine. Because of

Low-density lipoprotein (LDL) carries cholesterol to the body cells. High-density lipoprotein (HDL) reabsorbs the LDL from specific cells called macrophages and carries it to the liver.

Your doctor can measure the presence of both these lipoproteins in your blood and, based on the relationship between LDL and HDL cholesterol, determine if any risk factors exist.

An elevated LDL cholesterol level or a depressed HDL cholesterol level can pose a health risk. The risk of a heart attack is greatest if, at the same time, the level of LDL cholesterol is high and the level of HDL cholesterol is low.

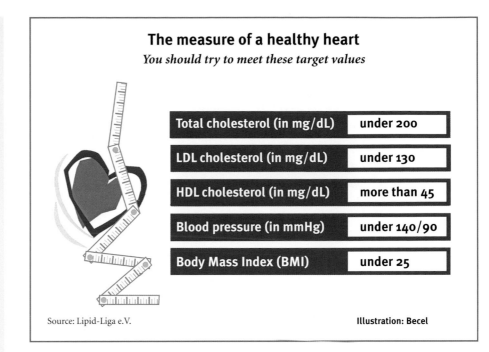

The measure of a healthy heart
You should try to meet these target values

Total cholesterol (in mg/dL)	under 200
LDL cholesterol (in mg/dL)	under 130
HDL cholesterol (in mg/dL)	more than 45
Blood pressure (in mmHg)	under 140/90
Body Mass Index (BMI)	under 25

Source: Lipid-Liga e.V.   Illustration: Becel

this particular ability to collect excess cholesterol, HDL remains distinct from all other types of lipoproteins in the blood: HDL prevents atherosclerotic deposits from occurring in blood vessels. Therefore, the higher the concentration of blood HDL, the better.

Triglycerides

Triglycerides—neutral fats—represent a third group of important blood fats that can play a role in the development of atherosclerosis.

Triglycerides are the primary component of the fats we ingest with our food. Fatty tissue within the body is largely made up of triglycerides, as they constitute the body's most important energy reserve. In the case of inherited disorders, excess weight or a poor diet, the concentration of triglycerides in the blood rises, particularly if alcohol, quickly absorbed carbohydrates and simple sugars are consumed.

Evaluating the risk posed by triglycerides isn't easy, as only specific forms promote heart attacks. But measuring the amount of triglycerides allows your doctor to assess how fat is metabolized in your body.

In the event of a significant increase in triglyceride values— over 1000 mg/dL (11.2 mmol/L)— the blood's fluidity is adversely affected, in particular in the capillaries.

Elevated triglyceride levels can be lowered quickly and effectively by

➤ abstaining from alcohol

➤ avoiding easily absorbed sugars—for example, those found in soft drinks, confectionery and products based on flour (especially highly processed white flour)—and eating fiber-rich carbohydrates such as vegetables, grains and legumes instead

➤ reducing excess weight

➤ increasing physical activity

Lipometabolic Disorders

What causes elevated blood cholesterol levels is well known, and this is important, as some individuals have a heart attack even if their LDL cholesterol level is only slightly elevated. In rare instances, congenital metabolic disorders are responsible for elevated cholesterol levels. Most of these can be attributed to slight biochemical changes, although only when additional risk factors come into play does the concentration of LDL cholesterol actually rise to harmful levels.

A particularly pronounced increase in LDL cholesterol needs to be monitored if a specific genetic defect results in no LDL absorption points (receptors) forming on the cells. In these rare, purely genetic cases, which affect only one in a million people, there are absolutely no LDL absorption points. In this instance, called **familial homozygote hypercholesterolemia**, a heart attack can occur before age 15.

In the case of the more common multigenerational form called **familial hypercholesterolemia,** which affects 1 in every 500 people, the number of LDL receptors is reduced by half. Without appropriate treatment, the first heart attack most often occurs between the ages of 40 and 60. If left untreated, this kind of lipometabolic disorder will lead to a heart attack in almost every case.

A completely different type of genetic disorder modifies the protein component of LDL in such a way that it can no longer be metabolized through the cells' absorption points. This disease, **familial defective apolipoprotein B100,** also causes chronically high LDL blood cholesterol values.

In most instances, the genetic modification of the way in which enzymes and proteins form does minimal damage to the lipometabolic process and doesn't lead to a significant increase in LDL cholesterol. Only when other factors are taken into account— such as excess weight, diabetes, a diet high in fat or calories, the consumption of too many saturated fatty acids, thyroid disorders or even specific medications—does LDL blood cholesterol increase to the point that it poses a health risk from a condition called **polygene hypercholesterolemia.**

Another type of lipometabolic disorder, **apolipoprotein E4 polymorphism,** results in more than the usual amount of dietary cholesterol being transferred to the body from the intestine. Because of this exceptionally high supply of cholesterol, the liver can do nothing more than reabsorb the cholesterol from the blood, which results in an increase in the level of LDL cholesterol.

In addition to the lipometabolic disorders identified so far, there are other types of high LDL cholesterol that are genetically predetermined and pose a significant risk of heart attack. Although the increase in LDL cholesterol might be minimal or nonexistent, the risk of heart attack is great. This lipometabolic disorder is most often diagnosed among people who have had a heart attack before the age of 60—about 1 in 100 people. Generally, early detection can be done only by a doctor.

As these examples show, the cardiovascular risk posed by lipometabolic disorders isn't linked solely to a higher LDL cholesterol level. Moreover, a high concentration of LDL cholesterol can be caused by other types of metabolic diseases, such as bile disorders, hypofunction of the thyroid or kidney disorders. A whole range of medications can also lead to higher LDL cholesterol levels.

Diet can also influence blood lipid values. If the dietary ratio is out of balance because more calories are consumed than are burned on a daily basis, and if more animal fats, saturated fatty acids and foods high in cholesterol are consumed, then LDL cholesterol levels can rise. In 40% of all cases of illness, a rise in cholesterol could be traced back to a poor diet. And the principal cause was not the cholesterol content of food but the type of fat that was consumed (see page 16 and following).

Whatever the reason for the higher levels, a change in diet is always required as a fundamental factor in the treatment of high LDL cholesterol values.

Lower concentrations of HDL cholesterol can also be caused by genetic makeup and are monitored in conjunction with lipometabolic disorders accompanied by high triglyceride levels and excess weight.

Risk Factors at a Glance

LDL cholesterol

If your doctor refers to a markedly high blood cholesterol level, this generally means that the concentration of LDL cholesterol is high. And only this factor promotes the development of atherosclerosis. In contrast, HDL cholesterol plays a protective role.

Knowing your total cholesterol value won't allow you to determine the cardiovascular risk, since HDL and LDL cholesterol values are both taken into account when calculating the total cholesterol value. Therefore, a high value can just as easily be the result of too much LDL cholesterol as too much HDL cholesterol. However, the implications for the risk of heart attack are completely opposite.

Without first consulting your doctor on how you can have a positive effect on your cholesterol values, you shouldn't take any decisive measures, since any change to your diet can alter the relationship between LDL and HDL cholesterol and in some situations even have a negative impact.

Nicotine

Smoking cigarettes facilitates the development of atherosclerosis and counts as one of the biggest risk factors. Smoking cigars and a pipe pose less of a risk because the smoke is not inhaled to the same extent.

Cholesterol Values—Healthy or Critical?

Optimal LDL and HDL cholesterol levels always depend on additional risk factors. According to the American Heart Association, the risk of cardiovascular disease is minimal if LDL cholesterol remains below the following values:

Fewer than two risk factors	LDL cholesterol < 160 mg/dL
Two or more risk factors	LDL cholesterol < 130 mg/dL
Existing cardiovascular problems	LDL cholesterol < 100 mg/dL

Additional risk factors at a glance
Excess weight · High blood pressure · Nicotine consumption · Lipometabolic disorders · Diabetes mellitus · Insufficient physical activity

For each of these conditions, the ratio of LDL cholesterol to HDL cholesterol should be less than a factor of 3. In other words, the measured LDL cholesterol value should not be higher than the measured HDL value multiplied by 3. If no other risk factors are present, then a ratio as high as 4 (LDL:HDL = 4:1) is considered satisfactory. It's been agreed internationally that cholesterol-reducing medication should be prescribed once the following LDL cholesterol values have been reached:

Fewer than two risk factors	LDL cholesterol > 190 mg/dL
Two or more risk factors	LDL cholesterol > 160 mg/dL
Existing cardiovascular problems	LDL cholesterol > 130 mg/dL

Excess Weight

Excess weight has a negative influence on lipometabolism. The greater the variation from a healthy average body weight, the higher the LDL cholesterol values, the lower the HDL cholesterol values and the higher the concentration of triglycerides in the blood will be. Moreover, being overweight also contributes to the development of other risk factors, such as diabetes, lipometabolic disorders and high blood pressure.

Losing weight will help increase your HDL cholesterol level and protect the body against storing cholesterol. Excess weight and what you can do to shed excess pounds in a sensible way are discussed on page 22.

High Blood Pressure

High blood pressure—considered critical at levels over 140/90 mmHg—pushes the blood through the arteries with such force that the sensitive artery walls can be damaged. And it's exactly in those damaged areas that changes leading to atherosclerosis can easily develop.

Should deposits form in the arteries, the high blood pressure can cause bits of the deposits to dislodge and be carried away, only to end up clogging the artery at some point farther along.

Diet

It was long believed that cholesterol consumed through food raised blood cholesterol levels. We now know that two other conditions account for dietary cholesterol raising LDL values, as cholesterol is primarily found in high-fat, animal-based products.

When these kinds of foods are regularly consumed in large quantities, energy intake quickly exceeds energy requirements. In addition, the surplus of undesirable fatty acids places a burden on lipometabolism. Both are decisive factors in the rise of LDL values. Just how strong the effect will be varies from person to person. In particular, a thoughtless diet consisting of fast food and meat-based meals can significantly raise the risk of atherosclerosis. More information on diet as a risk factor can be found on page 16.

Stress

Many people aren't even aware that they're under stress every day. The unconscious burden caused by pressure in the workplace, within the family or during spare time leads to the release of stress hormones that have a negative impact on blood pressure and the immune system's defenses. Careful attention must be paid to maintaining a balance through adequate rest and sleep, conscious relaxation techniques or light sports activities.

Diabetes

Diabetes can have a negative impact on lipo- and sugar metabolism, thereby facilitating the development of atherosclerosis. Have your doctor check your blood sugar values. After fasting, the values should not exceed 100 mg/dL (5.55 mmol/L). Two hours after a meal (post-prandial), you should reach a blood sugar value of 120 mg/dL (6.6 mmol/L). If blood sugar concentrations exceed these levels, then follow up with your doctor as to how you can effectively and permanently reduce them. A change in diet and weight loss are the most frequently recommended measures to reduce blood sugar to a safe and healthy level.

Lack of Exercise

Movement regulates and normalizes many metabolic processes, including lipometabolism and blood pressure. Moderate physical activity—roughly 30 to 60 minutes, three to four times a week—has a number of beneficial effects that help reduce atherosclerosis: Exercise improves cardiovascular functions, helps de-stress, prevents excess weight and raises HDL blood cholesterol values.

Therapeutic Objectives

The main objective in treating high cholesterol is always to lower the level of harmful LDL cholesterol. Regardless of the different causes of high blood cholesterol, a change in diet and lifestyle is the most sensible therapeutic approach. Studies indicate that reducing cholesterol in this manner is the most effective way to significantly lower the risk of heart attack.

But it doesn't make a lot of sense to focus solely on LDL blood cholesterol. All risk factors need to be taken into account and largely eliminated if you want to prevent a heart attack.

The basis of any treatment is always proper diet, even in a serious case of high LDL cholesterol. The higher the basic values, the better the results achieved when LDL cholesterol is reduced.

Bear in mind that a diet that lowers LDL cholesterol can also lead to less medication. The lower the dose, the better the tolerance. This is especially important given the fact that you'll have to take medication for your whole life.

Lowering LDL cholesterol

The following measures are implemented in stages to lower LDL cholesterol values:

➤ A proper diet and changes to lifestyle (stop smoking, more physical exercise, less stress).

➤ Medications to reduce LDL cholesterol.

➤ In severe cases, LDL apheresis, a process similar to dialysis, to remove LDL cholesterol from the blood.

Raising HDL cholesterol

The following changes can help raise HDL cholesterol:

➤ Losing weight—every kilogram helps.

➤ Quitting smoking is a very decisive measure. By stopping, you'll not only eliminate the risk factor of cigarette smoking, which alone has a serious impact on cardiovascular health, but also raise HDL cholesterol levels.

➤ Increasing physical activity. HDL rises 1 mg/dL (0.02 mmol/L) on average for every half mile (800 meters) of endurance running each week. Lack of exercise, on the other hand, contributes to numerous and early heart attacks. So even simple physical activities make sense, even if there's no immediate improvement in the level of HDL cholesterol.

➤ Consuming moderate amounts of alcohol—unless other health concerns caution against it. Consult your doctor. "Moderate" means consuming less than ½ oz (15 g) of alcohol per day, roughly one 12 oz (375 mL) bottle of 5.5% beer, a 6 oz (175 mL) glass of wine or a 1½ oz (45 mL) shot of spirits. If high triglyceride levels are the cause of your low HDL cholesterol levels, alcohol will cause them to go only lower.

➤ Treating the lipometabolic disorders that accompany low HDL cholesterol. The higher the triglyceride levels, the lower the HDL cholesterol levels.

➤ Introducing medication to reduce LDL cholesterol, which can also have a positive effect on HDL cholesterol.

The Right Diet Strategy to Combat High Cholesterol

The essential elements of a diet strategy against high levels of LDL cholesterol include

➤ losing excess weight

➤ reducing the amount of fat consumed, or, rather, consuming more vegetable than animal fats

➤ consuming fewer foods rich in cholesterol

A slight change in diet is all it takes to achieve these goals. Read the following pages to learn more about how the "right" cardiovascular-friendly diet can help reduce LDL cholesterol.

Getting the right amount of energy is important

The proper diet to combat high LDL cholesterol includes getting the right amount of energy. This means consuming an appropriate number of calories to maintain your body weight or to slowly reduce your weight if necessary.

In the following discussions on the positive effect of different foods, it's understood that energy intake never exceeds individual requirements to any great extent. If it does, no favorable outcome can be expected, even if the meal plan follows all the rules of healthy cooking.

You can calculate your own energy needs according to this simple formula:

body weight (kilograms) × 30, in the case of light exercise

This result represents a rough benchmark, since many other factors can influence your energy needs, including the choice of foods and the relative proportions of nutrients, your physical build and basal metabolism, and your level of physical activity, whether that be in sports or heavy physical labour.

Consuming fewer animal fats is key

Saturated fatty acids found primarily in animal-based food products are the one dietary factor with the most negative effect on LDL blood cholesterol values. The degree to which they influence LDL cholesterol will vary from person to person.

Eating an abundance of animal fats results in harmful levels of LDL blood cholesterol. The LDL absorption points become overloaded, so the excess is returned to the blood. You can avoid this situation by restricting the consumption of specific animal-based foods.

Choose foods that have a high ratio of mono- and polyunsaturated fatty acids. One good way to have a favorable impact on blood cholesterol values is to eat deep-sea fish on a regular basis. Fish oils called omega-3 fatty acids help prevent atherosclerosis because they have a stabilizing effect on the heart muscle cells and help reduce high triglyceride levels. At least two fish-based meals a week is recommended.

Choosing foods low in cholesterol makes sense

Approximately 50% of dietary cholesterol is absorbed by the body during digestion. More than 400 to 500 mg of dietary cholesterol per day can't be transferred from the intestine to the blood, so it's eliminated in the stool. But this is only a fraction of the total cholesterol produced by the body itself every day. The effects of ingested cholesterol on LDL cholesterol levels are more likely to be classified as minor, which is why dietary cholesterol is no longer the demon it once was.

Nevertheless, it still makes sense to take a critical look at your meal plan for products rich in cholesterol and to limit their consumption. These are often animal-based products rich in saturated fatty acids. And, as we noted before, eating lots of these types of foods raises the risk of atherosclerosis. In general, when it comes to dietary cholesterol, the same points of reference apply to people who have high cholesterol as to anyone else: Cholesterol intake should not exceed 300 mg per day.

The critical nutrient—fat

With an energy density of 9.3 calories per gram, fat is the biggest supplier of energy. Every type of dietary fat, whether from an animal or vegetable source, is a triglyceride (neutral fat). Indeed, triglycerides differ according to their building blocks—the fatty acids.

Saturated fatty acids: Found primarily in animal-based foods such as milk, butter, lard and meat, and less commonly in vegetable products such as coconut oil.

Monounsaturated fatty acids: Found in both animal- and vegetable-based foods. Olive, canola and safflower oil consist largely of monounsaturated fatty acids.

Polyunsaturated fatty acids: Must be obtained from food since body cells can't produce them themselves. Polyunsaturated fatty acids are an important component in the formation of hormones and cells. Both the unsaturated linoleic fatty acid, with its double bond, and the polyunsaturated linolenic fatty acid have to be supplied through food. Omega-3 fatty acids, often referred to as fish oil, are polyunsaturated and are most commonly found in deep-sea fish. There are only a few vegetable sources of omega-3 fatty acids, one of which is alpha-linolenic acid in the form of flax (linseed) oil, canola oil and soy oil.

Alpha-linolenic acid can be transformed to a small degree into "fish oil." Dark green vegetables such as spinach, broccoli and kale, as well as lentils and walnuts, are also rich in linolenic acid, but given the fact that vegetables and legumes are low in fat, they won't be able to meet your fat needs.

Double-bonded linoleic acid is found in vegetable oils and fats such as diet margarine. Safflower oil, canola oil, soy oil and wheat germ oil are especially rich in linoleic acid.

Trans-fatty acids: Occur when naturally occurring fatty acids are transformed into so-called trans-fatty acids—when vegetable oils are solidified, for example, to produce conventional margarine, or through the bacterial enzyme present in the stomachs of ruminants (mainly cows).

It's generally agreed that trans-fatty acids contribute to an increase in LDL cholesterol and a decrease in HDL cholesterol. Trans-fatty acids are being eliminated in North America and Europe, but small amounts can be found in butter and solid margarine, as well as in processed foods, fast food, deep-fried chicken and various snacks. New labelling requirements also mean that they have to be listed, but you should still watch for such terms as "partially hydrogenated" or "hydrogenated" fat.

Diet margarine contains no trans-fatty acids.

How Different Nutrients Affect LDL and HDL Cholesterol

Sugar

Sugar doesn't affect LDL values, but it does affect lipometabolism if large quantities of sugar-rich foods are consumed. When large amounts of simple sugars—fructose, glucose and raw sugar—are consumed, triglyceride levels rise. For this reason, soft drinks, fruit juices, sweets, cakes and other white-flour products should be consumed only in moderation.

Protein

Vegetable protein from soy products lowers LDL blood cholesterol levels because it activates the absorption points on body cells. This results in a decrease in LDL values in the blood. The higher the basic values of LDL concentration, the greater the decrease.

Fiber

Not all fiber obtained from food affects lipometabolism, but certain fibers directly contribute to a drop in LDL cholesterol—the soluble fiber in oat bran can reduce LDL cholesterol by up to 15%. In addition, daily consumption of sources of pectin (in apples and citrus fruit) and guar (a vegetable thickener) reduces LDL cholesterol. By eating more than 10 g a day of these fibers, you can reduce LDL values by roughly 21 mg/dL (0.54 mmol/L) for the pectin from three to four mid-sized apples or 11 mg/dL (0.28 mmol/L) for guar, respectively.

Caution is needed if you're taking cholesterol-reducing medication. Oat bran and pectin expand in the intestine, where they can also bond with a medication's active ingredients and neutralize their effect.

Alcohol

Social drinking of one or two glasses of alcoholic beverages can slightly raise the level of HDL cholesterol—which is why drinking moderate amounts of alcohol is recommended in cases where HDL cholesterol levels are low. But caution is called for if triglyceride levels are high. In this case, alcohol consumption should be limited, since it raises triglyceride values. Furthermore, the positive effect of alcohol on HDL cholesterol admittedly conflicts with its unhealthy side effects.

Coffee

There's no proof of a connection between high coffee consumption and the occurrence of coronary heart disease. Only in individual cases has it been shown that coffee prepared in the Scandinavian method, where the ground coffee is left to steep longer in the boiling water, did LDL cholesterol levels rise by up to 10%. In contrast, filtered coffee and espresso have no effect on cholesterol levels.

How Different Nutrients Affect LDL and HDL Cholesterol

Absorption (of nutrients)	Effect on LDL cholesterol	Effect on HDL cholesterol
Carbohydrates that quickly enter the bloodstream (simple sugars)	∅	∅
Soy protein	↓	∅
Less fat	↓	↓
Fewer saturated fatty acids (animal-based products)	↓	↓
More monounsaturated fatty acids (as a substitute for saturated fatty acids)	↓	↓
Increased supply of polyunsaturated and omega-6 fatty acids (as a substitute for saturated fatty acids)	↓	↓
Omega-6 fatty acids	↓	∅
Omega-3 fatty acids (fish oils)	∅	If these reduce triglyceride levels, HDL cholesterol rises
Less cholesterol	↓	∅
High fiber intake	↓	∅
Alcohol	∅	↑
Excess weight	↑	↓

↑ = increasing   ↓ = decreasing   ∅ = no effect

Caution: Saturated Fats

The following table lists examples of animal-based products that can raise LDL cholesterol levels due to their high saturated fatty acid content.

To compare the foods shown, consider the amount of each product you actually consume. While ½ cup (125 mL) of whole (4%) milk has only about 4 g of saturated fatty acids, drinking 1 quart (1 L) a day represents more than 40 g. If you replace this amount with low-fat milk with a fat content of 1%, you can avoid more than 30 g of fatty acids a day. Meanwhile, mayonnaise may contain 45.8 g of saturated fatty acids in ⅓ cup (75 mL)—but you'll hardly eat that in a day.

Food and serving size	Saturated fatty acids
Whole (4%) milk, ½ cup (125 mL)	4.0 g
Low-fat (2%) yogurt, ½ cup (125 mL)	1.8 g
Cottage cheese (4%), ½ cup	4.7 g
Brie, 1 oz	7.9 g
Diet Swiss cheese, 1 oz	2.0 g
Parmesan cheese, grated, 1 tbsp (15 mL)	1.5 g
Swiss cheese, 1 oz	7.8 g
Chicken breast (skinless boneless), 3½ oz (100 g)	3.5 g
Lean beef (rib roast or steak), 3½ oz (100 g)	13.7 g
Pork chop, 3½ oz (100 g)	15.2 g
Beef salami, 3½ oz (100 g)	19.9 g

Food and serving size	Saturated fatty acids
Extra-lean ground beef, 3½ oz (100 g)	16.0 g
Extra-lean ham, 3½ oz (100 g)	5.5 g
Pork sausage links, 3½ oz (100 g)	32.4 g
Canned tuna packed in water, 3½ oz (100 g)	0.4
Fresh salmon (cooked), 3½ oz (100 g)	7.5 g
Brownie with chocolate icing, 1 medium	5.0 g
Cheesecake, 1 piece	16.3 g
Chocolate chip cookie, 1 medium	2.2 g
White cake with chocolate frosting, 1 piece	11.0 g
Mayonnaise, 1 tbsp (15 mL)	11.1 g

The Fat-Modified Diet Plan

According to the most recent findings, a fat-modified diet can

➤ actively contribute to a decrease in LDL cholesterol levels

➤ prevent an increase in LDL values at an early stage

➤ stabilize the arteries so they're better able to protect themselves against any changes due to atherosclerosis

Bear in mind that it always takes a few weeks before any new dietary measures can have a positive or negative effect on LDL cholesterol levels. The pork chop you ate two days ago doesn't help explain a high LDL cholesterol level. So stick to your new diet plan even if your next checkup still doesn't show any changes.

Since a fat-modified diet is recommended for medical reasons in the case of high LDL cholesterol levels, the following dietary plan is based on the recommendations of the European Atherosclerosis Society. It does not mean completely eliminating all animal-based products from your diet, but, rather, maintaining the right proportion between foods. The main objective of these measures is to have a positive influence on blood cholesterol and to prevent atherosclerosis from developing.

How much is a healthy amount?

The following dietary amounts are recommended for reducing high cholesterol, more specifically high LDL cholesterol values:

Carbohydrates	50% to 60 %
Protein	10% to 20 %
Total fat	less than 30%
saturated fatty acids	7% to 10%
monounsaturated fatty acids	10% to 15%
polyunsaturated fatty acids	7% to 10%
Fiber	35 g per day
Cholesterol	less than 300 mg per day

Based on typical eating habits, the following measures are recommended to maintain a good relationship between the intake of fat and other nutrients:

➤ Reduce total fat consumption.

➤ Consume fewer animal-based products with high levels of saturated fatty acids and cholesterol. Instead, eat animal-based products low in saturated fatty acids, such as fish, turkey or chicken (without the skin), veal and game.

➤ Consume foods with higher levels of mono- and polyunsaturated fatty acids, in particular vegetable oils, more often.

➤ Consume lots of carbohydrate- and fiber-rich foods, such as grains, potatoes, vegetables, legumes, fruit, and dark, whole-grain breads.

When cooking

➤ Pay more attention to the quality rather than the quantity of the fat chosen. Only 30% of the daily caloric requirement should be in the form of fat. This represents 65 to 80 g of total fat.

➤ Use vegetable oils.

➤ Limit the total amount of fat consumed daily, especially animal fats. At most, only half of the total amount of fat should come from animal-based foods, the other half from vegetable sources.

➤ Consume fewer "fatty" animal-based foods, thereby limiting fat, saturated fatty acids and cholesterol intake.

➤ Choose low-fat meat and sausages, milk and dairy products.

➤ Avoid obvious *and* hidden fats. Hidden fats can be found in products such as processed meats, cheese and milk, as well as in sauces and many prepared snacks and meals.

➤ Choose low-fat cooking methods such as grilling and steaming.

➤ Replace butter with diet margarine with a high level of polyunsaturated fatty acids and no trans fats.

There's no need to radically change your diet—small adjustments work too. For example, on average, fat makes up 35% of the North American diet. To get it down to the recommended 30%, you need to reduce daily consumption by only about a seventh—an amount so small it won't affect your eating pleasure.

The measures mentioned opposite are aimed at optimizing fat consumption, but in the end it's the right combination that makes the difference. If your diet is varied enough, you'll get a balanced intake of carbohydrates, protein, fat, vitamins, minerals and trace elements. Emphasis should be placed on carbohydrate- and fiber-rich foods, such as vegetables, legumes, potatoes and bread, as well as other grains and fruit.

Controlling Excess Weight

One of the simplest ways to reduce LDL cholesterol is to control body weight. We already know that losing weight—even just a few pounds—has a positive effect on cholesterol values and also helps to improve related conditions, such as high blood pressure and lipometabolic disorders. Deciding to lose weight, and how much, is best determined in consultation with your doctor. If you're slightly overweight (a BMI of 25 to 29.9), you'll need to lose at least 6 to 10 pounds (3 to 5 kilograms). If you're seriously overweight (a BMI of 30 or more), you'll need to lose 10 to 20 pounds (5 to 10 kilograms).

Use the Body Mass Index (BMI), which measures body weight in relation to height, to find out if your weight is normal.

$$BMI = \frac{body\ weight\ in\ lbs}{(height\ in\ inches)^2} \times 703$$

$$BMI = \frac{body\ weight\ in\ kg}{(height\ in\ meters)^2} \times 10{,}000$$

These numbers are not to be used for children, teenagers, the elderly or pregnant women.

How much energy do I need?

The days of meticulously counting calories are long gone. Rolls of fat lost through starvation would generally reappear in problem areas once the diet was over. Most often, the weight is regained.

If you're trying a short-term dietary "cure," certain minimal requirements must be respected to avoid any serious complications. This is especially important for those who have already had a heart attack. In general, a self-directed restricted diet should never be followed for more than two weeks and only after consulting your doctor. Daily minimal requirements include 50 g of protein and 70 g of carbohydrates. Consuming less than the indicated minimal amount of carbohydrates will lead to excessive water loss through the kidneys and the collapse of the circulatory system.

Today we talk about eating a variety of foods low in fat. Energy needs vary from one person to the next. Follow the formula "15 calories per pound (30 calories per kilogram) of body weight per day." To lose weight, multiply your weight by 30 calories and subtract 500 calories. Under no circumstances should you ever consume less than 1,200 calories a day. Crash diets place a heavy strain on the cardiovascular system and have no long-term effect. Ideally, you should lose 2 to 4 pounds (1 to 2 kilograms) per month over a 3- to 6-month period or 12 months at most.

Reaching a desirable weight

When it comes to losing weight, most people automatically think this means sacrifice. Now is the time to change this way of thinking. You don't have to follow a boring diet or avoid your favorite foods. The most effective and realistic way to reach the weight you desire is to reduce fat intake and burn more energy by increasing physical activity.

By sensibly changing your diet as already discussed, you'll be able to eat a variety of healthy foods and feel full without having to forgo a few treats. In principle, everything is allowed—what's crucial is the right amount. If you exceed your energy requirements by just 30 calories a day, 2 pounds (1 kilogram) of new fatty tissue will have built up in a year. If it's 100 calories daily, nearly 8 pounds (3.5 kilograms) of fat will have built up.

Take a good look at your meal plan and your daily activities to identify any problems that are easy to correct. Here are a few tips to help you lose weight:

➤ Set small, realistic goals you can reach; for example, losing 2 pounds (1 kilogram) a month.

➤ Avoid distractions such as watching television or reading while eating. These activities can cause you to unconsciously eat larger servings than you need to feel full.

➤ Drink a glass of water or eat some raw vegetables or a salad to fill your stomach before eating.

➤ Make your meals look appetizing even when you're eating alone. Set the table in an attractive way so that eating is also a pleasure.

➤ Try to determine if you're actually hungry or if you just feel like eating.

➤ Chew your food well.

➤ Quench your thirst by drinking calorie-free drinks such as mineral water, herbal and fruit teas (with added lemon or lime juice) or diet soft drinks with artificial sweeteners.

➤ Never go grocery shopping on an empty stomach, and stick to your shopping list. Buy only as much as you'll need for one or two days.

➤ "Light" doesn't always mean sugar- or fat-free. Carefully read the list of ingredients. If fat is the first ingredient, the product is high in calories. If sugar is the last ingredient on the list, then the sugar content is essentially negligible.

Getting Physically Active

Regular exercise is fun, increases your sense of well-being and helps to control weight. It can also have a positive effect on many of the risk factors for heart attack, as well as on lipometabolic disorders, high blood pressure and diabetes. Therefore, increased and regular physical activity plays an essential role in preventing a heart attack. By increasing your level of physical activity, you can also expect a rise in HDL cholesterol. On the other hand, LDL cholesterol is not directly affected, though if physical activity contributes to weight loss, then LDL cholesterol values will clearly drop independently of any health concerns.

You don't need to become a competitive athlete—simple measures will also work to increase physical activity. Admittedly, not every type of sport is advisable. You should start with an exercise program of light to medium difficulty and slowly increase the time you spend exercising. If you haven't exercised in a long time, consult your doctor first. And give your body time to get used to the physical exertion again.

Endurance sports are ideal for improving the cardiovascular system and for burning fat. The longer the exercise, the more fat is taken from the body's reserves. The best fat-burning exercises are those

A combination of endurance sports and weight training is ideal. For example, walk briskly for 30 minutes four times a week and do some weight training once a week.

Sports that don't stress the joints—such as walking, easy exercises, cycling, swimming and dancing—are appropriate.

that last longer than 20 to 30 minutes. You should also be able to maintain this pace without losing your breath, and your pulse rate shouldn't exceed 130 beats per minute.

Activities that involve a sudden change in direction, pressure or impact put stress on the joints. If you are overweight or have any knee or back problems, you should avoid these types of sports, including jogging, tennis, soccer and many other sports involving a ball.

Weight training promotes building muscle. Since muscle burns more energy than fat, the amount of energy used remains high. Weight training does little to help reduce your weight, since building muscle mass hardly affects body weight. You may even gain weight—but your body will clearly be firmer and trimmer.

A Few Notes on Nutrition

Up until now, we've discussed fat only as a supplier of energy. Of greater importance for the body is a balanced diet of the energy-bearing nutrients —protein, fat and carbohydrates—and essential vitamins, minerals and trace elements. Here's a brief overview.

Carbohydrates

The body prefers carbohydrates as its energy provider, since their short or long "chains" of building blocks are a quick and immediate source of fuel for many cells. The best way to remain mentally and physically alert through the whole day is to eat meals with a high proportion of foods—grains and grain products (such as pasta and bread), potatoes, brown rice and vegetables—that supply complex carbohydrates. Legumes and fresh fruit are also good sources. In general, choose unprocessed or minimally processed foods, since these also deliver the minerals and vitamins necessary to feel healthier and more energetic.

Also rich in carbohydrates are foods containing sugar, such as granulated sugar, candy, soft drinks and fruit beverages, as well as fruit nectars or baked goods made with white flour, such as baguettes, pretzels and cakes. Given that these "simple sugars" can block the breakdown of fat in the blood, they should be eaten in moderation.

Fiber

The more fiber a meal contains, the more effectively fat is burned. The ability of fiber to help burn fat is based on the positive effect fiber has on blood cholesterol, which leads back to lipometabolism. Fiber is contained in legumes, oats, pasta, brown rice, potatoes, vegetables and fruit.

Carbohydrate-Rich Foods

➕ whole-grain and related products (for example, oatmeal, brown rice, certain types of bread and baked goods, pastas, granola mixes, etc.), potatoes, vegetables, fresh fruit, legumes

➖ sugar, jams, chocolate, confectionery, cakes and baked goods, sweet drinks, fruit beverages, baked goods made from white flour, sweetened granola mixes, prepared products with potatoes, prepared fruit products, many prepared foods

Eating the recommended amount of fiber (30 to 35 grams a day) can prevent digestive problems and promote healthy intestinal flora—the best foundation for good health.

Fat

The theme of fat and the negative health effects of consuming large amounts of it are like a red thread running through this book. It's important to remember, however, that the human organism can't live without fat. It serves as fuel for the heart and muscle cells, carries the fat-soluble vitamins A, D, E and K, keeps the skin smooth and supports many other bodily functions. What's important is consuming the right kind of fat in the right amounts.

How Much Fat Is Enough?

At most, 30%, or 60 to 80 grams, of your daily energy requirements should come from fat. This translates to 1 tsp (2 mL) of oil for cooking and frying plus 1 tbsp (15 mL) as a spread per person per day. Salads shouldn't have more than 1 tbsp (15 mL) of oil per serving per person. To avoid consuming too many "hidden" fats, choose cheeses that have a fat content below 15% to 20% and limit meats, sausages, fast foods and snacks.

What kind of fat is best?

Each type of fat consists of different fatty acids: saturated, mono- and polyunsaturated. Vegetable oils are rich in mono- and polyunsaturated fatty acids and are mostly cholesterol free. On the other hand, animal-based products contain mostly saturated fatty acids, with the exception of fish, which contain predominantly unsaturated fatty acids, including omega-3 fatty acids—which are good for the cardiovascular system.

To feel healthier and more productive, include in your diet foods that contain mostly unsaturated fatty acids. For cooking or frying or in salads, use good-quality vegetable oils, but sparingly.

Protein

Protein should meet 10% to 20% of your daily energy requirements. Since protein is an essential building block of all body cells, you need to eat protein-rich foods every day. Generally speaking, however, we consume protein-rich foods in quantities that exceed the recommended amount. Since the most popular sources of protein are animal based—milk and dairy products, cheese, meat and eggs—consuming these foods has an undesirable effect on lipometabolism. Many people are unaware that many vegetable products are also rich in protein, especially grains, legumes and nuts. Especially good for the body is the combination of vegetable and animal protein sources—potatoes and eggs; potatoes and cream cheese or yogurt; grains or legumes and

dairy products; and such internationally popular combos as potatoes and legumes, rice and legumes, or beans and corn.

Regularly include vegetarian meals in your meal plan, since the lipometabolism of animal sources of protein rich in fat means they should be eaten in moderation. Eat fish at least twice a week. Low-fat fish in particular deliver high-quality protein with little in the way of fat that is harmful to your health. The omega-3 fatty acids found in fish have a positive impact on blood cholesterol values and blood vessels. Moreover, fish is a source of iodine.

Protein-Rich Foods

➕ fish, shellfish (in moderation, given their cholesterol content), legumes, soy products, whole grains, skim milk products (0.1 to 1.5% fat), low-fat cheeses (less than 15% bf), sprouts, nuts

➖ preserved fish products, meat and meat products, duck, goose, poultry with the skin on, eggs, high-fat dairy products (more than 3.5% fat), high-fat cheeses (more than 22% bf)

Beneficial protein combinations

Potatoes and dairy products (for example, boiled potatoes with quark or puréed cottage cheese), grains and dairy products (for example, muesli with milk, whole-grain bread with cheese), beans and corn, or grains or potatoes with soy products.

Beverages

Your body needs at least 6 cups (1.5 L) of liquids every day to balance its need for water. Ideal beverages include mineral water, juice spritzers, and herbal and fruit teas. Fruit beverages, black tea and coffee can be enjoyed in moderation. Milk and milk-based beverages, on the other hand, should be viewed as foods containing energy and fat and are not appropriate for quenching thirst.

Vitamins and minerals

According to dietary recommendations, you should eat fresh fruit and vegetables at least five times a day. The more of these you eat every day, the more certain you can be that you're getting enough vitamins and other healthy vegetable matter as well as fiber. You can eat one serving of salad at each main meal plus at least one serving of vegetables at one of your main meals and have bell pepper, carrot, or other vegetable sticks as a snack between meals. Whether it's fruit or vegetables, enjoy them fresh or, if necessary, cooked quickly to preserve the valuable vitamins and health-protecting vegetable matter they contain.

The Nutrition Pyramid

Eat sparingly: Spreads such as butter or margarine. Vegetable oils are clearly more healthful for cooking and baking. Beware of hidden fats in sweets and prepared foods.

In moderation: Dairy products also contain carbohydrates. High-fat cheeses and products made from whole milk or cream are also high in fat. Select low-fat products instead.

2 to 3 times a week: Meat and poultry should be eaten only 2 to 3 times a week as a main course.
In moderation: cold cuts should be replaced as often as possible by low-fat cheese, vegetable spreads, herbs and vegetables.
At least 6 times a month: Consume plenty of fish because of its healthful fatty acids and iodine content.

Not always, but more often: Fresh fruit contains fructose. Eat up to 3 servings (about 4 oz/120 g per serving) a day as a snack.

Help yourself: Fresh vegetables can be eaten any time you're hungry. Vegetables should be the largest portion of on your plate at mealtimes.

Selecting grain products: Choose whole grains and whole-grain products, potatoes and legumes.

Practical Tips at a Glance

Low fat

➤ Steaming, stewing, sautéing in a nonstick skillet, braising, grilling or broiling, and stir-frying in a wok are all low-fat cooking methods that preserve vitamins (see page 30).

➤ Make olive oil and canola oil your first choice for cooking because the fatty acids they contain improve the relationship between polyunsaturated omega-6 fatty acids (lineic acid) and omega-3 fatty acids (linolenic acid).

➤ For dishes and dressings, use a variety of oils and vinegars with pronounced flavors. Since cold-pressed oils are more flavorful, you won't need to use as much.

➤ Avoid prepared salad dressings. Instead of creamy dressings, use oil and vinegar or yogurt. If you want a creamy dressing, use buttermilk or low-fat kefir, yogurt or sour cream instead of cream or regular sour cream, etc.

➤ Instead of thickening your sauces with fat and flour or with cream, purée some cooked vegetables to stir in. Here's a tip for a good gravy or sauce base: Braise or stew a lot of fresh vegetables. Dark gravies will become more flavorful if you add carrots, tomatoes, onions, celery and leek. For light gravies, use the white part of the leek, onions, a little celery or carrots.

➤ Soy products such as soy milk are good vegetable alternatives to sour cream and crème fraîche. If these aren't available, use buttermilk or low-fat kefir, yogurt or sour cream to round out your sauce without any noticeable change in taste. To prevent the yogurt or any of the substitutes from becoming runny or separating in the hot sauce, in a small bowl, stir 3 to 4 tablespoons (45 to 60 mL) of the stock or gravy (or some cornstarch) into the yogurt before stirring into the sauce.

➤ For desserts, use low-fat quark, puréed cottage cheese or strained yogurt instead of the full-fat varieties, add a few splashes of sparkling mineral water, and whisk to create a light and creamy dessert or component. This way, you can avoid using whipped cream, which is added to many desserts to make them fluffier.

➤ Combining low-fat quark, puréed cottage cheese or strained yogurt and plain low-fat yogurt in a 1:1 ratio offers a light base for quark-based foods and desserts.

➤ For baking, choose low-fat pastries and doughs such as phyllo, strudel, yeast dough or quark-and-oil pastry, batter or dough.

➤ To compensate for consuming too much energy and fat, eat fewer calories, in particular calories from fat, the next day.

Health consciousness

➤ The smaller the item to be cooked, the shorter the cooking time. Cut vegetables into small strips or cubes. If using a wok, cut the meat into thin strips.

➤ Frozen vegetables are a great alternative to fresh products. Avoid any prepared vegetables, such as vegetables in a cream sauce or with butter. Read the nutrients listed on the packaging—you'll be surprised to see how much fat there is.

➤ Spices and fresh herbs improve any meal and help save on salt. Add fresh herbs to a warm meal just before serving; otherwise, they'll lose their flavor.

➤ Use whole-grain products. Actual whole grains aren't necessary. For example, try finely ground whole wheat or graham crackers, whole-grain rolls and whole-grain crispbreads. You'll also increase your fiber intake.

➤ Brown rice has a nutty flavor that gives meals a particular taste.

➤ If you want to use whole-grain, egg-free noodles, try whole-grain spelt noodles, which have a mild flavor.

➤ If you are consciously increasing your fiber intake by eating more fruit and vegetables or whole-grain breads, there's nothing to say you can't occasionally eat a bagel or baguette or Italian bread made from white flour.

➤ Essential nutrients from fresh, natural foods are best for your body. The most important thing is a variety of foods that include three servings of vegetables and two small servings of fruit every day.

➤ Unprocessed or partially processed foods still contain their original fiber and many essential nutrients. This is why it's better to have fresh fruit instead of juice, brown rice instead of white, boiled potatoes instead of French fries and whole-grain bread instead of baguette.

➤ Use prepared foods sparingly and only if they don't contain too much fat, sugar or salt. Check the list of ingredients on the packaging.

➤ Given that dietary cholesterol plays a secondary role in raising LDL cholesterol levels, it's all right to have 2 to 3 eggs per week, including recipes that call for eggs. Remember also that foods such as casseroles, egg noodles, cakes and baked goods also contain eggs.

➤ Iodine deficiency can still be a problem in some areas. Use iodized salt when cooking if you don't suffer from thyroid problems.

➤ Alcohol can have both a positive and a negative impact on health. Alcohol used in cooking evaporates when heated. The finished meal contains some of the tasty flavor but no alcohol. Wine can enhance some meals.

➤ If you usually use mineral water or tea to quench your thirst, having a glass of wine with a meal poses no problem.

Nuts: A Delicious Snack between Meals

Because nuts are high in fat, many people with high blood cholesterol are unsure about whether they can eat nuts as part of a fat-modified diet.

First, the good news: You can eat nuts from time to time as a delicious between-meals snack or as a garnish to enhance exotic dishes. Nuts are rich in healthy mono- and polyunsaturated fatty acids, contain no cholesterol and are good sources of vitamins and good-quality protein.

Now the bad news: Despite everything, their high fat content must be taken into account as part of a fat-modified diet.

Pistachios have proved to be particularly healthy vis-à-vis

cholesterol levels. They contain the lowest amount of fat of all nuts, with a 10:1 ratio of unsaturated to saturated fatty acids. Because of this, they boost "good" HDL cholesterol and help decrease "bad" LDL cholesterol. Different studies have shown that regular consumption of green pistachios reduces LDL cholesterol as well as the risk of heart attack by 30% to 50%. Pistachios are also rich in vitamin B, magnesium and folic acid, which makes them "good food for the nerves." But beware: A handful of pistachios (approximately 45 nuts, or 1 oz/25 g) has 160 calories and 13 g of fat (of which 11 g are unsaturated fatty acids).

Foods suitable for a fat-modified diet

Meats: Veal, lean beef, skinless poultry (chicken, turkey, quail, pheasant), game (rabbit, venison, moose, buffalo)

Processed meats: Cold cuts containing up to 20% fat (check the label), ham, turkey, chicken

Cooked meats: Roast beef, skinless roasted poultry, ham with the fatty rind removed

Soups: Low-fat stock, homemade clear meat stock, vegetable stock

Fish: Cod, flounder, halibut, shellfish, plaice, salmon, sole, ocean perch, red snapper, turbot, trout, whitefish, perch, pickerel, pike

Eggs: Whites, cholesterol-free egg substitute

Milk and dairy products: Low-fat milk (skim, 1% or 2% fat), buttermilk, low-fat dairy products (1% to 2% fat) such as yogurt and sour cream, skim milk quark, low-fat cottage cheese, low-fat cream cheese

Grains: Buckwheat, spelt, barley, oats, millet, brown rice, rye, wheat

Breads: All types, and in particular in existing cases of hyper-Ftriglyceridemia, whole wheat and rye bread, flax seed bread, sunflower seed bread, whole-grain bread, soy bread

Pastas: All pastas made without egg yolks

Potatoes: All types of dishes prepared with low-fat milk, no egg yolks and good-quality vegetable fats

Cakes and pastries: Yeast-based and, in the case of hypertriglyceridemia, those types prepared with vegetable fats, low-fat milk and no egg yolks

Legumes: Beans, lentils, peas, soybeans

Vegetables: All types, preferably raw or in a salad

Fruit: All types except avocados

Desserts: Fruit and fruit-based desserts, milk pudding made with low-fat milk, sorbet and granita, chocolate desserts based on unsweetened cocoa powder

Beverages: Coffee (in moderation), tea, mineral water, fruit and vegetable juices, spritzers made with one part pure fruit juice to four parts of mineral water, diet soft drinks with artificial sweetener and, in the case of hypercholesterolemia, regular soft drinks

Foods that can be eaten as part of a fat-modified diet when their fat, saturated fatty acids and/or cholesterol content are taken into account

Meats: Pork, beef, mutton, lamb, ground beef, bacon, duck, goose, mature chickens, offal (liver, heart, kidneys, sweetbread, brain), canned meat products

Processed and sausage meats: All types of sausages with a fat content exceeding 20%, smoked pork or beef sausage, smoked sausage spread, salami, cold cuts, blood sausage, liverwurst, meat loaf, wieners

Fish: Herring, eel, mackerel, tuna, calamari, carp, oysters, crab, lobster, shrimp, caviar, canned fish in a sauce, breaded fish

Eggs: Egg yolks, foods and meals prepared with egg yolk (such as egg noodles), scrambled eggs, fried eggs, omelets

Milk and dairy products: Whole and partially skimmed milk and dairy products, such as homogenized milk, cream, yogurt, sour cream, quark, crème fraîche, cheeses containing more than 15% bf

Dumplings: All types

Pastas: Pastas containing eggs

Cakes and pastries: Shortcake, pies, phyllo pastries and strudels, loaf cakes, frosted cakes, donuts

Nuts: All types

Fruit: Avocado

Confectionery: Chocolate and chocolate bars, pralines, nut brittles, marzipan, nougat, chocolate syrup, caramels

Sweet dishes: Pastry confections, cream confections made with whole milk or cream

Fats: Oils, margarine with a low or high polyunsaturated fat content, butter, lard, coconut oil, palm kernel oil, mayonnaise, creamy dressing, bacon, suet

Beverages: When triglyceride levels are also high, beverages containing alcohol and soft drinks and spritzers containing sugar

Low-Fat Cooking Methods

Lowering your cholesterol level means changing your habits. Old standbys for how you cook need to be reviewed and adjusted. The information below should make it easy to switch to the right cooking method.

Grilling or broiling

Grilling or broiling at 500°F (260°C) is a low-fat way of cooking and browning that adds flavor and crispness.

What you need:

You can choose a charcoal, gas or electric grill or barbecue, or an oven with a broiler or grill. Or use a table grill, a grilling pan or an electric grilling skewer.

Appropriate ingredients:

Unsalted, lean meat, sausages, fish, vegetables, potatoes, fruit.

Here's how:

Preheat the grill or broiler according to the manufacturers' instructions.

Place the food you are grilling on the heated cooking surface, on a broiling or grilling pan or thread onto a skewer. Brown the food until it's just cooked.

Steaming

Steaming at roughly 212°F (100°C) is the gentlest cooking method. No cooking liquid or fat comes in contact with the food, which retains its characteristic flavor and fresh color.

What you need:

To steam, you'll need a Chinese bamboo steamer, a perforated steamer insert or a flexible metal insert made to fit various sizes of pans.

Appropriate ingredients:

Broccoli, cauliflower, peas, beans, fennel, potatoes, leeks, carrots, beets, asparagus, fish fillets, trout, mackerel, poultry breasts and thighs.

Here's how:

Cover the bottom of a pot with 1 to 2 inches (2.5 to 5 cm) of water, stock or wine.

Put the food in the steamer and place in or over a pot or a wok with a lid so that the steamer will fit without touching the liquid.

Cover and allow the liquid to come to a boil.

Cooking has begun once there's steam. Turn down the heat and cook until done.

Stewing

Stewing cooks the food in its own juices or a little liquid and requires very little fat or none at all. The cooking temperature is roughly 212°F (100ºC). Vitamins and minerals are largely preserved.

What you need:

A good-quality, heavy-bottomed pan, or a nonstick pan that conducts heat well and has a tight-fitting lid, or a pressure cooker are all fine. Tried and true alternatives include a clay roasting pot, a roasting bag, parchment paper and roasting or aluminum foil.

Appropriate ingredients:

Beans, carrots, bell peppers, mushrooms, tomatoes, zucchini, fruit, fish fillets, whole fish, poultry parts.

Here's how:

Wash the food and place, dripping wet, in the pot, wrap in parchment or foil, or sauté lightly with a little bit of fat.

Pour water or stock over the food. Cover and cook on low heat.

If using parchment, foil or a clay roasting pot, cook the food in the oven at about 275°F (140°C). Remove the parchment or foil packets from the oven along with the rack and open carefully, preferably over the sink—they're very hot.

Sautéing

You can sauté using no or very little fat. The optimal cooking temperature is between 275°F (140°C) and 400°F (200°C). At these high temperatures, the pores close and the food remains juicy.

What you need:
Nonstick, scratch-proof skillets or frying pans with or without a lid are ideal. Invest in skillets, frying pans and saucepans made from nickel-free, multi-layer materials that conduct heat quickly and evenly.

Appropriate ingredients:
Steaks, cutlets, medallions, chops, fish fillets, vegetables, potatoes, eggs.

Here's how:
Heat the skillet, frying pan or saucepan. Brush lightly with oil.

Place the dry food in the skillet or saucepan and brown on all sides. Depending on the type of food, lower the heat and cook until done.

Remove the food, loosen the roasting juices by cooking them in a little liquid as you scrape any browned bits from the bottom and use to prepare a sauce, if desired.

Braising

This cooking method is a combination of sautéing at 325°F (160°C) to 400°F (200°C) and stewing in a small amount of liquid at 200°F (100°C).

What you need:
A Dutch oven or flat pan with a close-fitting lid, a roasting pan, or a skillet or frying pan with a cover are all appropriate, especially if you can cook using very little liquid or no fat.

Appropriate ingredients:
Pork, beef or lamb chunks, pot roasts and roulades, braising vegetables such as cabbage, stuffed bell peppers and eggplants.

Here's how:
Heat a little fat and brown the food on all sides;

Add the other ingredients, such as vegetables, spices and dried herbs;

Pour in a little stock, wine or water, cover and simmer gently until done.

Stir-frying in a wok

Cooking in a wok or large skillet or frying pan is called stir-frying and is a healthy cooking method that helps preserve flavor. Finely chopped ingredients are prepared using a little fat and are constantly stirred.

What you need:
For a gas range, you'll need a conventional wok with a curved bottom. For electric burners, you'll need a flat-bottomed wok. Woks are made from cast iron, cast iron with a scratch-free enamel coating, stainless steel or copper. A large skillet or frying pan will do the job but doesn't distribute the heat in exactly the same way or permit you to push ingredients up the sides and away from the heat.

Appropriate ingredients:
All vegetables, fish, seafood, poultry and lean meat.

Here's how:
Finely slice, dice or julienne the ingredients into thin strips.

Heat a minimum amount of oil. Add the larger or harder ingredients first, then the smaller or softer ones with a shorter cooking time, and sauté, stirring constantly.

Add any spices or flavorings, then pour in some liquid and cook until done. Keep some cornstarch mixed with water or soy sauce on hand if the sauce needs some thickening; pour in and bring to a boil at the end.

Breakfast and Snacks

Fresh Fruit Salad with Poppy seed Yogurt

Fat	●	20 min.
Cholesterol	1 mg	
Fiber	●●	

Per serving: approx. 202 calories
7 g protein · 5 g fat · 34 g carbohydrates

MAKES 2 SERVINGS
2 tbsp (30 mL) poppy seeds
½ cup (50 mL) skim milk
⅔ cup (150 mL/150 g) low-fat yogurt
1 tsp (5 mL) vanilla sugar
1 small red apple
1 small banana
1 tbsp (15 mL) freshly squeezed
    lemon juice
⅔ cup (155 mL /100 g) green grapes
1 orange

1 In a small saucepan, bring the poppy seeds and milk to a boil. Pour the mixture into a small bowl; let cool. Combine with the yogurt and sugar, stir well, and set aside to cool.

2 Quarter and core the apple and cut into wedges. Peel and slice the banana. Combine with the apple and drizzle immediately with the lemon juice.

3 Halve and remove any seeds from the grapes. Peel the orange. Cut into wedges, reserving any juice, and stir into the poppy seed yogurt.

4 Carefully mix all the fruit with the poppy seed yogurt and serve immediately.

‼ **TIP** You can use other fruit. Let your taste buds, the season and what's in the market be your guide.

Muesli with Creamy Cheese

Fat	●	15 min.
Cholesterol	7 mg	
Fiber	●●●	

Per serving: approx. 392 calories
19 g protein · 6 g fat · 65 g carbohydrates

MAKES 2 SERVINGS
¾ cup + 2 tbsp (200 mL/200 g) low-fat quark, puréed cottage cheese or strained yogurt
1 cup (250 mL/100 g) mixed frozen berries
2 tbsp (30 mL) thawed frozen apple juice concentrate or pear nectar
¼ tsp (1 mL) vanilla
⅓ cup (75 mL/50 g) sultanas (golden raisins)
1 cup (250 mL/100 g) mixed grain flakes

1 Add 3 to 4 tbsp (90 to 120 mL) water to the quark and stir until creamy (skip or reduce for cottage cheese or strained yogurt). Thaw the berries in a small bowl in the microwave; set a few berries aside. Mash the remaining berries and combine with the quark, apple concentrate or pear nectar, and vanilla.

2 Wash the sultanas in hot water, dry on a paper towel and mix with the grain flakes.

3 Arrange the raisins and grain flakes on top of the quark mixture and garnish with the reserved berries.

‼ **TIP** A blend of grain flakes is available in health food stores. You can also use only one type of grain, such as old-fashioned rolled oats or spelt flakes.

Banana Tofu with Fruit

Fat	–	15 min.
Cholesterol	–	
Fiber	●	

Per serving: approx. 157 calories
4 g protein · 3 g fat · 35 g carbohydrates

MAKES 2 SERVINGS
⅔ cup (150 mL/150 g) silken tofu
1 banana
1 to 2 tbsp (15 to 30 mL) maple syrup or granulated sugar
1 cup (250 mL/150 g) green or red grapes
1 cup (250 mL/150 g) strawberries
2 tbsp (30 mL) corn flakes cereal

1 Using a fork or a hand-held blender, mash the tofu. Peel and mash the banana. Combine the banana, tofu and maple syrup or sugar to form a smooth pudding.

2 Slice the grapes and remove any pits. Carefully wash the strawberries, hull, drain and dice. Stir into the banana tofu and serve garnished with corn flakes.

‼ **TIP** You can buy quark, cottage cheese and yogurt with different amounts of fat—which affects not only the fat and therefore the calories the product contains, but also the amount of cholesterol. For example, ½ cup (125 mL/100 g) of quark with 20% milk fat by weight (40% by dry weight) contains roughly 153 calories and 31 g of cholesterol. The same amount of skim milk quark contains approximately 72 calories and 1 mg of cholesterol. The same applies to all dairy products, so always choose the low- or non-fat types.

Fresh Fruit Salad with Poppy Seed Yogurt, top
Muesli with Creamy Cheese, bottom left
Banana Tofu with Fruit, bottom right

Pineapple Yogurt with Flax Seeds

Fat	●●●	10 min.
Cholesterol	–	
Fiber	●●●	

Per serving: approx. 315 calories
11 g protein · 11 g fat · 44 g carbohydrates

Makes 2 servings

1 cup (250 mL/250 g) low-fat yogurt
3 tbsp (45 mL) crushed or lightly
   ground flax seeds
Juice of ½ lemon
2 tbsp (30 mL) granulated sugar
¼ tsp (1 mL) vanilla
2 tbsp (30 mL) ground almonds
½ tsp (2 mL) ground cinnamon
½ tsp (2 mL) ground allspice
10 oz (300 g) fresh pineapple (about
   ½ cleaned fruit)

1 In a medium bowl, combine the yogurt, flax seeds and lemon juice. Stir in the sugar, vanilla, almonds, cinnamon and allspice; combine well.

2 Peel, core and finely dice pineapple. Mix with the yogurt and serve immediately.

‼ **TIP** You can now buy pineapple all year. They're usually picked still unripe and won't achieve the same quality as fruit that's been harvested ripe, so buy only sweet-smelling pineapples with fresh, green leaves. Store in the refrigerator and use as quickly as possible.

Soy Muesli with Pears

Fat	+	20 min.
Cholesterol	–	
Fiber	●●●	

Per serving: approx. 423 calories
13 g protein · 17 g fat · 57 g carbohydrates

Makes 2 servings

2 tbsp (30 mL) ground hazelnuts
2 tbsp (30 mL) large-flake rolled
   oats
2 tbsp (30 mL) raisins
¾ cup + 2 tbsp (200 mL/200 g)
   plain soy milk
2 tbsp (30 mL) cashews
2 tbsp (30 mL) pear nectar
2 ripe pears (about 8 oz/250 g)
⅔ cup (150 mL/150 g) low-fat yogurt
2 tbsp (30 mL) crushed or lightly
   ground flax seeds

1 In a medium bowl, combine the hazelnuts, rolled oats and raisins. Stir in the soy milk and let sit for 10 to 15 minutes.

2 Coarsely chop the cashews and brown in a small, dry nonstick skillet on low heat. Remove and set aside.

3 Stir the pear nectar into the rolled oat mixture. Peel, core and finely dice pears. Combine the pears, yogurt and flax seeds with the rolled oat mixture. Sprinkle with cashews and serve.

‼ **TIP** You can combine the hazelnuts, rolled oats, raisins and soy milk the night before and let sit overnight.

‼ **TIP** The slightly bitter cashews should be stored in a dry, dark place, preferably in the refrigerator. They contain a lot of protein but no cholesterol and very little fat compared to other nuts.

Millet Muesli with Raisins

Fat	●●	25 min.
Cholesterol	5 mg	
Fiber	●●	

Per serving: approx. 420 calories
12 g protein · 7 g fat · 75 g carbohydrates

Makes 2 servings

¾ cup + 2 tbsp (200 mL/200 g) skim
   or 1% milk
⅓ cup (75 mL/70 g) millet
2 tbsp (30 mL) raisins
6 dried unsulphured apricots
1 apple (such as Gala or Granny
   Smith)
2 tbsp (30 mL) freshly squeezed
   lemon juice
⅔ cup (150 mL/150 g) low-fat yogurt
6 amaretti biscuits

1 Bring the milk and millet to a boil, stir in the raisins, cover and cook on low heat.

2 Meanwhile, finely slice the apricots. Peel the apple, finely dice and drizzle immediately with the lemon juice. Fold the apricot strips, diced apple and yogurt into the millet.

3 Crumble the amaretti and sprinkle over the muesli.

‼ **TIP** Once largely forgotten, millet is becoming more widely available. It contains a good quantity of valuable vegetable protein, all kinds of minerals—in particular magnesium and potassium—and its high iron content makes it essential for those who eat little or no meat.

‼ **TIP** Ameretti are small, airy, crisp Italian macaroons flavored with bitter-almond paste.

**Banana Yogurt with Flax Seeds, top
Soy Muesli with Pears, bottom left
Millet Muesli with Raisins, bottom
right**

Oat Germ with Kiwis and Strawberries

Fat	++	15 min.
Cholesterol	8 mg	
Fiber	●●●	

Per serving: approx. 640 calories
16 g protein · 22 g fat · 96 g carbohydrates

MAKES 2 SERVINGS
¼ cup (50 mL) oat germ
2 tbsp (30 mL) raisins
1 cup (250 mL/250 g) skim or
    1% milk
1 to 2 tbsp (15 to 30 mL) liquid honey
1¼ cup (300 mL/200 g) strawberries
2 kiwis
2 tbsp (30 mL) pecans or walnuts

1 Combine the oat germ with the raisins, milk and honey and let sit for 10 to 15 minutes.

2 Carefully wash the strawberries, drain, hull and cut into wedges. Peel the kiwis, quarter, remove the hard center and dice. Coarsely chop the pecans.

3 Stir the strawberries and kiwis into the oat germ mixture. Garnish with the nuts and serve.

!! **TIP** Oats in all forms are ideal if your cholesterol is too high. They contain large amounts of essential fatty and amino acids, and the outer layer of the whole grain is rich in soluble fiber, which explains why oat germ is especially recommended for a cholesterol-friendly diet.

Oat Bran Flakes with Peaches

Fat	●●	5 min.
Cholesterol	6 mg	
Fiber	●●	

Per serving: approx. 286 calories
10 g protein · 7 g fat · 43 g carbohydrates

MAKES 2 SERVINGS
2 heaping tbsp (30 mL/20 g) shelled
    pistachios
2 peaches or other seasonal fruit,
    such as nectarines or apricots
1¼ cups (300 mL/60 g) oat bran
    flakes cereal
2 tbsp (30 mL) pear nectar
1 cup (250 mL/250 g) low-fat kefir or
    yogurt

1 Toast the pistachios in a small, dry nonstick skillet on low heat until golden. Remove and set aside.

2 Wash the peaches in hot water, halve, pit and dice. Combine with the oat bran flakes and pear nectar. Pour in the kefir, sprinkle with pistachios and serve immediately so the oats remain crunchy.

!! **TIP** Products with oat bran, such as oat bran flakes or toasted oat cereal, can't be forgotten in a cholesterol-friendly diet. Oats contain fiber that is particularly easy for the body to process. Soluble fiber stimulates digestion and attaches itself to harmful cholesterol to eliminate it. It's important to drink plenty of fluids with products high in such fiber—immediately after eating, drink a glass of mineral water flavored with fruit juice.

A Bowl of Buckwheat with Fruit

Fat	–	25 min.
Cholesterol	3 mg	
Fiber	●●●	

Per serving: approx. 393 calories
12 g protein · 3 g fat · 78 g carbohydrates

MAKES 2 SERVINGS
¾ cup + 2 tbsp (200 mL) skim or
    1% milk
½ tsp (2 mL) lemon zest
½ vanilla bean
½ cup (125 mL/100 g) buckwheat
    groats
1 small mango (about 8 oz/250 g
    prepared)
2 tbsp (30 mL) granulated sugar
⅔ cup (150 mL/150 g) low-fat yogurt
1⅔ cups (400 mL/200 g) raspberries

1 Combine the milk and lemon zest. Slice the vanilla bean open lengthwise, scrape out the seeds and stir into the milk.

2 Rinse the buckwheat with cold water and drain. Bring to a boil with the milk, cover and simmer on low heat for 15 minutes or until all the liquid has been absorbed.

3 Peel and finely dice mango. Combine the buckwheat, mango, sugar and yogurt. Carefully wash the raspberries, drain well and sprinkle over the buckwheat.

Oat Germ with Kiwis and
Strawberries, top
Oat Bran Flakes with Peaches,
bottom left
A Bowl of Buckwheat with Fruit,
bottom right

Celery Root–Cream Cheese Spread

Fat	–	10 min.
Cholesterol	–	
Fiber	●	

Per serving: approx. 130 calories
5 g protein · 3 g fat · 22 g carbohydrates

MAKES 2 SERVINGS
¾ cup (175 mL /100 g) celery root
1 tbsp (15 mL) freshly squeezed
   lemon juice
¼ cup (50 mL/50 g) low-fat cream
   cheese
Pinch freshly ground nutmeg
Salt and freshly ground white
   pepper
1 tbsp (15 mL) chopped walnuts

1 Peel and finely chop celery root. Toss immediately with the lemon juice to prevent discoloration. Stir in the cream cheese, season with the nutmeg, salt and pepper and let sit to combine flavors. Sprinkle with walnuts and serve.

!! **TIP** Goes well with sandwich bread.

!! **TIP** By regulation, standard North American cream cheeses contain not less than 33% milk fat by weight, but it is now possible to choose from a wide variety of fat-reduced products that contain 20%, 5% or virtually no milk fat at all. These products are often labelled "light", "made with buttermilk" (or yogurt), "sport" or "fitness."

Kidney Bean Spread

Fat	●	10 min.
Cholesterol	–	
Fiber	●●●	

Per serving: approx. 446 calories
30 g protein · 4 g fat · 77 g carbohydrates

MAKES 2 SERVINGS
1 can (19 oz/540 mL) red kidney
   beans
1 small onion
1 clove garlic
1 tsp (15 mL) sunflower or canola oil
1 tsp (5 mL) freshly squeezed lemon
   juice or white wine vinegar
Salt and freshly ground black
   pepper
Pinch cayenne pepper
1 tbsp (15 mL) chopped fresh parsley

1 Rinse the kidney beans and drain well.

2 Peel and mince onion and garlic. Heat the oil in a nonstick skillet. On low heat, cook the onion until translucent; add the garlic and sauté lightly.

3 With a blender or food processor, purée the kidney beans. Mix the bean purée with the onions and garlic. Season with lemon juice, salt, pepper and cayenne. Garnish with parsley and serve.

!! **FYI** Can be stored, covered, for up to 3 days in the refrigerator.

!! **TIP** This spread goes well with flatbreads or French bread, but it's perfect for flour tortillas (whole wheat is preferred). Cover the tortillas with bean spread, garnish with 1 or 2 thin tomato slices and a few strips of lettuce, and roll or fold as desired.

Sweet Apple Spread

Fat	–	10 min.
Cholesterol	7 mg	
Fiber	●	

Per serving: approx. 126 calories
6 g protein · 3 g fat · 17 g carbohydrates

MAKES 2 SERVINGS
3 heaping tbsp (45 mL) wheat germ
1 large apple (about 5 oz/150 g
   cleaned)
1 tbsp (15 mL) freshly squeezed
   lemon juice
¼ cup (50mL/50 g) low-fat cream
   cheese
1 tsp (5 mL) vanilla sugar
Pinch ground cloves
Ground cinnamon

1 On medium heat, toast the wheat germ in a dry nonstick skillet for 2 to 3 minutes, stirring constantly. Leave to cool on a plate (it would continue to brown in the hot pan).

2 Peel, core and chop apple. Use a blender or food processor to purée the apple and lemon juice.

3 Stir in the wheat germ and cream cheese until creamy. Season with the vanilla sugar, cloves and cinnamon.

!! **TIP** Toast, crispbread or French bread go well with this spread.

!! **TIP** Wheat germ is the most valuable part of the grain. It delivers protein, essential fatty acids, lecithin, B vitamins, vitamin E, minerals and trace elements, and it's rich in fiber.

Kidney Bean Spread, top
Sweet Apple Spread, bottom

Almond-Cress Spread

Fat	●	10 min.
Cholesterol	3 mg	
Fiber	●	

Per serving: approx. 95 calories
7 g protein · 6 g fat · 3 g carbohydrates

MAKES 2 SERVINGS
10 whole almonds (or 2 tbsp/
   30 mL/20 g ground)
¼ bunch chives
1 bunch pepper cress or watercress
½ cup (125 mL/100 g) creamy low-
   fat quark, puréed cottage cheese
   or strained yogurt
Salt and freshly ground white
   pepper

1 Grind the almonds until fine in a blender or food processor. Chop the chives finely. Using kitchen scissors, trim the cress; rinse and drain well.

2 Combine the almonds, quark, chives and cress (reserving some for a garnish), stirring to form a creamy paste. Season with salt and pepper. Garnish with the reserved chives and cress.

!! **TIP** This spread goes well with any whole-grain or rye bread.

!! **TIP** Nuts and seeds taste best when lightly roasted. Toast in a dry skillet until golden.

Herbed Yeast Flake Paste

Fat	●●●	10 min.
Cholesterol	9 mg	
Fiber	●	

Per serving: approx. 116 calories
2 g protein · 11 g fat · 1 g carbohydrates

MAKES 2 SERVINGS
3 tbsp (45 mL/40 g) diet margarine
⅓ cup (75 mL) fine yeast flakes
¼ cup (50 mL /50 g) sour cream
¼ tsp (1 mL) vegetable stock powder
2 tbsp (30 mL) chopped fresh herbs,
   such as parsley and chives
Freshly ground black pepper

1 Combine the margarine, yeast flakes, sour cream, stock powder and herbs in a small mixing bowl; stir until creamy. Season well with pepper and refrigerate for 10 minutes, until firm.

!! **TIP** Whole-grain breads and raw vegetables— cucumber slices with cress or tomato slices with basil—go well with this spread.

!! **TIP** In preparing this spread, use a diet margarine containing plant sterols. Studies have shown that LDL cholesterol will decrease by 10% to 15% in a short time if you substitute about 1½ tbsp (22 mL /20 g) of this type of margarine for other fat-based spreads daily.

Smoked Fish Spread

Fat	–	10 min.
Cholesterol	–	
Fiber	–	

Per serving: approx. 54 calories
9 g protein · 1 g fat · 3 g carbohydrates

MAKES 2 SERVINGS
½ cup (125 mL/100 g) low-fat quark,
   puréed cottage cheese or strained
   yogurt
1 oz (25 g) smoked fish, such as
   Kieler sprats, mackerel or trout
   (fillets or canned)
½ tsp (2 mL) prepared horseradish
½ tsp (2 mL) Dijon mustard
½ small onion
Salt
Freshly ground black pepper

1 With a blender or food processor, purée the quark, smoked fish, horseradish and mustard until smooth and creamy. Add mineral water as needed.

2 Peel the onion, mince and fold into the cream (do not purée). Season with salt and pepper.

!! **TIP** This spread goes well with whole-grain bread or rolls. It also goes well with radishes, tomatoes or other types of vegetables.

Almond-Cress Spread, top
Herbed Yeast Flake Paste, bottom
left
Smoked Fish Spread, bottom right

Soy-Hazelnut Cream

Fat	+	5 min.
Cholesterol	−	
Fiber	−	

Per serving: approx. 190 calories
5 g protein · 15 g fat · 8 g carbohydrates

MAKES 2 SERVINGS
3 tsp (45 mL) hazelnut butter or
  puréed hazelnuts
3 tbsp (45 mL) plain soy milk
1 tbsp (15 mL) low-fat quark, puréed
  cottage cheese or strained yogurt
½ tsp (2 mL) freshly squeezed
  lemon juice
1 tbsp (15 mL) liquid honey or a few
  drops liquid sweetener

1 Combine the hazelnut butter, soy milk, quark and lemon juice; stir until creamy. Sweeten with honey or sweetener.

!! **TIP** Use sparingly on bread or crispbread. Garnish with fresh fruit, such as slices of banana or kiwi.

Mediterranean Spread

Fat	●	15 min.
Cholesterol	−	
Fiber	●●●	

Per serving: approx. 81 calories
3 g protein · 6 g fat · 3 g carbohydrates

MAKES 2 SERVINGS
¼ cup (50 mL/40 g) sunflower seeds
12 green olives, pitted
1 clove garlic
½ cup (125 mL/100 g) plain soy
  milk, creamy low-fat quark,
  puréed cottage cheese or strained
  yogurt
1 heaping tsp (5 mL) capers
½ tsp (2 mL) balsamic vinegar

1 On low heat, toast the sunflower seeds in a dry nonstick skillet until golden. Remove from the heat and set aside.

2 Drain olives, if necessary, and cut them in half. Peel and coarsely chop garlic. Use a blender or food processor to purée the soy milk or quark, olives, capers, garlic, vinegar and sunflower seeds until creamy.

!! **TIP** This flavorful spread goes best with white bread. Use it as you would other spreads, such as diet margarine, but sparingly. Spread thinly and garnish with a few tomato slices.

Radish-Tofu Spread

Fat	●	10 min.
Cholesterol	−	
Fiber	●●	

Per serving: approx. 244 calories
10 g protein · 4 g fat · 43 g carbohydrates

MAKES 2 SERVINGS
3½ oz (100 g) smoked or extra-firm
  flavored tofu
4 radishes
1 tbsp (15 mL) freshly squeezed
  lemon juice
1 tbsp (15 mL) plain soy milk or
  low-fat yogurt
¼ bunch chives
Freshly ground white pepper

1 Coarsely dice the tofu. Wash and quarter the radishes.

2 With a blender or food processor, purée the tofu and radishes with the lemon juice and soy milk or yogurt. Finely slice the chives and stir into the milk. Season the spread well with pepper.

!! **TIP** This spread goes especially well with dark rye or pumpernickel bread.

!! **FYI** Plain soy milk is low fat, cholesterol free and neutral tasting. You can use it as you would cream, milk, sour cream or yogurt to make spreads, salad dressings, desserts, soups and sauces, or for vegetable gratins and casserole dishes.

Mediterranean Spread, top
Radish-Tofu Spread, bottom

Cottage Cheese with Peppers and Curry

Fat	●	10 min.
Cholesterol	8 mg	
Fiber	●●	

Per serving: approx. 286 calories
19 g protein · 5 g fat · 44 g carbohydrates

MAKES 2 SERVINGS
⅔ cup (150 mL/150 g) low-fat
   cottage cheese
1 tsp (5 mL) curry powder
2 to 3 small gherkins
4 black olives, pitted
½ red bell pepper
Salt and freshly ground black
   pepper
2 whole-grain rolls

1 Combine the cottage cheese
and curry powder. Finely dice
the gherkin and olives. Halve and
clean the red pepper. Dice one
half; slice the other half into
strips.

2 Stir the diced pepper, gherkin
and olives into the cottage
cheese. Season well with salt and
pepper.

3 Cut the whole-grain rolls in
half. Spread each half with
cottage cheese mixture and garnish with pepper strips.

!! TIP If you like spicy
foods, you can also slice
half a chili pepper and
combine it with the cottage
cheese. Or add a pinch of an
Asian chili sauce, such as sambal
oelek, to spice it up.

Low-Fat Liptauer

Fat	–	15 min.
Cholesterol	–	
Fiber	●	

Per serving: approx. 61 calories
9 g protein · 2 g fat · 2 g carbohydrates

MAKES ENOUGH SPREAD FOR
4 TO 5 ROLLS
3 oz (80 g) limburger or romadur
   cheese (10% mf), low-fat cream
   cheese, neufchâtel or boursin
⅔ cup (150 mL/150 g) creamy low-
   fat quark, puréed cottage cheese
   or strained yogurt
1 tsp (5 mL) hot paprika
1 tsp (5 mL) anchovy paste
1 tsp (5 mL) dry mustard
½ small red bell pepper
1 small red onion
1 gherkin
1 tsp (5 mL) capers
Salt and freshly ground pepper

1 Dice the limburger or cream
cheese. In a food processor,
purée with the quark. Stir in the
paprika, anchovy paste and
mustard.

2 Finely mince the pepper,
onion and gherkin. Chop the
capers. Combine with the cheese
and season well with salt and
pepper.

!! TIP Cover slices of coarse
rye or whole-grain bread
with the Liptauer spread.
Slice a small red onion into thin
rings to use as a garnish or use
finely chopped chives.

!! TIP This spread can be
stored in an air-tight
container in the refrigerator for several days.

Apple Cheese with Onion Rings

Fat	–	15 min.
Cholesterol	–	
Fiber	●	

Per serving: approx. 188 calories
13 g protein · 3 g fat · 27 g carbohydrates

MAKES 2 SERVINGS
1 small onion
1 small apple (about 3½ oz/
   100 g cleaned)
1 tsp (5 mL) canola oil
2 tsp (10 mL) granulated sugar
Freshly ground black pepper
⅔ cup (150 mL/150 g) creamy low-
   fat quark, puréed cottage cheese
   or strained yogurt
Salt
4 crispbreads

1 Peel the onion and finely slice
into rings. Peel, quarter and
core the apple; cut the quarters
into slivers approximately 1 inch
(2.5 cm) long.

2 Using a brush, coat a skillet
with the oil and cook the
onion rings on low heat until
lightly browned. Remove and set
aside. Add the sugar and apple
slivers to the same pan and stir
until tender and golden. Season
well with pepper and let cool.

3 Fold the apples into the quark
and season with salt. Spread
the apple cheese over the crispbreads. Sprinkle with ground
pepper and garnish with onion
rings.

Cottage Cheese with Peppers and
Curry, top
Low-Fat Liptauer, bottom left
Apple Cheese with Onion Rings,
bottom right

Marjoram Millet Spread

Fat	+	25 min.
Cholesterol	2 mg	
Fiber	●●●	

Per serving: approx. 425 calories
10 g protein · 16 g fat · 59 g carbohydrates

MAKES 2 SERVINGS
½ cup (125 mL) vegetable stock
¼ cup (50 mL/50 g) millet
1 small red onion
⅓ cup (75 mL, about 2 oz/60 g) mushrooms
1 tbsp (15 mL) canola oil
1 tsp (5 mL) dried marjoram
1 tsp (5 mL) dried thyme
½ tsp (2 mL) salt
½ tsp (2 mL) green peppercorns
3 tbsp (45 mL/40 g) diet margarine
1 to 2 tomatoes
2 slices whole-grain bread

1 Combine the vegetable stock and millet and bring to a boil. Lower the heat and cook for 20 minutes, until tender.

2 Meanwhile, peel and finely chop onion. Clean and finely dice mushrooms. Heat the oil in a nonstick skillet. On low heat, cook the onions until translucent. Add the diced mushrooms and cook for 1 to 2 minutes. Stir in the marjoram and thyme.

3 In a blender or food processor, combine the millet, mushrooms, salt, peppercorns and margarine; purée to form a fine paste.

4 Slice the tomatoes. Spread the bread slices with the paste and garnish with the tomato slices.

!! **TIP** This recipe can be doubled and stored in a tightly sealed jar in the refrigerator for up to 1 week.

Strawberry Cheese with Corn Flakes

Fat	–	10 min.
Cholesterol	–	
Fiber	●	

Per serving: approx. 175 calories
18 g protein · 1 g fat · 24 g carbohydrates

MAKES 2 SERVINGS
1¼ cup (200 mL/200 g) strawberries
1 tbsp (15 mL) maple syrup or 1 tsp (5 mL) vanilla sugar
Freshly ground black pepper
1 cup (250 mL/250 g) low-fat quark, puréed cottage cheese or strained yogurt
2 tbsp (30 mL) chopped fresh lemon balm
4 tbsp (50 mL) corn flakes cereal or old-fashioned rolled oats

1 Carefully wash, drain and hull strawberries. Set two aside for garnishing. Mash the remaining fruit with a fork or food processor.

2 Stir in the maple syrup or vanilla sugar and season well with pepper. Stir in the quark until smooth and fold in the lemon balm. Sprinkle with corn-flakes or rolled oats and serve.

!! **TIP** Go ahead and season the strawberry quark with black pepper to taste—it will balance the sweetness of the fruit.

Pumpernickel with Oranges and Cheese

Fat	●	15 min.
Cholesterol	11 mg	
Fiber	●●●	

Per serving: approx. 304 calories
24 g protein · 5 g fat · 41 g carbohydrates

MAKES 2 SERVINGS
½ cup (125 mL/100 g) low-fat quark, puréed cottage cheese or strained yogurt
2 tbsp (30 mL) orange marmalade
4 slices pumpernickel
3½ oz (100 g) Gouda, limburger or romadur cheese (10% to 12% mf), neufchâtel or low-fat cream cheese
Freshly ground black pepper
1 orange
Freshly ground coriander seeds

1 Combine the quark and orange marmalade with a splash of mineral water; stir until creamy. Spread over the pumpernickel slices. Thinly slice the Gouda or cream cheese; season well with pepper.

2 Peel the orange. Cut each segment out from the pith. Distribute the orange segments over the cheese and sprinkle with ground coriander.

!! **TIP** Partially skimmed cream cheese (sometimes known as neufchâtel) contains relatively little cholesterol, about 22 mg per oz (30 g). Partially skimmed limburger (perhaps the closest relation to the hard-to-find German romadur cheese) and Gouda and three-quarter skimmed Tilsit are also available; all can be used in a cholesterol-reduced diet.

Strawberry Cheese with Corn Flakes, top
Marjoram Millet Spread, bottom left
Pumpernickel with Oranges and Cheese, bottom right

Salmon Cream on Dark Rye

Fat	+	20 min.
Cholesterol	44 mg	
Fiber	●●●	

Per serving: approx. 437 calories
30 g protein · 15 g fat · 46 g carbohydrates

MAKES 2 SERVINGS
3 whole juniper berries
1 piece lemon zest
7 oz (200 g) salmon fillet
2 tbsp (30 mL) freshly squeezed
    lemon juice, divided
¼ cup (50 mL/50 g) low-fat quark,
    puréed cottage cheese or strained
    yogurt
Salt and freshly ground pepper
3 basil leaves
1 small red bell pepper
4 slices dark rye bread

1 Crush the juniper berries and combine with the lemon zest and some water in a small saucepan with a steamer attachment. Bring to a boil.

2 Skin the salmon and place in the steamer. Cook for 10 minutes, remove and let cool.

3 Shred the fish and purée with 1 tbsp (15 mL) lemon juice and the quark. Stir in the remaining lemon juice, salt and pepper. Slice the basil leaves into fine strips and mix half into the cream.

4 Slice the pepper into strips. Spread the salmon cream on the bread slices and garnish with the remaining basil and pepper strips.

!! **TIP** The salmon cream can be stored, sealed, in the refrigerator for 2 to 3 days. It's cool, light and delightful as an appetizer or as part of a cold buffet.

Turkey Breast and Fresh Figs on Spelt Slices

Fat	●●	15 min.
Cholesterol	75 mg	
Fiber	●●	

Per serving: approx. 330 calories
34 g protein · 7 g fat · 33 g carbohydrates

MAKES 2 SERVINGS:
2 pieces (about 3½ oz/100 g each)
    turkey breast
Salt and freshly ground black
    pepper
2 ripe figs
1 tbsp (15 mL) olive or canola oil
1 tbsp (15 mL) soy sauce
1 tbsp (15 mL) Worcestershire sauce
2 thick or 4 thin slices spelt bread

1 Remove any fat or sinew from the breast, lightly pound flat and season with salt and pepper. Carefully clean the figs and slice thinly.

2 On medium heat, heat the oil in a nonstick skillet and cook the turkey for 3 to 4 minutes a side, until golden. Remove and set aside. Warm the fig slices in the oil left over in the skillet.

3 Mix the soy and Worcestershire sauce with 2 tbsp (30 mL) water. Stir into the figs and reduce.

4 Place a piece of turkey on a thick slice of spelt bread. Pour the figs and sauce over and serve. Or put the turkey and figs on 2 thick slices and cover with the other 2 slices of bread. Quickly press together and wrap in aluminum foil or plastic wrap for a takeout lunch.

Whole-Grain Bread with Roast Beef

Fat	●	10 min.
Cholesterol	35 mg	
Fiber	●	

Per serving: approx. 255 calories
16 g protein · 6 g fat · 35 g carbohydrates

MAKES 2 SERVINGS
2 slices whole-grain bread
2 tsp (10 mL/10 g) diet margarine
2 tbsp (30 mL) freshly chopped
    mixed Italian herbs, such as pars-
    ley, oregano, marjoram and
    rosemary
Salt and freshly ground black
    pepper
1 piece (about 2 inches/ 5 cm)
    cucumber
3½ oz (100 g) thinly sliced roast
    beef
2 tsp (10 mL) prepared horseradish
2 tbsp (30 mL) chopped chives or
    watercress

1 Toast the whole-grain bread. Stir the diet margarine and herbs until smooth. Season with salt and pepper. Spread over the bread slices.

2 Thinly peel the cucumber, halve lengthwise, remove seeds and cut into thin slices. Arrange over the herb spread.

3 Roll the slices of roast beef to form small cones, add a little horseradish to each cone and arrange on the bread. Sprinkle with chives or cress and serve.

!! **VARIATION** You can use other herbs, such as herbes de Provence, dill or a salad mix.

Salmon Cream on Dark Rye, top
Turkey Breast and Fresh Figs on
Spelt Slices, bottom left
Whole-Grain Bread with Roast Beef,
bottom right

Tofu Spread with Mushrooms

Fat	●●	
Cholesterol	–	
Fiber	●●	20 min.

Per serving: approx. 196 calories
9 g protein · 8 g fat · 22 g carbohydrates

MAKES 2 SERVINGS
3½ oz (100 g) soft smoked
 or flavored tofu
1 tbsp (15 mL) soy sauce
Freshly ground coriander
 seeds
2 slices whole-grain bread
3½ oz (100 g) mushrooms
 (cremini preferred)
1 clove garlic
1 tbsp (15 mL) olive oil
2 green (spring) onions
Salt and freshly ground
 black pepper

1 With a blender or food processor, purée the tofu and season with soy sauce and coriander. Spread over the bread slices.

2 Clean and coarsely chop mushrooms. Peel the garlic and crush in a garlic press.

3 On medium heat, heat the oil in a non-stick skillet. Cook the mushrooms and garlic, stirring constantly. Finely slice the green onions. Distribute the cooked mushrooms and green onions over the bread, pressing lightly down into the spread. Season well with salt and pepper and serve.

TIP Instead of coriander, you can use caraway seeds for this spread.

Open-Faced Tofu Sandwich with Tomatoes and Basil

Fat	●●	
Cholesterol	–	
Fiber	●●●	15 min.

Per serving: approx. 262 calories
10 g protein · 8 g fat · 37 g carbohydrates

MAKES 2 SERVINGS
3½ oz (100 g) firm smoked
 or extra-firm flavored tofu
1 shallot
1 tsp (5 mL) olive oil
Freshly ground black
 pepper
1 tbsp (15 mL) mild bal-
 samic vinegar
1 ripe beefsteak tomato
 (about 5 oz/150 g)
6 basil leaves
2 slices dark rye bread
Salt

1 Cut the tofu into 6 thin slices. Peel the shallot and finely slice into rings.

2 On medium heat, heat the olive oil in a nonstick skillet. Sauté the tofu slices and shallot until brown on both sides. Season with pepper. Pour in the vinegar, remove from the heat and let the flavors combine.

3 Halve and slice the tomato. Rub the basil leaves to release their flavor and place on the bread slices, alternating with the tofu and tomato slices. Sprinkle the shallot rings on top. Season with salt and more pepper.

TIP You can also toast the rye bread and rub it with garlic.

Flax Seed Bread with Lox

Fat	●●●	10 min.
Cholesterol	13 mg	
Fiber	●●	

Per serving: approx. 326 calories
28 g protein · 10 g fat · 37 g carbohydrates

MAKES 2 SERVINGS
4 thin slices flax seed bread
½ cup (125 mL/100 g) low-fat quark, puréed cottage cheese or strained yogurt
2 tbsp (30 mL) plain soy milk
Salt and freshly ground black pepper
1 tsp (5 mL) anchovy paste
1 to 2 tsp (5 to 10 mL) freshly squeezed lemon juice
1 small bunch pepper cress or watercress
2 oz (50 g) lox (cured, or smoked, salmon)
10 snow peas or 2 green (spring) onions

1 Toast the bread slices. Combine the quark with the soy milk, salt, pepper, anchovy paste and lemon juice; stir until smooth.

2 Trim the cress, coarsely chop and fold in. Spread the mixture over the bread slices and garnish with the lox slices. Season with pepper.

3 Slice the snow peas or green onions into strips. Distribute the strips over the sandwiches.

Mango Quark on Flax Seed Rolls

Fat	–	10 min.
Cholesterol	–	
Fiber	●●	

Per serving: approx. 284 calories
13 g protein · 3 g fat · 50 g carbohydrates

MAKES 2 SERVINGS
2 flax seed rolls
½ mango (about 5 oz/150 g prepared)
½ cup (125 mL/100 g) low-fat quark, puréed cottage cheese or strained yogurt
1 tbsp (15 mL) granulated sugar
Pinch ground cinnamon
1 tbsp (15 mL) sliced almonds
10 red or black grapes
2 sprigs mint

1 Cut the rolls in half and toast. Cut the mango flesh into sections and remove from the peel. Purée one-third with the quark, sugar and cinnamon.

2 Finely dice the remaining mango and fold into the purée (or reserve some to sprinkle over the rolls). Spread the cream over the rolls. On low heat, toast the almonds in a dry non-stick skillet until golden. Sprinkle over the rolls.

3 Wash and slice grapes, removing any pits. Sprinkle over the rolls. Garnish with mint sprigs.

TIP Mango quark also tastes great on its own as a snack.

Soups, Salads and Dips

Mushroom Vinaigrette

Fat	●●●	5 min.
Cholesterol	–	
Fiber	–	

Per serving: approx. 97 calories
0 g protein · 10 g fat · 2 g carbohydrates

MAKES 2 SERVINGS
1 mushroom
1 clove garlic
1 tbsp (15 mL) sunflower oil
4 tbsp (60 mL) sherry vinegar
Salt and freshly ground white
　pepper
1 pinch granulated sugar

1 Clean and mince the mushroom. Peel the garlic.

2 Mix the oil, vinegar, 1 tbsp (15 mL) water, salt and pepper. Crush the garlic in a garlic press and mix in. Stir in the sugar. Mix in the minced mushroom.

!! **TIP** Mushroom vinaigrette tastes great with lamb's lettuce (corn salad, or mâche), but it also goes well with all leafy salads.

!! **TARRAGON VINAIGRETTE** Instead of the mushroom, use dried or fresh tarragon, ½ tsp (2 mL) dry mustard and ½ tsp (2 mL) condensed milk and mix with a blender. This is also a great dip for artichokes.

Light Yogurt Mayonnaise

Fat	●	5 min.
Cholesterol	–	
Fiber	–	

Per serving: approx. 82 calories
3 g protein · 5 g fat · 5 g carbohydrates

MAKES 2 SERVINGS
1 tbsp (15 mL) sunflower or corn oil
1 tsp (5 mL) medium-hot prepared
　mustard
½ tsp (2 mL) granulated sugar or
　4 drops liquid sweetener
½ tsp (2 mL) vegetable stock
　powder
1 clove garlic
⅔ cup (150mL/150 g) low-fat yogurt

1 Whisk together the oil, mustard, sugar or sweetener, and stock powder. Peel the garlic, crush in a garlic press and stir in. Gradually whisk in the yogurt, stirring constantly until the sauce is creamy.

!! **TIP** Instead of using garlic, you can try other seasonings, such as curry powder, horseradish, soy sauce or fresh herbs.

!! **TIP** Yogurt mayonnaise makes a perfect accompaniment for cooked vegetables—cauliflower, broccoli, zucchini, turnips, kohlrabi or carrots—and can also serve as a dressing for vegetable, potato, pasta and rice salads.

Apple-Soy Mayonnaise with Mustard

Fat	–	5 min.
Cholesterol	–	
Fiber	–	

Per serving: approx. 52 calories
2 g protein · 2 g fat · 7 g carbohydrates

MAKES 2 SERVINGS
1 small apple
⅓ cup + 2 tbsp (100 mL/100 g) plain
　soy milk
1 tsp (5 mL) tomato paste
2 tsp (10 mL) Dijon mustard
1 tsp (5 mL) freshly squeezed lemon
　juice
Salt and freshly ground white
　pepper
½ tsp (2 mL) granulated sugar or
　4 drops liquid sweetener

1 Peel, core and coarsely dice the apple.

2 In a blender or food processor, purée the apple, soy milk, tomato paste, mustard and lemon juice. Stir in the salt, pepper and sugar or sweetener.

!! **FYI** Dijon mustard gives apple-soy mayonnaise a spicy bite that resembles horseradish—which is why it serves particularly well as a dip for grain-and-vegetable patties; as a dressing for rice, pasta or potato salads with vegetables; or with lox or smoked fish, lightly smoked pork, low-fat cold cuts or ham.

Mushroom Vinaigrette, top
Light Yogurt Mayonnaise, bottom
left
Apple-Soy Mayonnaise with
Mustard, bottom right

Anchovy–Cream Cheese Dip for Raw Vegetables

Fat	●	5 min.
Cholesterol	23 mg	
Fiber	–	

Per serving: approx. 123 calories
13 g protein · 5 g fat · 3 g carbohydrates

MAKES 2 SERVINGS
½ cup (125 mL/100 g) low-fat cream cheese
½ cup (50 mL/50 g) low-fat quark, puréed cottage cheese
   or strained yogurt
4 anchovy fillets
1 tbsp (15 mL) capers
½ tsp (2 mL) sweet paprika
1 tbsp (15 mL) gin (optional)
Sweet paprika and capers

1 In a small mixing bowl, use a hand-held blender (or use a regular blender or food processor) to purée the cream cheese with the quark, anchovies, capers and paprika, gin, if using, or 1 tbsp (15 mL) water, until it forms a smooth yet firm cream. If the cream is too firm, add a little liquid from the capers.

2 Serve the dip in a small bowl, dust with a little paprika and garnish with a few chopped capers.

TIP Sticks made from raw vegetables, such as carrots, zucchini, kohlrabi, peppers, celery, fennel and cucumbers, are ideal for dipping. Serve the raw vegetable sticks and anchovy–cream cheese dip as an appetizer with crackers.

TIP Spread the anchovy–cream cheese dip over hearty dark bread and garnish with finely grated carrot.

Tuna Sauce for Cooked Vegetables

Fat	●	5 min.
Cholesterol	30 mg	
Fiber	–	

Per serving: approx. 125 calories
20 g protein · 4 g fat · 1 g carbohydrates

MAKES 2 SERVINGS
1 can (6 oz/170 g) tuna packed in water
¼ cup (50 mL) clear vegetable stock
⅓ cup + 2 tbsp (100 mL) condensed milk (4%)
1 tbsp (15 mL) capers
1 tbsp (15 mL) freshly squeezed lemon juice
Salt and freshly ground black pepper

1 Drain the tuna, reserving the liquid. With a blender or food procesor, purée the tuna, vegetable stock, condensed milk and capers, adding the reserved liquid as needed to thin the mixture. Season well with lemon juice, salt and pepper, and chill until ready to serve.

TIP The best way to use this sauce is over warm vegetables—carrot, kohlrabi, zucchini and fennel wedges or sticks, and green beans—cooked or stewed in a little vegetable stock but still tender-crisp. To serve, arrange the vegetables on a plate, pour the tuna sauce over and sprinkle with finely sliced green onions. Multigrain or white bread goes best with this sauce.

Anchovy–Cream Cheese Dip for Raw Vegetables, top
Tuna Sauce for Cooked Vegetables, bottom

Corn Salad (Mâche) with Puréed Mango

Fat	●●●	20 min.
Cholesterol	–	
Fiber	●	

Per serving: approx. 160 calories
3 g protein · 14 g fat · 11 g carbohydrates

MAKES 2 SERVINGS
5 oz (150 g) corn salad (mâche, or lamb's lettuce)
2 to 3 tbsp (30 to 45 mL) white balsamic vinegar, divided
½ mango (about 3½ oz/100 g cleaned)
1 tbsp (15 mL) olive oil
½ tsp (2 tsp) liquid honey
Pinch grated fresh ginger
2 tbsp (30 mL) vegetable stock
Salt and freshly ground white pepper
2 tbsp (30 mL) pine nuts

1 Thoroughly wash the corn salad and spin dry. Divide between two plates. Sprinkle with 1 tbsp (15 mL) vinegar.

2 Cut the flesh of the mango into sections and remove from the peel. With a blender or food processor, purée the mango, olive oil, honey, ginger and vegetable stock. Season with the remaining vinegar, salt and pepper. Spoon over the greens.

3 Coarsely chop the pine nuts and toast on low heat in a dry nonstick skillet until golden; sprinkle over the salad and serve.

!! TIP Canned mango or fresh peaches can also be used.

Potato-Pear Salad

Fat	–	45 min.
Cholesterol	–	
Fiber	●●●	

Per serving: approx. 231 calories
6 g protein · 1 g fat · 49 g carbohydrates

MAKES 2 SERVINGS
1 lb (500 g) small potatoes (such as fingerling, Kipfler or baby Yukon Golds)
4 tbsp (60 mL) white wine vinegar
3 tbsp (45 mL) soy milk
1 tbsp (15 mL) maple syrup or granulated sugar
Salt and freshly ground white pepper
2 small or 1 large ripe pear
1 red bell pepper

1 Wash the potatoes and cook for 20 to 25 minutes with the skins on. Let cool slightly, peel and slice thinly.

2 To make the dressing, combine the vinegar, soy milk and maple syrup or sugar. Season with salt and pepper and mix with the potatoes.

3 Peel the pears, cut into wedges, core and dice. Dice the pepper. Fold in.

!! TIP Try sprinkling this salad with 1 to 2 tbsp (15 to 30 ML) pumpkinseed oil—an Austrian specialty available in specialty markets. It's rich in vitamin E and omega-3 fats and gives salads a particularly fine, nutty flavor.

Red Cabbage with Orange Dressing

Fat	●●	55 min.
Cholesterol	–	
Fiber	●●	

Per serving: approx. 179 calories
4 g protein · 7 g fat · 27 g carbohydrates

MAKES 2 SERVINGS
½ small red cabbage (about 10 oz/ 300 g)
1 orange
2 plums
2 tbsp (30 mL) raisins
Salt and freshly ground black pepper
½ tsp (2 mL) ground allspice
1 tbsp (15 mL) walnut oil
2 tbsp (30 mL) chopped walnuts

1 Trim the outer leaves and center stalk of the cabbage. Using a mandoline or sharp knife, finely slice the cabbage.

2 Halve the orange; peel and dice the fruit of one half. Halve, pit and cut the plums into thin wedges. Mix the cabbage with the diced orange, plums and raisins.

3 Squeeze the juice of the other orange half. To prepare the dressing, mix the orange juice, salt, pepper, allspice and oil. Pour over the red cabbage, toss well and let the flavors blend for 30 minutes.

4 Before serving, toast the walnuts in a dry nonstick skillet and sprinkle over the red cabbage.

!! TIP Nuts should be toasted before the salad is assembled otherwise it will wilt from the dressing.

Corn Salad (Mâche) with Puréed Mango, top
Potato-Pear Salad, bottom left
Red Cabbage with Orange Dressing, bottom right

Bulgur Salad with Turkey

Fat	●	25 min.
Cholesterol	31 mg	
Fiber	●●●	

Per serving: approx. 333 calories
22 g protein · 6 g fat · 53 g carbohydrates

FOR 2 TO 3 SERVINGS

¾ cup (175 mL/150 g) bulgur (finely ground wheat groats)
1¼ cups (300 mL) vegetable stock or water and salt
½ tsp (2 mL) hot paprika
1 tsp (5 mL) dried oregano
5 oz (150 g) turkey cutlet
Freshly ground black pepper
1 tbsp (15 mL) olive oil
3 tbsp (45 mL) white balsamic or white wine vinegar
1 tbsp (15 mL) lemon oil or 1 tbsp (15 mL) canola oil and the zest of ½ lemon
1 yellow bell pepper
1 beefsteak tomato
1 red onion
2 tbsp (30 mL) chopped chives

1 Bring the bulgur, stock or salted water, paprika and oregano to a boil. Cook on low heat for 20 minutes, until all the liquid has been absorbed.

2 Remove any fat or sinews from the turkey cutlet, lightly pound flat and season with salt and pepper. On medium heat, heat the olive oil in a nonstick skillet and sauté the cutlet on each side for 4 to 5 minutes, until golden. Set aside.

3 To make the dressing, cook the juices left in the skillet with a little water. Stir in the vinegar and lemon oil, scraping up any brown bits, and season.

4 Slice the turkey. Dice the yellow pepper. Blanch the tomato, for 1 minute in boiling water, peel and dice. Peel the onion and finely slice into rings. In a bowl, combine the bulgur, turkey, vegetables and dressing. Sprinkle with chives and serve.

Sprout Salad with Millet

Fat	●●	35 min.
Cholesterol	56 mg	
Fiber	●●	

Per serving: approx. 161 calories
15 g protein · 8 g fat · 9 g carbohydrates

MAKES 2 SERVINGS

1¼ cups (300 mL) vegetable stock
½ cup (125 mL/100 g) millet
1 tbsp (15 mL) soy sauce
2 tbsp (30 mL) white wine vinegar
¼ inch (0.5 cm) piece fresh ginger
1 tbsp (15 mL) olive oil
3½ oz (100 g) cremini mushrooms
7 oz (200 g) bean sprouts (about 2 cups/500mL)
Freshly ground black pepper
3 tbsp (45 mL) chopped chives

1 Bring the stock to a boil. Turn down the heat, add the millet and cook, covered, for 25 minutes, until all the liquid has been absorbed.

2 For the dressing, mix the soy sauce and vinegar. Peel, grate and stir in the ginger. Whisk in the olive oil.

3 Clean the mushrooms and slice finely. Chop the sprouts coarsely. Mix the mushroom and sprouts with the dressing, season with pepper and let the flavors combine for a minute or two. Fold in the millet. Divide between two plates, sprinkle with chives and serve.

!! **VARIATIONS** You can also use radishes or green (spring) onions. And instead of millet, use bulgur or rice. What's important is that the salad contain enough fiber—it helps lower cholesterol.

Lettuce Hearts with Shiitakes

Fat	●●●	25 min.
Cholesterol	–	
Fiber	●●●	

Per serving: approx. 493 calories
13 g protein · 12 g fat · 101 g carbohydrates

MAKES 2 SERVINGS

2 lettuce hearts
2 shallots
8 oz (250 g) shiitake or oyster mushrooms
1 orange
1 tbsp (15 mL) canola oil
Freshly ground black pepper
Chopped fresh coriander
2 tbsp (30 mL) white wine vinegar
1 tsp (5 mL) tomato paste
Salt and freshly ground black pepper
1 tbsp (15 mL) olive oil
1 small bunch pepper cress or watercress

1 Tear the lettuce hearts, wash, spin dry, and spread out on two plates.

2 Peel the shallots and dice finely. Clean the mushrooms and trim off the hard stems. Tear (do not cut!) the caps into ½ inch (1 cm) pieces. Squeeze the juice from the orange.

3 Heat the canola oil in a large nonstick skillet until very hot. Sauté the shallots, mushrooms, pepper and coriander, stirring constantly. Pour in the orange juice and white wine vinegar, and immediately remove from the heat.

4 Whisk the tomato paste, salt, pepper and olive oil. Distribute the mushrooms and orange sauce over the lettuce leaves. Drizzle with the dressing. Cut the cress into fine pieces over the salad.

**Bulgur Salad with Turkey, top
Sprout Salad with Millet, bottom left
Lettuce Hearts with Shiitakes, bottom right**

Salmon Tartare on Zucchini Carpaccio

Fat	●●	20 min.
Cholesterol	16 mg	
Fiber	–	

Per serving: approx. 149 calories
14 g protein · 8 g fat · 6 g carbohydrates

MAKES 2 SERVINGS
1 shallot
2½ oz (75 g) lox (cured, or smoked, salmon)
Salt and freshly ground black pepper
2 tsp (10 mL) freshly squeezed lemon juice
3 tbsp (45 mL) chopped fresh dill, divided
1 small zucchini
2 tbsp (30 mL) cider vinegar
¼ cup (150 mL/50 g) low-fat yogurt
2 black olives

1 Peel the shallot and dice very finely. Trim any brown edges off the salmon (these are fatty and taste oily). Finely dice the salmon and combine with the shallot, salt, pepper, lemon juice and 1 tbsp (15 mL) dill. Cover and let the flavors combine for 15 minutes.

2 Slice the zucchini paper-thin on a mandoline. Arrange on two plates and drizzle with the cider vinegar.

3 Place a round cookie cutter or mold, 2½ inches (6 cm) in diameter, in the center of the zucchini slices and carefully fill with the tartare. Pat down firmly and carefully lift the mold.

4 Combine the yogurt, salt and remaining dill, and distribute around the tartar. Garnish with the olives and serve.

Beet Carpaccio with Goat's Milk Cream Cheese

Fat	●●●	25 min.
Cholesterol	18 mg	
Fiber	●	

Per serving: approx. 209 calories
17 g protein · 12 g fat · 10 g carbohydrates

MAKES 2 SERVINGS
8 oz (250 g) cooked beets
Chopped fresh coriander
Freshly ground white pepper
Cider-balsamic vinegar
8 fennel seeds
2 tsp (10 mL) prepared horseradish

FOR THE CREAM CHEESE
3½-oz (100 g) log goat's milk cheese (25% mf) or goat's milk cream cheese
2 tbsp (30 mL/30 g) soy milk
4 tbsp (60 mL/60 g) low-fat quark, puréed cottage cheese or strained yogurt
Salt and freshly ground black pepper

1 Finely slice the beets on a mandoline and divide between two large plates. Sprinkle with coriander and pepper, and drizzle with vinegar. Coarsely chop the fennel seeds and divide between the plates. Cover with plastic wrap and allow the flavors to blend for at least 15 minutes.

2 Using a fork, mash the goat's milk or cream cheese. Stir in the soy milk and quark until smooth. Season with salt and pepper.

3 Before serving, place 1 dollop of cream cheese and 3 tiny dollops of horseradish in the center of each slice of beet.

!! **TIP** Serve with whole-grain baguette or rye rolls.

!! **TIP** If you can't find cider-balsamic vinegar, mix balsamic and cider vinegars in equal proportions.

Salmon Tartare on Zucchini Carpaccio, top
Red Beet Carpaccio with Goat's Milk Cream Cheese, bottom

Tomato Soup with Banana

Fat	+	15 min.
Cholesterol	6 mg	
Fiber	●●●	

Per serving: approx. 233 calories
5 g protein · 15 g fat · 19 g carbohydrates

MAKES 2 SERVINGS
1 small onion (about 2 oz/50 g)
1 medium banana (about 5 oz/150 g)
1 tbsp (15 mL) sunflower oil
1 can (28 oz/796 mL) tomatoes,
    strained to leave about 1 lb
    (500 g) and puréed
2 cups (500 mL) chicken or beef
    stock
2 tbsp (30 mL) half-and-half (10%)
    cream
Salt and freshly ground white
    pepper
2 tsp (10) shredded or fresh grated
    coconut

1 Peel and dice onion. Peel the banana and slice into thin rounds.

2 On low heat, heat the oil in a skillet and cook the onion until translucent. Add the banana slices, sauté slightly and mash gently (or reserve to use as a garnish).

3 Transfer the tomato purée to a saucepan, stir in the stock and cook on low heat for 5 minutes. Stir in the onion, banana, cream, salt and pepper. Sprinkle with coconut and serve.

‼ TIP A good accompaniment to toast.

‼ TIP Shredded or grated coconut tastes even better when it's toasted in a dry nonstick skillet on low heat until golden.

Creamy Mixed Vegetables

Fat	●●	15 min.
Cholesterol	3 mg	
Fiber	●●●	

Per serving: approx. 107 calories
1 g protein · 7 g fat · 9 g carbohydrates

MAKES 2 SERVINGS
3 to 4 oz (100 g) raw vegetables or
    leftover cooked vegetables
1 cooked potato or 1 tbsp (15 mL)
    instant potato flakes
1 tbsp (15 mL) sunflower oil
2 tsp (10 mL) vegetable stock
    powder
Fresh herbs, such as parsley, chives,
    cress

1 Coarsely grate or mince the raw vegetables. Coarsely dice the potato.

2 Bring the vegetables, oil, stock and 2 cups (500 mL) water to a boil, and cook for 5 to 10 minutes. Use a blender or food processor to purée the vegetables, diced potato or potato flakes.

3 Finely chop the herbs, sprinkle on the soup and serve immediately.

‼ TIP Depending on the vegetables you are using, this soup can be seasoned in a number of ways. A mixture of leek, kohlrabi, carrots and celery can be seasoned with freshly ground white or black pepper; spinach and red cabbage with nutmeg; cauliflower and broccoli with minced garlic. The soup can be enhanced as desired by adding 1 to 2 tbsp (15 to 30 mL) plain soy milk or low-fat yogurt.

Onion Soup with Mushrooms

Fat	–	30 min.
Cholesterol	13 mg	
Fiber	●●●	

Per serving: approx. 117 calories
4 g protein · 3 g fat · 15 g carbohydrates

MAKES 2 SERVINGS
7 oz (200 g) onions (about
    1⅓ cups/325 mL sliced)
3½ oz (100 g) mushrooms (about
    ½ cup/125 mL sliced)
3 cups (750 mL) beef stock
2 tsp (10 mL) Dijon mustard
¼ cup (50 mL/20 g) small pasta or
    noodles
Salt and freshly ground black
    pepper
½ bunch parsley

1 Peel, halve and slice the onions into thin strips. Clean the mushrooms and slice thinly.

2 In a saucepan, on low heat, bring the stock to a boil and simmer the onions for 5 minutes. Stir in the mushrooms and cook for 5 minutes. Stir in the mustard. Add the noodles and cook for 5 minutes, until done. Season with salt and pepper.

3 Finely chop the parsley. Put the soup in two bowls, sprinkle with parsley and serve.

Tomato Soup with Banana, top
Creamy Mixed Vegetables, bottom
left
Onion Soup with Mushrooms,
bottom right

Tomato Soup Provençale

Fat	●●●	30 min.
Cholesterol	1 mg	
Fiber	●●	

Per serving: approx. 148 calories
3 g protein · 11 g fat · 8 g carbohydrates

MAKES 2 SERVINGS
1 lb (500 g) plum tomatoes
1 medium onion
2 tbsp (15 mL) olive oil
1 clove garlic
¾ cup + 2 tbsp (200 mL) vegetable
    stock
Salt and freshly ground black
    pepper
Herbes de Provence or 4 to 6 sprigs
    lavender (with blossoms, if
    possible)

1 Cut an X in the bottom of the
tomatoes, blanch in boiling
water for 1 minute, peel and dice
coarsely.

2 Peel and finely dice the onion.
Heat the oil in a saucepan. On
low heat, cook the onion until
translucent. Peel the garlic and
crush in a garlic press.

3 Stir in the tomato and stock.
Season with salt, pepper and
herbes de Provence (or pluck the
leaves and the blossoms of lavender. Set aside the blossoms, finely
chop the leaves and stir into the
soup). Cover and simmer on low
heat for 20 minutes.

4 Adjust the seasoning with salt
and pepper, sprinkle with
lavender blossoms (if using)
and serve.

!! **TIP** This soup is also
good cold. Cover and
store overnight in the
refrigerator.

Quick Minestrone with Pesto

Fat	●●	15 min.
Cholesterol	7 mg	
Fiber	●	

Per serving: approx. 154 calories
8 g protein · 7 g fat · 11 g carbohydrates

MAKES 2 SERVINGS
10 oz (300 g) frozen mixed
    vegetables
1¼ cups (300 mL) vegetable stock
Salt and freshly ground white
    pepper
2 tbsp (30 mL) prepared pesto
2 tbsp (30 mL) freshly grated
    Parmesan cheese

1 Place the frozen vegetables in
a saucepan and pour in the
stock. Bring to a boil, cover and
simmer on medium heat for 10
minutes.

2 Season the soup with salt and
pepper and put into two
bowls. Garnish each bowl with
1 tbsp (15 mL) pesto and 1 tbsp
(15 mL) Parmesan.

!! **TIP** You can buy the
beloved basil paste from
Liguria already prepared
or you can make your own pesto
quickly and easily. Toast 2 tbsp
(30 mL) pine nuts in a skillet
until golden. Peel 3 cloves garlic
and chop coarsely. Combine the
pine nuts, garlic and 1 large
bunch basil leaves (about
2 cups/500 mL) in a mortar,
blender or food processor.
Grind to a paste with about
½ cup (125 mL) olive oil. Spoon
into a small bowl and stir in
⅓ cup (75 mL/50 g) freshly
grated Parmesan. Store any
remaining pesto in a small glass
jar with a screw-top lid, cover
with olive oil and seal tightly.
Store in the refrigerator for up
to 2 weeks.

Barley Soup with Peas

Fat	●●	25 min.
Cholesterol	3 mg	
Fiber	●●●	

Per serving: approx. 323 calories
11 g protein · 8 g fat · 49 g carbohydrates

MAKES 2 SERVINGS
7 tbsp (105 mL/100 g) barley
2 cloves garlic
1 tbsp (15 mL) canola oil
2½ cups (625 mL) vegetable stock
1 tsp (5 mL) hot paprika
1½ cups (375 mL/200 g) frozen peas
Salt and freshly ground pepper
2 tbsp (30 mL) chopped chives

1 Thoroughly rinse the barley
in cold water.

2 Peel the garlic and slice into
fine rounds. Over medium
heat, heat the oil in a nonstick
saucepan and sauté garlic until
golden. Add the barley and cook
until translucent.

3 Pour in the stock and season
with paprika. Turn down the
heat, cover the soup and simmer
for 10 to 15 minutes, until barley
is tender. Add the frozen peas
and cook for a further 3 to
5 minutes.

4 Season well with salt and
pepper, sprinkle with chives
and serve.

Tomato Soup Provençale, top
Quick Minestrone with Pesto,
bottom left
Barley Soup with Peas, bottom right

East Indian Chicken Soup

Fat	++	30 min.
Cholesterol	30 mg	
Fiber	●	

Per serving: approx. 641 calories
36 g protein · 26 g fat · 65 g carbohydrates

MAKES 2 SERVINGS
4 oz (125 g) chicken breast
1 small onion
¼-inch (0.5 cm) piece fresh ginger
1 tbsp (15 mL) vegetable oil
1 tbsp (15 mL) whole wheat flour
1 tbsp (15 mL) curry powder
2 cups (500 mL) chicken stock
1 small apple
Salt and freshly ground black pepper
2 tbsp (30 mL) chopped fresh coriander or parsley

1 Finely dice the chicken breast. Peel the onion and ginger; dice finely.

2 Heat the oil in a nonstick saucepan. On medium heat, sauté the chicken and onion until golden. Add the ginger and cook slightly. Dust with flour and stir well. Stir in the curry powder and chicken stock. Bring to a boil, turn down the heat and simmer for 10 minutes.

3 Meanwhile, peel, core and finely dice the apple. Add to the soup and simmer for 2 minutes, until tender. Season with salt and pepper, sprinkle with chopped coriander or parsley and serve.

!! **VARIATION** To make this soup a bit more exotic, add slices of banana to the soup with the pieces of apple.

Dill Soup with Millet

Fat	●	35 min.
Cholesterol	6 mg	
Fiber	●●●	

Per serving: approx. 208 calories
6 g protein · 5 g fat · 33 g carbohydrates

MAKES 2 SERVINGS
6 tbsp (90 mL/80 g) millet
2½ cups (625 mL) chicken or vegetable stock
1 leek
1 bunch dill
Salt and freshly ground black pepper
1 to 2 tbsp (15 to 30 mL) freshly squeezed lemon juice
2 tbsp (30 mL) sour cream

1 Toast the millet in a dry nonstick skillet on low heat until the little balls "jump." Pour in the stock and bring to a boil. Simmer on low heat for 10 minutes.

2 Meanwhile, cut the leek lengthwise, wash thoroughly and slice. Finely chop the dill. Stir the leek and half the dill to the soup and simmer for another 20 minutes.

3 Stir in salt, pepper and lemon juice, and remove from the stove. Stir the sour cream until smooth and fold into the soup (which should not cook any longer). Ladle into two warm bowls, sprinkle with the remaining dill and serve.

!! **TIP** Whole-grain croutons are great with this soup. Take 1 slice of whole-grain bread, about ¼ inch (1 cm) thick, spread with a thin layer of diet margarine, wrap in plastic wrap and let stand for 10 minutes with a weight resting on top. Cut into ¼-inch (1 cm) cubes and sauté in a dry nonstick skillet until crisp.

!! **VARIATION** Instead of millet, you can prepare this soup with the same amount of bulgur or buckwheat. These grains will give you the fiber you need.

East Indian Chicken Soup, top
Dill Soup with Millet, bottom

Potato-Mushroom Soup with Cinnamon Croutons

Fat	●●	35 min.
Cholesterol	3 mg	
Fiber	●●●	

Per serving: approx. 203 calories
4 g protein · 8 g fat · 27 g carbohydrates

MAKES 2 SERVINGS
1 small onion
2 small potatoes (8 oz/250 g)
1 tbsp (15 mL) olive oil
2 cups (500 mL) vegetable stock
2 oz (50 g) fresh chanterelles or 1 oz (25 g) dried porcini (cèpes)
Salt and freshly ground white pepper
2 tbsp (30 mL) chopped chives

FOR THE CROUTONS
1 tsp (5 mL) diet margarine
½ tsp (2 mL) ground cinnamon
1 thin slice rye bread

1 Peel and finely dice onion. Peel the potatoes and cut into roughly ¼ inch (1 cm) cubes. Heat the oil in a nonstick saucepan. On low heat, cook the onions until translucent and pour in the stock. Add the potato and cook for 10 minutes.

2 Clean the mushrooms and cut into strips (dried mushrooms will need to be soaked in hot water for 20 minutes to rehydrate).

3 To prepare the croutons, mix the diet margarine and the cinnamon and spread over the bread. Dice the bread. Heat a small dry nonstick skillet and sauté until crisp.

4 Coarsely purée the soup—chunks of potato should still be visible. Season with salt and pepper, sprinkle with chives and croutons and serve.

Creamy Squash Soup

Fat	●●	35 min.
Cholesterol	5 mg	
Fiber	●●●	

Per serving: approx. 188 calories
4 g protein · 8 g fat · 21 g carbohydrates

MAKES 4 SERVINGS
2 shallots
2 medium carrots
1 lb (500 g) cleaned orange squash, such as hokkaido, butternut or turban
1 tbsp (15 mL) vegetable oil
4 cups (1 L) vegetable stock
Juice from ½ orange
Salt and freshly ground black pepper
Pinch cayenne pepper
4 tbsp (60 mL) soy milk or low-fat yogurt

1 Peel and dice the shallots. Peel and slice carrots. Peel, seed and dice squash.

2 Heat the oil in a nonstick saucepan and cook the shallot on low heat until translucent. Stir in the squash and cook for a minute. Pour in the stock. Add the carrots and cook for 15 minutes.

3 Remove a few carrot rounds, dice and set aside. Purée the soup until smooth. Stir in orange juice, salt, pepper and cayenne.

4 Ladle into four warm bowls, spoon some diced carrot into the center of each and drizzle 1 tbsp (15 mL) soy milk around the carrots.

Cream of Pepper Soup with Soy Milk

Fat	●●●	30 min.
Cholesterol	–	
Fiber	●●●	

Per serving: approx. 172 calories
10 g protein · 11 g fat · 10 g carbohydrates

MAKES 2 SERVINGS
1 yellow bell pepper
1 red bell pepper
1 shallot
1 tbsp (15 mL) canola oil
2½ cups (625 mL) plain soy milk
1 tbsp (15 mL) white balsamic vinegar or white wine vinegar
Salt and freshly ground black pepper
Hot pepper sauce
2 tbsp (30 mL) chopped chives

1 Clean and coarsely chop the peppers. Peel and finely dice the shallot.

2 Heat the oil in a deep non-stick saucepan and cook the shallot on low heat until translucent. Add the peppers and cook slightly. Pour in the soy milk and cook, uncovered, for 20 minutes, stirring often.

3 Purée the soup until smooth, strain through a sieve to remove any remaining pepper skins and reheat. Season well with vinegar, salt, pepper and few drops of hot pepper sauce. Sprinkle with chives and serve.

!! **TIP** You can also use all red or all yellow peppers. If you like spicy foods, slice a jalapeño pepper and cook it with the bell peppers.

Potato-Mushroom Soup with Cinnamon Croutons, top
Creamy Winter Squash Soup, bottom left
Cream of Pepper Soup with Soy Milk, bottom right

Vegetables and Legumes

Potato Curry

Fat   ●   40 min.
Cholesterol   –
Fiber   ●●●

Per serving: approx. 247 calories
9 g protein · 6 g fat · 39 g carbohydrates

MAKES 2 SERVINGS
3 waxy potatoes (about 1 lb/500 g), such as Yukon golds
1 medium carrot
1 tbsp (15 mL) canola oil
1 tbsp (15 mL) vegetable stock (or more, as required)
2 medium tomatoes
1 small leek
1 clove garlic
½ inch (1 cm) piece fresh ginger
1 small green chili pepper
2 tsp (10 mL) garam masala
⅔ cup (150 mL/150 g) skim milk yogurt
¼ tsp (1 mL) whole wheat flour
1 tbsp (15 mL) freshly squeezed lemon juice
Salt and freshly ground black pepper
2 sprigs mint

1 Peel the potatoes and carrots; cut into 1 inch (2.5 cm) cubes. On medium heat, heat the oil in a nonstick skillet and sauté the potatoes and carrots for 20 minutes, stirring often. Stir in the vegetable stock.

2 Meanwhile, cut an X in the bottom of the tomatoes and blanch for 1 minute in boiling water. Peel, quarter, gently squeeze out the seeds and dice the flesh. Slice the leek lengthwise, wash thoroughly, and slice the white and pale green parts.

3 Peel and finely chop garlic and ginger. Slice the chili lengthwise and scrape out the seeds, if desired. Chop finely and add to the potatoes and carrots along with the garlic, ginger and leek. Sauté lightly. Stir in the garam masala.

4 Combine the yogurt with the flour and stir until smooth, then add to the vegetable mixture. Stir in the tomatoes. Cook on low heat for 10 minutes. Season with lemon juice, salt and pepper. Finely slice or chop mint leaves; sprinkle over the curry and serve.

!! **TIP** The chili pepper makes this curry quite fiery. If you like milder curry, leave it out or deseed it.

Potato-Tomato Gratin

Fat   ●●●   15 min.
Cholesterol   25 mg   (+ 30 min. baking)
Fiber   ●●

Per serving: approx. 294 calories
14 g protein · 13 g fat · 28 g carbohydrates

LARGE OVENPROOF DISH

MAKES 2 SERVINGS
2 or 3 waxy potatoes (about 14 oz/400 g), such as Yukon golds
2 beefsteak tomatoes (about 14 oz/400 g)
4 anchovy fillets in oil
1 to 2 cloves garlic
Salt and freshly ground black pepper
¼ tsp (1 mL) dried thyme
¼ tsp (1 mL) dried oregano
1 tbsp (15 mL) olive oil
2 oz (50 g) grated Gouda or Edam cheese (reduced-fat preferred)

1 Wash the potatoes and cook with the skins on for 20 to 25 minutes; let cool. Meanwhile, preheat the oven to 400°F (200°C). Peel the potatoes and slice into rounds. Slice the tomatoes. Drain and coarsely chop anchovy fillets. Peel and mince garlic.

2 Layer the potato slices in the casserole dish; sprinkle with salt and thyme. Distribute the tomato slices overtop, then the anchovies and garlic. Season with salt, pepper and oregano. Drizzle with oil.

3 Cover the dish and bake in the preheated oven for 20 minutes. Remove the cover, sprinkle with the cheese and bake for another 10 minutes.

!! **TIP** This dish can be served as a main course with a leafy salad of choice. It's also an excellent side dish with lightly roasted fish or meat.

!! **TIP** Choose a potato that keeps its shape when it's cooked instead of mealy (floury) mashing or baking types.

Potato Curry, top
Potato-Tomato Gratin, bottom

Potato-Bean Stir-Fry

Fat	●●●	45 min.
Cholesterol	–	
Fiber	●●●	

Per serving: approx. 305 calories
8 g protein · 13 g fat · 32 g carbohydrates

MAKES 2 SERVINGS
3 or 4 small waxy potatoes (about 14 oz/400 g), such as
 Yukon golds
1½ cups (375 mL/200 g) green beans
5 cooked or canned artichoke hearts
1 small onion
2 cloves garlic
½ bunch flat-leaf (Italian) parsley
2 tbsp (30 mL) olive oil
Salt and freshly ground black pepper
1 tbsp (15 mL) pine nuts
1 tsp (5 mL) green peppercorns
1 tbsp (15 mL) balsamic vinegar

1 Thoroughly wash the potatoes and cook with the skins on for 20 to 25 minutes; let cool. Peel the potatoes and halve lengthwise.

2 Clean and finely chop beans; boil in salted water or steam for 8 minutes, until tender-crisp. Transfer to a sieve, plunge in ice water and drain well.

3 Drain and quarter the artichoke hearts. Peel, halve and slice onion into fine strips. Peel and finely chop garlic. Coarsely chop parsley.

4 Heat the oil in a large skillet or wok. On medium heat, cook the potatoes, turning and sautéing each side until golden. Season with salt and pepper. Move the potato slices to the side of the skillet. Stir the onion and garlic into the center and lightly sauté. Add the beans and pine nuts and sauté for 5 minutes, stirring occasionally. Add the artichokes and green peppercorns and heat thoroughly. Stir in the vinegar and parsley and serve.

TIP You can combine the potatoes with the vegetables before adding the artichokes.

Puréed Squash with Tomato

Fat	–	30 min.
Cholesterol	–	
Fiber	●●●	

Per serving: approx. 71 calories
3 g protein · 1 g fat · 13 g carbohydrates

MAKES 2 SERVINGS
14 to 16 oz (400 to 500 g) cleaned orange squash, such as
 butternut or hokkaido
½ tsp (2 mL) ground caraway seeds
1 tomato
Salt and freshly ground black pepper
Hot pepper sauce
1 tbsp (15 mL) chopped fresh basil

1 Peel, clean and dice squash. Place in a saucepan and cover with water. Season with caraway, cover, and simmer on low heat for 20 minutes, until tender.

2 Meanwhile, cut an X in the bottom of the tomato, blanch in boiling water for 1 minute, peel, gently squeeze out the seeds and dice the flesh. Keep warm.

3 Drain the squash, reserving some of the cooking liquid. Purée in a blender or food processor, adding liquid as needed to make a smooth mixture. Season with salt, pepper and a few dashes of hot pepper sauce. Transfer the puréed squash to a serving dish, fold in the basil and tomato and serve hot.

TIP Grilled meat or chickpea patties (see recipe, page 102) go well with this dish.

VEGETABLES AND LEGUMES

Potato-Bean Stir-Fry, top
Puréed Squash with Tomato, bottom

East Indian–Style Vegetables with Yogurt

Fat	●●●	50 min.
Cholesterol	–	
Fiber	●●●	

Per serving: approx. 226 calories
9 g protein · 14 g fat · 16 g carbohydrates

MAKES 2 SERVINGS
1 red chili pepper
¼ inch (0.5 cm) piece fresh ginger
1 clove garlic
1 medium onion
1½ medium zucchini (about 8 oz/250 g)
1 small Japanese eggplant (about 8 oz/ 250 g)
1¼ cups (300 mL/125 g) green beans
⅔ cup (150 mL/150 g) skim milk yogurt
1 tsp (5 mL) whole wheat flour
1 tbsp (15 mL) ground almonds
1 tbsp (15 mL) tomato paste
⅓ cup (75 mL) vegetable stock
2 tbsp (30 mL) soy oil
1 to 2 tsp (5 to 10 mL) garam masala
½ to 1 tsp (2 to 5 mL) ground cumin
Salt
Fresh coriander

1 Slice the chili lengthwise and remove seeds, if desired; chop finely. Peel and finely chop ginger and garlic. Peel and dice onion. Cut the zucchini, eggplant and beans into bite-sized pieces. Combine the yogurt, flour, almonds, tomato paste and stock; stir until smooth.

2 Heat the oil in a skillet. On low heat, cook the onion, chili, ginger and garlic, stirring constantly, for 2 minutes. Stir in the garam masala and cumin, and cook until fragrant. Stir in the yogurt mixture.

3 Add the vegetables, mix well and simmer, covered, on low heat, stirring occasionally, for 20 minutes. Season with salt. Coarsely chop coriander, sprinkle overtop and serve.

!! **TIP** Basmati rice goes well with this dish. Cook about ⅓ cup (75 mL/2 oz/60 g) per serving according to package instructions.

Cauliflower with Herb Sauce

Fat	●●	25 min.
Cholesterol	177 mg	
Fiber	●●	

Per serving: approx. 189 calories
19 g protein · 9 g fat · 9 g carbohydrates

MAKES 2 SERVINGS
1 small cauliflower (about 1 lb/500 g)
1 egg
½ bunch parsley
½ bunch chives
¾ cup + 2 tbsp (200 mL/200 g) creamy low-fat quark, puréed cottage cheese or strained yogurt
½ tsp (2 mL) prepared horseradish
½ tsp (2 mL) medium-hot prepared mustard
Salt and freshly ground white pepper
2 oz (60 g) cooked ham
1 tbsp (15 mL) freshly grated Parmesan cheese

1 Cut the cauliflower into florets; cook in salted water for 10 minutes. Add the egg and cook for another 8 to 10 minutes, until firm.

2 Finely chop the parsley and chives. Combine the quark with the horseradish, water as needed and mustard, stirring until creamy. Stir in the herbs, reserving 1 tbsp (15 mL). Season with salt and pepper. Finely dice the ham.

3 Drain the cauliflower. Plunge the egg in ice water, peel and dice. In a small bowl, combine the diced ham and egg with the Parmesan and reserved herbs.

4 Arrange the cauliflower on two plates, garnish with the herb sauce and sprinkle with the diced ham and egg mixture.

!! **TIP** Boiled potatoes go well with this dish. Use 1 medium-sized Yukon gold or 2 small red potatoes (about 5 oz/150 g) per serving, which will add 105 calories.

East Indian–Style Vegetables with Yogurt, top
Cauliflower with Herb Sauce, bottom

TVP and Zucchini Casserole

Fat	+		35 min.
Cholesterol	29 mg		(+ 35 to 40 min. baking)
Fiber	●●●		

Per serving: approx. 305 calories
29 g protein · 15 g fat · 12 g carbohydrates

MEDIUM-SIZED OVENPROOF DISH

MAKES 2 SERVINGS
1 cup (250 mL) vegetable stock
½ cup (125 mL/60 g) texturized vegetable protein (TVP)
   slices
2 cloves garlic
1 tsp (5 mL) herbes de Provence
2 small zucchini (about 8 oz/250 g)
5 large green olives, pitted
½ bunch parsley
2 medium tomatoes (about 8 oz/250 g)
½ tsp (2 mL) dried sage
Salt and freshly ground black pepper
1 onion
1 tsp (5 mL) olive oil
4 oz (125 g) mozzarella (low-fat preferred)

1 Heat the stock and pour over the TVP slices. Peel the garlic and crush in a garlic press. Stir in the herbes de Provence and let sit for 10 minutes.

2 Slice the zucchini into thin rounds. Coarsely chop the olives. Finely chop parsley. Combine the zucchini, tomatoes, olives and parsley. Season well with sage, salt and pepper.

3 Preheat the oven to 350°F (180°C). Peel and finely dice onion. Heat the olive oil in a nonstick skillet. Lower the heat and cook the onion until translucent. Stir in the TVP slices and sauté for 4 minutes, stirring constantly.

4 Place the vegetables and TVP slices in alternating layers in the casserole dish, ending with a layer of zucchini. Cover and bake for 35 minutes. Slice the mozzarella. Remove the cover and distribute the mozzarella over the casserole; bake until the cheese has melted, about 10 minutes more.

FYI Texturized soy products—slices, chunks or small crumbles—are steeped in double their amount of water, vegetable or yeast stock before use. This gives the soy a meatlike consistency and allows it to be used as a meat substitute. This product is fat and cholesterol free and quite tasteless, so season it well.

TVP Curry with Bananas

Fat	●●		20 min.
Cholesterol	10 mg		(+ 25 min. soaking)
Fiber	●●●		

Per serving: approx. 240 calories
15 g protein · 9 g fat · 26 g carbohydrates

MAKES 2 SERVINGS
1 cup (250 mL) vegetable stock
½ cup (125 mL/60 g) texturized vegetable protein (TVP)
   chunks
1 small onion
1 small apple
1 large banana
1 tbsp (15 mL) freshly squeezed lemon juice
1 tbsp (15 mL) sunflower oil
1 tsp (5 mL) raisins
¼ cup (50 mL/50 g) sour cream
1 heaping tsp (5 mL) curry powder
Salt and freshly ground white pepper
Cayenne pepper
Freshly squeezed lemon juice

1 Heat the stock and add the TVP chunks. Cover and soak overnight or at least 25 minutes.

2 Drain the TVP chunks, reserving the liquid. Halve the chunks. Peel and finely chop onion. Peel, quarter, core and dice apple. Peel the banana and slice into rounds. Mix the apple and banana with the lemon juice.

3 Heat the oil in a skillet. On low heat, cook the onion until translucent. On medium heat, add the TVP pieces and sauté on all sides for 5 minutes, turning constantly. Stir in the diced apple, banana rounds and raisins and cook, covered, for 4 minutes.

4 Mix the sour cream and curry powder into the reserved soaking liquid. Pour into the skillet and heat through, stirring constantly, but don't bring to a boil. Season with salt, pepper, cayenne and lemon juice to taste.

TIP Rice goes well with this dish.

TVP Curry with Bananas, top
TVP and Zucchini Casserole, bottom

Baked Eggplant with Tzatziki

Fat	+		25 min.
Cholesterol	25 mg		(+ 45 min. baking)
Fiber	●●●		

Per serving: approx. 236 calories
6 g protein · 18 g fat · 12 g carbohydrates

PREHEAT OVEN TO 400°F (200°C)
LARGE OVENPROOF DISH

MAKES 2 SERVINGS
1 small eggplant (about 14 oz/400 g)
2 cloves garlic
2 tbsp (30 mL) olive oil
Salt and freshly ground black pepper
1 small bunch parsley

FOR THE TZATZIKI
1 cucumber
Salt
⅔ cup (150 mL/150 g) Greek-style yogurt or
    low-fat sour cream
1 clove garlic
Freshly ground white pepper
¼ bunch fresh dill

1 Wash and coarsely dice eggplant. Peel and finely chop garlic.

2 Place the eggplant, garlic and oil in the casserole dish, sprinkle with salt and pepper and mix well. Bake, covered, in the preheated oven for 45 minutes.

3 To make the tzatziki, peel and finely grate the cucumber. Sprinkle with salt and let sit. Drain and gently wring out as much excess liquid as you can. Mix with the yogurt or sour cream. Peel the garlic and crush in a garlic press. Season with pepper. Finely chop dill and fold in.

4 Coarsely chop the parsley. Combine with the eggplant and serve with tzatziki.

!! **TIP** Flatbreads or French bread go well with this dish.

Bulgarian-Style Peppers with Sheep's Milk Cheese

Fat	●●●		30 min.
Cholesterol	19 mg		
Fiber	●●●		

Per serving: approx. 185 calories
11 g protein · 13 g fat · 5 g carbohydrates

MAKES 2 SERVINGS
2 large red bell peppers (about 14 oz/400 g)
1 tbsp (15 mL) olive oil
Salt and freshly ground black pepper
4 oz (125 g) sheep's milk cheese (22% mf), such as
    halloumi or feta

1 Quarter the peppers lengthwise, remove the seeds and cut into strips. Heat the oil in a skillet. Lightly sauté the pepper strips, then cook, covered, on medium heat for 10 minutes, stirring occasionally.

2 Season with salt and pepper. Crumble the cheese and sprinkle overtop, cover and allow the cheese to melt slightly.

!! **TIP** Baguette or mashed potatoes go well with this dish.

!! **TIP** If you can't stand (or digest) the pepper skins, broil or bake first, skin side up, until the peppers turn brown and form blisters. Wrap in a damp tea towel until you can handle the peppers and peel them.

Baked Eggplant with Tzatziki, top
Bulgarian-Style Peppers with Sheep's Milk Cheese, bottom

White Beans in Tomato-Sage Sauce

Fat	●●	80 min.
Cholesterol	1 mg	
Fiber	●●●	

Per serving: approx. 264 calories
15 g protein · 7 g fat · 37 g carbohydrates

MAKES 2 SERVINGS

¾ cup (175 mL/160 g) large dried lima or other white beans
1 sprig fresh or 1 tsp (5 mL) dried savory
1 tsp (5 mL) salt

FOR THE SAUCE
2 cloves garlic
1 tbsp (15 mL) olive oil
4 fresh sage leaves or 1 tsp (5 mL) dried sage
1 cup (250 mL/250 g) puréed tomatoes
1 tsp (5 mL) vegetable stock powder
¼ tsp (1 mL) dried thyme
Freshly ground white pepper

1 Wash the beans and soak overnight in 2 cups (500 mL) cold water. The next day, cook the beans, soaking liquid and savory for 1 hour on medium heat. Stir in the salt.

2 To prepare the sauce, peel the garlic. Just before the beans are done, heat the oil in a skillet and lightly sauté the sage. Crush the garlic with a garlic press and add to skillet. Pour in the puréed tomatoes, ⅔ cup (150 mL) water and the stock powder. Stir in the thyme and pepper and bring to a boil.

3 Drain the beans and remove the savory sprig. Mix the beans with the sauce, cover and cook on low heat for 20 minutes.

!! **TIP** Grilled meat goes well with this dish, as does baguette or flatbread for dipping in the sauce.

Red Lentils with Carrots and Leek

Fat	●●●	40 min.
Cholesterol	3 mg	
Fiber	●●●	

Per serving: approx. 309 calories
15 g protein · 13 g fat · 33 g carbohydrates

MAKES 2 SERVINGS

2 medium carrots (about 5 oz/150 g)
1 leek (about 5 oz/150 g)
1 clove garlic
½ cup (125 mL/100 g) red lentils
1 tbsp (15 mL) sunflower oil
1 tsp (5 mL) turmeric
¼ tsp (1 mL) ground coriander seeds
¼ tsp (1 mL) ground black cumin
1 cup (250 mL) vegetable stock
1 tbsp (15 mL) dark (toasted) sesame oil
2 heaping tbsp (30 mL) low-fat sour cream or yogurt
2 tbsp (30 mL) chopped chives

1 Peel and coarsely grate the carrots. Carefully clean and finely slice the leek into rings. Peel and finely chop garlic. Place the red lentils in a sieve and rinse in cold running water.

2 Heat the oil in a skillet. On medium heat, lightly sauté the carrots. Add the garlic and sauté. Stir in the leek, lentils, turmeric, coriander, cumin and stock. Bring to a boil, cover, and cook on low heat for 15 minutes, until all the liquid has been absorbed.

3 Mix in the sesame oil and ladle into two bowls. Garnish each serving with 1 tbsp (15 mL) sour cream or yogurt, sprinkle with chives and serve.

!! **TIP** Basmati rice goes well with this dish. For each serving, cook ⅓ cup (75 mL/60 g) rice in ⅔ cup (150 mL) water, which will yield 1 cup (250 mL/200 g) cooked rice and add another 205 calories.

White Beans in Tomato-Sage Sauce, top
Red Lentils with Carrots and Leek, bottom

Horseradish-Radish Ragout with Noodles

Fat	●●●	25 min.
Cholesterol	–	
Fiber	●●●	

Per serving: approx. 356 calories
12 g protein · 12 g fat · 54 g carbohydrates

MAKES 2 SERVINGS
1 cup (250 mL/100 g) vermicelli or angel's hair pasta
½ medium-sized horseradish root (about 10 oz/300 g)
1 bunch radishes
4 dried tomatoes
1 bunch green (spring) onions
2 tbsp (30 mL) vegetable oil
Freshly ground black pepper
Ground coriander seeds
3 tbsp (45 mL) balsamic vinegar
Soy sauce

1 Bring a pot of salted water to a boil. Add the vermicelli and cook for 3 minutes. Pour the noodles into a sieve, plunge in ice water and drain.

2 Clean and peel horseradish, halve lengthwise and slice. Wash and quarter the radishes. Finely slice the tomatoes into thin strips. Cut the root ends off the green onions and slice into rings.

3 Heat the oil in a nonstick skillet. On low heat, cook the green onions and tomatoes until starting to soften. Add the horseradish and radishes and cook for 2 minutes, stirring constantly, until the horseradish becomes slightly translucent.

4 Stir in the vermicelli and season with pepper, coriander and vinegar. Sprinkle with soy sauce to taste.

Buckwheat Crêpes with Soy Sprouts

Fat	+	35 min.
Cholesterol	151 mg	
Fiber	●●	

Per serving: approx. 288 calories
11 g protein · 15 g fat · 28 g carbohydrates

MAKES 2 SERVINGS
½ cup (125 mL/60 g) buckwheat flour
⅓ cup + 2 tbsp (100 mL) skim, 1% or 2% milk
1 egg
Pinch salt
1 cup (250 mL/100 g) soy sprouts
1 yellow bell pepper
1 clove garlic
2 tbsp (30 mL) olive oil, divided
2 tbsp (30 mL) sambal oelek (Indonesian chili sauce)

1 Combine the buckwheat flour, milk, egg and salt; stir until smooth. Cover the batter and let stand for 10 minutes.

2 Meanwhile, coarsely chop the soy sprouts. Halve, clean and dice pepper. Peel and finely slice garlic. Heat 1 tbsp (15 mL) oil in a nonstick skillet. On low heat, cook the pepper and garlic. Stir in the soy sprouts and cook lightly, then set aside.

3 In a 10-inch (25 cm) skillet or crêpe pan, heat 1½ tsp (7 mL) oil. Pour in half the batter and cook on each side until golden. Repeat with the remaining oil and batter. Transfer each crêpe to a plate.

4 Arrange vegetables in a semi-circle on half of each crêpe and fold over. Drizzle with 1 tbsp (15 mL) sambal oelek and serve.

!! VARIATION You can add tofu to the filling, if desired. Drain about 2 oz (50 g) of firm tofu, cut into slivers and sauté with the diced pepper.

Horseradish-Radish Ragout with Noodles, top
Buckwheat Crêpes with Soy Sprouts, bottom

Broccoli Quiche

Fat	–	45 min.
Cholesterol	–	(+ 20 min. baking)
Fiber	●●●	

Per serving: approx. 92 calories
12 g protein · 2 g fat · 11 g carbohydrates

PREHEAT OVEN TO 350°F (180°C)
9-INCH (23 CM) QUICHE PAN, GREASED

MAKES 8 SERVINGS
FOR THE CRUST
¾ cup (175 mL/100 g) whole-grain spelt flour
3 tbsp (45 mL/25 g) soy flour
1 tsp (5 mL) baking powder
Pinch salt
⅓ cup (75 mL/75 g) low-fat quark, puréed cottage cheese
    or strained yogurt
4 tbsp (60 mL) mineral water

FOR THE FILLING
1 lb (500 g) broccoli
⅓ cup + 2 tbsp (100 mL/100 g) low-fat quark, puréed cot-
    tage cheese or strained yogurt
2 to 3 tbsp (30 to 45 mL) 1% or 2% milk
½ tsp (2 mL) fennel seeds
Salt and freshly ground black pepper
1 tsp (5 mL) red peppercorns

FOR THE YOGURT SAUCE
⅔ cup (150 mL/150 g) low-fat yogurt
1 tsp (5 mL) paprika
Salt
1 to 2 tsp (5 to 10 mL) freshly squeezed lemon juice

1 Quickly knead together the ingredients for the crust and roll out (don't add flour or the dough will get crumbly) to fit the prepared pan. Transfer to the prepared pan and poke a few holes with a fork.

2 Bring plenty of salted water to a boil. Cut the broccoli into florets. Peel and slice the stems and cook for 3 minutes. Add the florets and blanch for a further 2 minutes. Remove and drain well.

3 Purée the broccoli stems and half the florets with the quark, milk and fennel seeds. Season with salt and pepper. Pour over the dough. Distribute the remaining florets over the purée and sprinkle with the peppercorns. Bake for 20 minutes in the pre-heated oven, until the edge of the crust is crisp.

4 Meanwhile, combine the yogurt, paprika, salt and lemon juice. Cut the quiche into 8 pieces and serve with the yogurt sauce.

Pepper Pie

Fat	●	55 min.
Cholesterol	2 mg	(+ 30 min. resting)
Fiber	●●	(+ 20 min. baking)

Per serving: approx. 129 calories
5 g protein · 4 g fat · 19 g carbohydrates

PREHEAT OVEN TO 350°F (180°C)
9-INCH (23 CM) QUICHE PAN, GREASED

MAKES 8 SERVINGS
1½ cups (375 mL/200 g) whole-grain spelt flour
⅓ cup (75 mL), skim, 1% or 2% milk
1 package (¼ oz/7 g/2¼ tsp) active dry yeast
Pinch granulated sugar
2 tbsp (30 mL) olive oil, divided
2 green (spring) onions
2 cloves garlic
1 small eggplant
1 small zucchini
1 red bell pepper
1 green bell pepper
1 tbsp (15 mL) tomato paste
1 to 2 tsp (5 to 10 mL) dried oregano
Salt and freshly ground black pepper

1 Place the flour in a large bowl and make a well in the center. Heat the milk to body temperature and mix with the yeast and sugar. Pour into the well, cover and let rise for 15 minutes.

2 Add 1 tbsp (15 mL) oil and ¼ cup (50 mL) water and knead to form a smooth dough. Shape the dough into a ball, cover and let rise for 15 minutes.

3 Meanwhile, trim the root ends and slice the green onions into rings. Clean and slice the eggplant and zucchini into ¼ inch (0.5 cm) rounds. Halve, clean and cut the peppers into strips.

4 Heat the remaining 1 tbsp (15 mL) oil in a large nonstick skillet. On medium heat, sauté the green onions, garlic, eggplant and zucchini. Dilute the tomato paste with ⅓ cup + 2 tbsp (100mL) water and pour over the vegetables. Season with oregano, salt and pepper, and reduce the sauce slightly.

5 Roll out the dough and fit into the prepared pan. Distribute the vegetables and pepper strips over-top. Bake in the preheated oven for 20 minutes. Cut into 8 wedges and serve.

Pepper Pie, top
Broccoli Quiche, bottom

Stuffed Peppers with Tofu

Fat	+	20 min.
Cholesterol	1 mg	(+ 45 min. baking)
Fiber	●●●	

Per serving: approx. 486 calories
18 g protein · 19 g fat · 66 g carbohydrates

PREHEAT OVEN TO 350°F (180°C)
OVENPROOF DISH WITH A TOP

MAKES 2 SERVINGS
3 large yellow bell peppers
4 oz (125 g) smoked or extra-firm flavored tofu
2 cloves garlic
2 green (spring) onions
4 large mushrooms, such as portobellos
4 dried tomatoes
2 tbsp (30 mL) canola oil
Salt and freshly ground black pepper
½ tsp (2 mL) hot paprika
½ cup (125 mL/100 g) brown rice
1 cup (250 mL) vegetable stock
2 tbsp (30 mL) soy milk or low-fat sour cream

1 Slice the tops off 2 peppers. Clean the cavities and set aside to fill later. Halve, clean and dice the remaining pepper and tops.

2 Finely dice and purée the tofu. Peel the garlic and crush in a garlic press. Trim the root ends and finely dice the green onions. Clean and finely slice mushrooms. Finely dice dried tomatoes.

3 Heat the oil in a nonstick skillet. On low heat, cook the garlic and green onions until fragrant. Stir in the mushrooms and tomatoes, and cook briefly. Stir in the tofu. Season with salt, pepper and paprika. Fill the peppers with this mixture.

4 Wash the rice and mix into the stock in the casserole dish. Add the diced and stuffed peppers. Cover and bake for 35 to 40 minutes. Remove the lid and bake for another 5 minutes, until the rice has absorbed all the liquid.

5 Arrange the peppers on two plates. Mix the soy milk with the rice and serve on the side.

Whole Wheat Fusilli with Broccoli

Fat	+	25 min.
Cholesterol	20 mg	
Fiber	●●●	

Per serving: approx. 455 calories
25 g protein · 16 g fat · 53 g carbohydrates

MAKES 2 SERVINGS
1½ cups (375 mL/350 g) broccoli (about ⅔ medium bunch)
Salt
2 cups (500 mL/150 g) whole wheat fusilli or other spiral-shaped pasta
1 bunch green (spring) onions
1 tbsp (15 mL) olive oil
3½ oz (100 g) sheep's milk cheese
1 to 2 tbsp (15 to 30 mL), skim, 1% or 2% milk
Freshly ground nutmeg
Freshly ground white pepper
2 tbsp (30 mL) chopped fresh parsley

1 Divide the broccoli into florets. Peel and finely dice stems. Heat plenty of salted water in a large saucepan and blanch the florets for 2 minutes. Remove and plunge in ice water so they keep their color.

2 Cook the fusilli in the boiling broccoli water according to package instructions, until just al dente. Drain well.

3 Trim the root ends and finely slice the green onions. Heat the oil in a nonstick skillet. On low heat, cook the green onions and broccoli stems, stirring constantly, until starting to soften. Stir in the florets and cook briefly.

4 Crumble the sheep's milk cheese, mix with the milk and mash with a fork. Season well with nutmeg and pepper. Stir the cheese into the broccoli. Fold in the pasta and sprinkle with parsley. Serve hot or at room temperature.

!! **VARIATION** Use half the amount of sheep's milk cheese and replace it with tofu. The meal will contain only 10 mg of cholesterol and 11 g of fat. Mash the tofu with a fork and combine with the cheese.

Stuffed Pepper with Tofu, top
Whole Wheat Fusilli with Broccoli, bottom

Vegetable Curry with Millet and Beans

Fat	●●	30 min.
Cholesterol	1 mg	
Fiber	●●●	

Per serving: approx. 322 calories
11 g protein · 9 g fat · 49 g carbohydrates

MAKES 2 SERVINGS

½ cup (125 mL/100 g) millet
1 cup (250 mL) vegetable stock, divided
1 medium onion
2 cups (500 mL/250 g) green beans
1 tbsp (15 mL) olive oil
1 tbsp (15 mL) curry powder
3 medium tomatoes
Salt and freshly ground black pepper
A few drops sambal oelek (Indonesian chili sauce)
2 tbsp (30 mL) chopped chives

1 In a saucepan, combine the millet with ¾ cup + 2 tbsp (200 mL) of the vegetable stock and bring to a boil. Cover and cook on low heat for 20 minutes, until all the liquid has been absorbed.

2 Meanwhile, peel and finely slice the onion into rings. Cut the beans into thirds or 1 inch (2.5 cm) pieces.

3 Heat the oil in a nonstick skillet. On medium heat, sauté the onion and beans for 4 to 5 minutes, stirring constantly. Dust with curry powder, stir well and pour in the remaining 2 tbsp (30mL) stock.

4 Dice the tomatoes. Stir into the onion-bean mixture. Season with salt, pepper and sambal oelek. Stir in the millet, garnish with chives and serve.

!! **VARIATION** You can also use tofu. Slice 3½ oz (100 g) of firm smoked or extra-firm flavored tofu into strips about 1 inch (2.5 cm) long and sauté with the beans.

Summer Vegetables with Cellophane Noodles and Tofu

Fat	+	35 min.
Cholesterol	–	
Fiber	●●●	

Per serving: approx. 383 calories
23 g protein · 18 g fat · 37 g carbohydrates

MAKES 2 SERVINGS

5 oz (150 g) firm tofu
1 tsp (5 mL) dried oregano
Freshly ground pepper
2 tbsp (30 mL) Asian fish sauce or soy sauce
4 cups (1 L/450 g) green beans
Salt
1 bunch green (spring) onions
1 yellow bell pepper
1 beefsteak tomato
2 oz (50 g) cellophane noodles
2 tbsp (30 mL) olive oil

1 Finely dice the tofu and combine with the oregano, pepper and fish sauce or soy sauce. Cover and let sit.

2 Clean and boil or steam beans until tender-crisp, 5 to 10 minutes. Drain and plunge in ice water so they keep their color.

3 Meanwhile, trim the root ends and finely slice the green onions. Halve, clean and finely slice pepper. Cut an X in the bottom of the tomato, blanch in boiling water for 1 minute, peel and dice finely.

4 Cook the cellophane noodles salted in boiling water for 3 minutes, drain and coarsely chop on a cutting board.

5 Heat the oil in a nonstick skillet. On medium heat, sauté the green onions and tofu. Add the pepper and tomato and cook for 2 minutes. Stir in the beans and noodles and heat through, stirring constantly.

!! **TIP** If your cholesterol level allows it, you can sprinkle diced mozzarella or sheep's milk cheese over the dish. The cholesterol content would go up to 38 to 46 mg per serving.

!! **TIP** Cellophane (or bean thread or glass) noodles are made from mung beans and are available in Asian stores and some supermarkets.

Vegetable Curry with Millet and Beans, top
Summer vegetables with Cellophane Noodles and Tofu, bottom

Meatless Cassoulet

Fat	●	15 to 20 min.
Cholesterol	2 mg	(+ 8 hr. soaking)
Fiber	●●●	(+ 2 hr. 30 min. baking)

Per serving: approx. 283 calories
14 g protein · 5 g fat · 44 g carbohydrates

OVENPROOF SAUCEPAN OR BAKING DISH

MAKES 2 TO 3 SERVINGS
¾ cup (375 mL/150 g) dried white kidney, navy or Great
   Northern beans
1 medium onion
2 cloves garlic
1 medium carrot
1 leek
1 tbsp (15mL) olive oil
1 tbsp (15 mL) tomato paste
Pepper
2 sprigs fresh thyme
2 whole cloves
2 cups (500 mL) vegetable stock, divided
2 slices whole-grain toast
Salt
Cider vinegar

1 Soak the dried beans in plenty of cold water for 8 hours or overnight, then drain.

2 Preheat the oven to 275°F (140°C). Peel and finely chop the onion and garlic. Peel and cut the carrot into ½ inch (1 cm) cubes. Slice the leek lengthwise, wash carefully, and slice white and pale green parts into fine rings.

3 Heat the oil in a nonstick skillet. On low heat, cook the onion and garlic until translucent. Add the carrot and leek and cook briefly. Add the tomato paste, cook briefly and mix well.

4 Arrange half the beans and 1 sprig of thyme in the saucepan or dish. Season with pepper. Layer in the vegetables and cloves, more pepper and the remaining sprig of thyme. Cover with the remaining beans. Pour in stock until the beans are covered. Coarsely crumble 1 slice of whole-grain toast and sprinkle overtop.

5 Bake in the preheated oven for 2 hours, occasionally adding stock if the dish starts to dry out. When the beans are tender, stir well and season with salt and a few dashes of cider vinegar. Crumble the remaining slice of toast and sprinkle overtop. Bake, uncovered, for another 30 minutes, until the bread is crisp. Serve hot from the dish.

Sautéed Mushrooms with Grains

Fat	+++	35 min.
Cholesterol	3 mg	
Fiber	●●●	

Per serving: approx. 694 calories
17 g protein · 37 g fat · 72 g carbohydrates

MAKES 2 SERVINGS
1 cup (250 mL/200 g) mix of 6 grains (such as barley,
   brown rice, buckwheat groats, spelt, millet, quinoa)
2 cups (500 mL) vegetable stock
1 ripe avocado
Juice from ½ lemon
1 medium onion
7 oz (200 g) oyster mushrooms
1 tbsp (15 mL) vegetable oil
Salt and freshly ground black pepper
2 tbsp (30 mL) chopped fresh parsley or chives

1 Rinse the mixed grains in cold water, mix with the stock in a saucepan and bring to a boil. Cover and cook on low heat for 30 minutes.

2 Meanwhile, peel and pit the avocado and slice finely. Drizzle immediately with lemon juice, cover and let sit. Peel and finely chop the onion. Clean the oyster mushrooms and halve or quarter the larger ones.

3 Heat the oil in a nonstick skillet. On low heat, cook the onion until translucent. Add the oyster mushrooms and cook on high heat for 3 minutes, stirring constantly. Stir in the grains, carefully fold in the avocado slices and cook for a further 2 minutes. Season with salt and pepper, sprinkle with parsley or chives and serve.

! ! **TIP** Avocados should be soft to the touch— only then are they full of flavor and easy to work with. Unripe avocados don't have much taste, but you can let them ripen on a windowsill.

VEGETABLES AND LEGUMES

Meatless Cassoulet, top
Sautéed Mushrooms with Grains, bottom

Curried Potatoes and Spinach

Fat	●●	40 min.
Cholesterol	1 mg	
Fiber	●●●	

Per serving: approx. 215 calories
8 g protein · 7 g fat · 30 g carbohydrates

MAKES 2 SERVINGS
7 oz (200 g) fresh spinach
1 medium onion
2 cloves garlic
14 oz (400 g) small potatoes such as Yukon golds
1 tbsp (15 mL) canola oil
2 tsp (10 mL) mustard seeds
1 tbsp (15 mL) Madras curry powder
⅔ cup (150 mL) water or vegetable stock
Salt and freshly ground black pepper
1 tbsp (15 mL) chopped chives

1 Wash the spinach and trim any large stems. Blanch for 3 minutes in a large saucepan or skillet with the water that's left on the leaves. Drain well and let cool. Squeeze out as much excess water as possible and chop coarsely.

2 Peel and finely slice the onion and garlic. Peel and slice the potatoes into thin rounds.

3 Heat the oil in a nonstick skillet. On low heat, briefly sauté the mustard seeds (careful—they jump). Add the onion and garlic and cook until translucent. Stir in the curry and potatoes and pour in the water or stock. Cover and cook until tender, about 12 minutes.

4 Stir in the spinach and simmer, covered, for 5 to 8 minutes, until the potatoes are tender. Season with salt and pepper and serve garnished with chives.

!! **VARIATION** You can add 1 to 2 tbsp (15 to 30 mL) raisins to the potatoes in the skillet. The sweet raisins will harmonize well with the curry.

Azuki Beans with Celery Root

Fat	●●●	2 hr.
Cholesterol	19 mg	(+ 8 hr. soaking)
Fiber	●●●	

Per serving: approx. 442 calories
19 g protein · 14 g fat · 60 g carbohydrates

MAKES 2 SERVINGS
⅔ cup (150 mL/150 g) azuki beans
2 cups (500 mL) vegetable stock
½ small celery root (about 8 oz/250 g)
1 tart apple
1 medium onion
1 tbsp (15 mL) canola oil
Salt and freshly ground black pepper
1 tbsp (15 mL) cider vinegar
⅓ cup + 2 tbsp (100 mL/100 g) sour cream
2 tbsp (30 mL) chopped walnuts

1 Soak the beans in cold water to cover for at least 8 hours. Drain and bring to a boil in the stock. Cover and cook on low heat for 2 hours, until all the liquid has been absorbed and the beans are tender.

2 Meanwhile, peel and finely dice the celery root. The celery root must be tossed with an acid such as lemon juice or vinegar, or it will discolour immediately. Peel, core and cut the apple into small wedges. Peel the onion and finely slice into rings.

3 Heat the oil in a nonstick skillet. On low heat, cook the onion rings until translucent. Add the celery root and cook until tender-crisp, stirring constantly. Stir in the beans and apple. Season with salt, pepper and vinegar. Fold in the sour cream, garnish with the walnuts and serve.

!! **TIP** Like all legumes, the azuki bean suits a cholesterol friendly diet—but of course you can use other beans in this dish.

Curried Potatoes and Spinach , top
Azuki Beans with Celery Root, bottom

Mung Beans with Kohlrabi and Peanuts

Fat	+		25 min.
Cholesterol	–		(+ 1 hr. soaking)
Fiber	●●●		

Per serving: approx. 523 calories
29 g protein · 16 g fat · 68 g carbohydrates

MAKES 2 SERVINGS
1 cup (250 mL/200 g) mung beans
1 tsp (5 mL) caraway seeds
1 small kohlrabi
2 vine-ripened tomatoes
2 cloves garlic
2 tbsp (30 mL) canola oil
2 tbsp (30 mL) fresh thyme leaves
2 tbsp (30 mL) soy milk
Salt and freshly ground black pepper
2 to 3 tbsp (30 to 45 mL) soy sauce
2 tbsp (30 mL/20 g) peanuts

1 In a saucepan, combine the mung beans, caraway seeds and 4 cups (1 L) of water and bring to a boil. Cook for 5 minutes, then cover and cook for 1 hour on low heat, until the beans are al dente. Drain.

2 Peel the kohlrabi and cut into thin strips 1 inch (2.5 cm) long. Cut an X in the bottom of the tomatoes, blanch for 1 minute in boiling water, peel and dice. Peel the garlic and crush in a garlic press.

3 Heat the oil in a nonstick skillet. On medium heat, cook the kohlrabi and garlic, stirring constantly, until tender-crisp. Add the beans, tomatoes and thyme leaves and cook for 5 minutes, stirring constantly.

4 Stir in the soy milk and season with salt, pepper and soy sauce. Coarsely chop the peanuts and fold in just before serving.

!! TIP Mung beans are just as cholesterol friendly as soybeans, so you should try to include them in your meal plan. They're available in Asian food stores and many supermarkets.

Yellow Lentils with Zucchini and Asparagus

Fat	●●●		20 min.
Cholesterol	2 mg		
Fiber	●●●		

Per serving: approx. 400 calories
23 g protein · 12 g fat · 48 g carbohydrates

MAKES 2 SERVINGS
⅔ cup (150 mL/150 g) yellow lentils or split peas
1¼ cups (300mL) vegetable stock
1 small zucchini (about 7 oz/200 g)
1 lb (500 g) white asparagus
2 cloves garlic
2 tbsp (30 mL) olive oil
1 tsp (5 mL) granulated sugar
3 tbsp (45 mL) white balsamic or white wine vinegar
Salt and freshly ground white pepper
2 tbsp (30 mL) chopped fresh basil

1 Bring the lentils and stock to a boil, cover and cook on medium heat for 10 to 15 minutes, until all the liquid has been absorbed and the lentils are tender.

2 Meanwhile, trim the zucchini, halve lengthwise and slice thinly. Peel any thick stalks of asparagus and cut on an angle into ½-inch (1 cm) pieces. Peel and dice garlic.

3 Heat the oil in a nonstick skillet. On low heat, cook the garlic until golden. Add the zucchini and asparagus and cook for 5 minutes, stirring constantly, until tender-crisp. Sprinkle with sugar and pour in the vinegar. Stir in the lentils and season with salt and pepper. Arrange on two plates, sprinkle with basil and serve.

!! TIP If you'd like a little meat, slice 3½ oz (100 g) of smoked turkey into strips, combine with the lentils and warm for 1 minute. Smoked turkey contains only 1 g of fat in 3½ oz (100 g).

Mung Beans with Kohlrabi and Peanuts, top
Yellow Lentils with Zucchini and Asparagus, bottom

Fish

Sole with Carrots in a Soy-Mustard Sauce

Fat	●●	20 min.
Cholesterol	76 mg	
Fiber	●●	

Per serving: approx. 229 calories
25 g protein · 9 g fat · 12 g carbohydrates

MAKES 2 SERVINGS
4 medium carrots (about 10 oz/300 g)
1 tbsp (40 mL) sunflower or corn oil
½ to ¼ cup (50 to 125 mL) vegetable stock or
    salted water, divided
Pinch granulated sugar
2 sole fillets (5 oz/125 g each)
½ tsp (2 mL) freshly squeezed lemon juice
Salt and freshly ground white pepper
⅓ cup + 2 tbsp (100 mL/100 g) plain soy milk
1 heaping tsp (5 mL) Dijon mustard
1 bunch chives

1 Peel and thinly slice carrots. Heat the oil in a saucepan and sauté the carrots briefly. On low heat, pour in half the stock or salted water, stir in the sugar, cover, and cook for 3 minutes.

2 Drizzle the sole fillets with lemon juice, season with salt and pepper, arrange on top of the carrots and cook, covered, on low for 6 minutes. Add stock as needed. Remove the fish and keep warm.

3 Combine the soy milk and mustard, add to the carrots and bring to a boil. Chop the chives. Arrange the carrots and fish on a plate and serve sprinkled with chives (you could also fold some chives in with the carrots).

TIP Rice or boiled potatoes go well with this dish.

Rolled Sole in an Herb-Cream Sauce

Fat	–	25 min.
Cholesterol	71 mg	
Fiber	–	

Per serving: approx. 144 calories
24 g protein · 1 g fat · 5 g carbohydrates

MAKES 2 SERVINGS
4 sole fillets (about 2 oz/60 g each)
⅓ cup + 2 tbsp (100 mL) condensed milk (4%)
⅓ cup + 2 tbsp (100 mL) white wine or water
1 package herb sauce (to make 1 cup/250 mL sauce)
Small wooden skewers

1 Wash the sole fillets and pat dry with a paper towel. Roll up each fillet and fasten with a small wooden skewer.

2 Whisk together the condensed milk, wine or water, and sauce powder. Transfer to a saucepan and bring to a boil. Place the fish rolls in the saucepan and cook for 15 minutes on low heat.

TIP Cooked long-grain rice mixed with wild rice and steamed broccoli taste good with this dish.

TIP You can also use fresh or frozen salmon fillets.

TIP If you've always prepared your sauces with butter (83% fat), crème fraîche (40% fat) or whipping cream (35% fat), this dish proves you can use such low-fat alternatives as condensed milk, sour cream (10% fat or lower) or plain soy milk (about 2% fat) just as easily and the meal will still taste wonderful.

Sole with Carrots in a Soy-Mustard Sauce, top
Rolled Sole in an Herb-Cream Sauce, bottom

Herring in a Light Sauce

Fat	+		15 min.
Cholesterol	13 mg		(+ 24 hr. marinating)
Fiber	●		

Per serving: approx. 329 calories
25 g protein · 18 g fat · 15 g carbohydrates

MAKES 2 SERVINGS
1 can (5 oz/150 g) Matjes or other small herring fillets
　packed in vegetable oil (4 oz/125 g, drained)

FOR THE SAUCE
1 small onion
1 medium-sized gherkin
1 small tart apple
1 tbsp (15 mL) white wine vinegar
¼ tsp (1 mL) Dijon mustard
¼ tsp (1 mL) prepared horseradish
¾ cup + 2 tbsp (200 mL/200 g) creamy low-fat quark,
　puréed cottage cheese or strained yogurt
⅓ cup (75mL/70 g) sour cream
1 tbsp (15 mL) pickle liquid
Freshly ground white pepper
Liquid sweetener or granulated sugar

1 Drain the herring. Peel and finely slice onion into rings. Finely dice the gherkin. Peel, core and quarter the apple; slice into thin pieces.

2 Mix the vinegar with the mustard and horseradish. Gradually stir in the quark and sour cream until creamy. Add the onion rings, diced gherkin and apple rounds. Season with pickle liquid, pepper and sweetener or a pinch of sugar.

3 Pour the sauce into a container with a lid, press in the herring fillets, seal the container and refrigerate for 24 hours, stirring occasionally. Or let the sauce sit and serve over the fillets.

 TIP Boiled potatoes garnished with parsley go well with this dish.

FYI Matjes herring are skinned and filleted and cured in a spiced sugar-vinegar brine. Compared to some preparations, Matjes are only lightly salted, so you won't need to rinse them. Part of the salt is absorbed by the sauce while it marinates, thereby reducing the salt content of the fish and eliminating the need to add salt. If you use saltier kippered or Digby herring fillets, you might want to soak them in water or milk to reduce the salt content.

Cod Fillets with Tomato-Dill Sauce

Fat	●		20 min.
Cholesterol	65 mg		
Fiber	●		

Per serving: approx. 210 calories
24 g protein · 6 g fat · 16 g carbohydrates

MAKES 2 SERVINGS
2 cod fillets (4 oz/125 g each)
1 tsp (5 mL) freshly squeezed lemon juice
Salt and freshly ground black pepper
1 tbsp (15 mL) sunflower oil
1 cup (250 mL/250 g) strained tomatoes
4 tbsp (60 mL/60 g) condensed milk (4%)
½ bunch fresh dill
Pinch granulated sugar

1 Wash the cod fillets, pat dry with a paper towel, drizzle with lemon juice and briefly let the flavors combine.

2 Pat the fillets dry and season with salt and pepper. Heat the oil in a skillet. Sauté the fish on medium heat for 4 minutes a side, until golden.

3 Combine the tomatoes and condensed milk in a small saucepan and bring to a boil, stirring constantly. Trim and finely chop dill. Season the sauce with salt, pepper and sugar and stir in the dill. Arrange the fillets on a plate and drizzle with sauce.

 TIP Mashed potatoes or rice go well with this dish.

TIP It's easier to turn tender fish fillets if you coat each side with flour before sautéing.

VARIATION You can use other tender fish fillets, such as salmon, sole, snapper or halibut.

Cod Fillets with Tomato-Dill Sauce, top
Herring in a Light Sauce, bottom

Steamed Trout with Spinach

Fat	● ●	30 min.
Cholesterol	88 mg	(+ 35 min. baking)
Fiber	●	

Per serving: approx. 246 calories
35 g protein · 9 g fat · 6 g carbohydrates

MAKES 2 SERVINGS
4 oz (125 g) spinach
2 small shallots
1 tsp (5 mL) olive oil
1 small clove garlic
Salt and freshly ground black pepper
2 dressed, skinless trout (about 10 oz/300 g each)
4 firm tomatoes
¼ cup (50 mL/50 g) sliced pitted black olives
1 tsp (5 mL) fresh thyme

1 Thoroughly wash the spinach, trim large stems and coarsely chop leaves. Peel and finely dice the shallots. Heat the olive oil in a saucepan and cook the shallots on low heat until translucent. Peel the garlic, crush in a garlic press and add. Add the spinach and cook until wilted. Season with salt and pepper, transfer to a sieve, drain over a bowl and squeeze out excess moisture.

2 Preheat the oven to 350°F (180°C). Wash the trout and pat dry with a paper towel, stuff with the spinach, and season with salt and pepper. Slice the tomatoes into thick rounds.

3 Lay two roasting bags on a baking sheet. Lay the tomato rounds flat in the bags, followed by the trout. Add the olives, thyme and a little spinach water, seal the bags and poke a few holes in the top with a needle. Bake for 35 minutes.

!! **TIP** It's faster to use frozen spinach—a great way to stuff trout.

Stuffed Trout in a Clay Pot

Fat	●	25 min.
Cholesterol	88 mg	(+ 35 min. baking)
Fiber	●	

Per serving: approx. 256 calories
35 g protein · 6 g fat · 17 g carbohydrates

CLAY ROASTING POT AND LID, SOAKED IN COLD WATER AT LEAST 20 MINUTES

MAKES 2 SERVINGS
1 bunch green (spring) onions, divided
½ bunch fresh dill
½ bunch flat-leaf (Italian) parsley
½ bunch basil
1 small slice good-quality bread
Salt and freshly ground white pepper
2 dressed trout (about 10 oz/300 g each)
2 small carrots
⅓ cup + 2 tbsp (100 mL) vegetable stock

1 Trim the root ends and finely slice the green onions into rings. Set aside a few of the herb leaves for garnishing; finely chop the rest. Dice the bread into small cubes.

2 In a small bowl, mix the chopped herbs, 1 tbsp (15 mL) green onions, bread cubes, salt and pepper. Rinse the trout in cold water and pat dry with a paper towel. Stuff with the bread mixture. Season the outside of the fish with salt and pepper.

3 Remove the clay pot from the water. Peel and finely slice the carrots into rounds; transfer to the clay pot along with the remaining green onions. Pour in the stock and arrange the stuffed trout on top.

4 Cover the clay pot and place on the bottom rack of a cold oven. Turn the oven on to 350°F (180°C) and bake for 35 minutes. Sprinkle with the remaining herbs and serve.

Steamed Trout with Spinach, top
Stuffed Trout in a Clay Roasting Pot, bottom

Char and Thyme in a Salt Crust

Fat	+	20 min.
Cholesterol	105 mg	(+ 25 min. baking)
Fiber	–	

Per serving: approx. 351 calories
37 g protein · 15 g fat · 17 g carbohydrates

PREHEAT OVEN TO 350°F (180°C)
BAKING SHEET, LINED WITH GREASED PARCHMENT PAPER

MAKES 2 SERVINGS
2 lbs (1 kg) salt
2 tbsp (30 mL) cornstarch
2 small char or rainbow trout, dressed
2 sprigs fresh thyme
1 large lemon

1 Place the salt in a large bowl. Whisk the cornstarch in ½ cup (250mL) water and stir into the salt. Mix with your hands until firm. Let stand for 10 minutes.

2 Wash the fish and pat dry with a paper towel. Place the thyme sprigs inside the stomach cavity. Slice the lemon into very thin rounds.

3 Lay the fish on the prepared pan. Cover completely with lemon slices and cover with the salt crust, sealing well.

4 Bake the fish in the preheated oven for 25 minutes, until the salt has completely hardened. Carefully break the crust with a hammer, scrape off any remaining salt and serve.

 TIP All kinds of things can be prepared in a salt crust, including chicken thighs and turkey breast. It's important that a layer of seasonings or lemon slices separate the fish or meat from the salt or the food will get too salty.

TIP Boiled potatoes and a tossed salad complete this meal perfectly.

Perch with Puy Lentils and Vegetables

Fat	●●●	40 min.
Cholesterol	35 mg	
Fiber	●●●	

Per serving: approx. 438 calories
41 g protein · 13 g fat · 39 g carbohydrates

MAKES 2 SERVINGS
1 small onion
2 tbsp (30 mL) canola oil, divided
½ cup (125 mL/125 g) puy lentils
¾ cup + 2 tbsp (200 mL) vegetable stock
1 perch fillet (about 8 oz/250 g)
1 tbsp (15 mL) freshly squeezed lemon juice
1 small carrot
1 small yellow bell pepper
Salt and freshly ground black pepper
Flour for dusting
1 to 2 tbsp (15 to 30 mL) balsamic vinegar
2 tbsp (30 mL) plain soy milk
2 tbsp (30 mL) chopped chives

1 Peel and finely dice onion. Heat 1 tbsp (15 mL) oil in a nonstick skillet. Cook the diced onion on low heat until translucent. Add the lentils and stock, cover, and simmer on medium heat for 20 minutes.

2 Meanwhile, halve the perch, drizzle with lemon juice, cover and let sit for 10 minutes. Peel and finely dice carrot. Halve, clean and finely dice pepper. Add the carrots and peppers to the lentils, and simmer for 10 minutes.

3 Pat the fish fillets dry with a paper towel, season with salt and pepper, and dust with flour. Heat the remaining oil in the nonstick skillet. Sauté the fish over medium heat on both sides until golden.

4 Season the lentil mixture with the vinegar and stir in the soy milk. Arrange the lentils and fish on two plates, garnish with chives and serve.

TIP The dark, shiny puy lentils from France are the finest and tastiest kind. They can be found in better supermarkets or in health food stores. You can also use green lentils.

Char and Thyme in a Salt Crust, top
Pike with Puy Lentils and Vegetables, bottom

Salmon Trout Cooked in Foil

Fat	●	15 min.
Cholesterol	85 mg	(+ 20 min. baking)
Fiber	●	

Per serving: approx. 383 calories
36 g protein · 6 g fat · 18 g carbohydrates

PREHEAT OVEN TO 350°F (180°C)
2 LARGE PIECES HEAVY-DUTY ALUMINUM FOIL, BRUSHED WITH
OLIVE OIL

MAKES 2 SERVINGS
2 tomatoes
2 green (spring) onions
2 tart apples
Salt and freshly ground white pepper
2 salmon trout fillets (about 5 oz/150 g each)
2 sprigs fresh tarragon
4 tbsp (60 mL) cider or apple juice

1 Slice the tomatoes into rounds. Trim the root ends and finely slice the green onions into rings. Core and cut the apple into rounds. Overlap the slices of tomato and apple in the center of the pieces of foil. Sprinkle with the green onions. Season with salt and pepper.

2 Wash the fillets in cold water and pat dry with a paper towel. Season with salt and pepper and arrange on the bed of tomato and apple slices. Pluck the leaves off the tarragon and sprinkle on top.

3 Bring up the foil on all sides, then drizzle the cider or apple juice over all. Seal tightly and place the packages on a baking sheet. Bake in the preheated oven for 20 minutes.

‼️ **TIP** You can use parchment paper instead of foil. Parchment is a little harder to use, but the results are the same. If you want to try it, use a thick paper and, to avoid any mishaps, lay out two sheets instead of one. Cutting the paper into large circles, folding and pleating works best as a seal.

Small Flatfish Rolls with Zucchini

Fat	●	35 min.
Cholesterol	89 mg	
Fiber	●●	

Per serving: approx. 223 calories
27 g protein · 6 g fat · 11 g carbohydrates

MAKES 2 SERVINGS
4 flatfish fillets (about 2½ oz/70 g each), such as sole or flounder
1 tbsp (15 mL) freshly squeezed lemon juice, divided
Salt and freshly ground white pepper
1 tbsp (15 mL) tomato paste
1 bunch fresh dill
1 small red onion
1 large zucchini (about 10 oz/300 g)
1 tsp (5 mL) olive oil
⅓ cup + 2 tbsp (100 mL) vegetable stock
1 to 2 tbsp (15 to 30 mL) instant potato flakes
Small wooden skewers

1 Wash the fillets in cold water and pat dry with a paper towel. Drizzle with a little of the lemon juice; season with salt and pepper. Spread a thin layer of tomato paste on top. Coarsely chop dill and sprinkle at least half over the fish. Roll up the fillets, pin with small wooden skewers and chill.

2 Peel and finely dice the onion. Coarsely grate the zucchini. Heat the oil in a saucepan. On low heat, cook the onion until translucent. Add the zucchini and cook until tender, then pour in the stock.

3 Season the vegetables with the remaining lemon juice, dill, salt and pepper. Arrange the rolls on top of the vegetables, cover tightly and cook on medium heat for 6 minutes.

4 Remove the rolls from the saucepan and arrange on two plates. Stir the potato flakes into the zucchini, bring to a boil and then pour around the rolls. Serve immediately.

‼️ **TIP** Binding sauces and soups with instant potato flakes is a quick, simple and low-calorie way to achieve a light creaminess.

Salmon Trout Cooked in Foil, top
Small Flatfish Rolls with Zucchini, bottom

Fish Kebabs with Zucchini and Pepper

Fat	+	20 min.
Cholesterol	100 mg	
Fiber	●	

Per serving: approx. 348 calories
29 g protein · 15 g fat · 2 g carbohydrates

PREHEAT BROILER OR GRILL
4 SKEWERS (SOAKED FOR AT LEAST 20 MINUTES IF WOODEN),
DIPPED IN OIL

MAKES 2 SERVINGS
1 tuna steak or halibut fillet (about 5 oz/250 g)
Salt and freshly ground white pepper
1 tsp (5 mL) turmeric
½ medium zucchini
1 small yellow bell pepper
2 large mushrooms
1 lemon
Oil for brushing

1 Preheat the broiler or grill. Season both sides of the tuna or halibut with salt, pepper and turmeric. Cut into ½ inch (1 cm) cubes.

2 Halve the zucchini lengthwise and cut into ½ inch (1 cm) half-moons. Halve and clean pepper; cut to form little diamonds or cubes. Clean the mushrooms, trim the stems and cut into quarters.

3 Thread alternating strips and cubes of the fish and vegetables on the prepared skewers, being careful to thread the fish against the grain. Brush lightly with oil and place under the preheated broiler or grill. Turn and grill until browned.

4 Slice the lemon into wedges and use them to garnish the kebabs as you serve them.

!! **TIP** You can also prepare the fish kebabs in a nonstick skillet. Brush a little oil in the pan and heat well. Sear the kebabs on all sides on high heat, then sauté on medium heat until the fish is cooked.

!! **TIP** Serve the tuna kebabs on a bed of watercress, arugula (rocket) or mâche (corn salad or lamb's lettuce). Wash and clean about 3½ oz (100 g) of the greens. Mix 2 tbsp (30 mL) lemon juice with salt and pepper and toss with the greens. Arrange the salad on two plates and lay the kebabs on top.

Perch Fillet with Dried Apricots

Fat	●	25 min.
Cholesterol	45 mg	
Fiber	●●	

Per serving: approx. 330 calories
32 g protein · 6 g fat · 33 g carbohydrates

MAKES 2 SERVINGS
10 dried apricots (unsulfured preferred)
1 perch or haddock fillet (about 8 to 10 oz/250 to 300 g)
1 tbsp (15 mL) freshly squeezed lemon juice
2 shallots
Salt and freshly ground black pepper
Flour for coating
1 tbsp (15 mL) vegetable oil
2 tbsp (30 mL) cider vinegar
2 tsp (10 mL) liquid honey
1 tbsp (15 mL) chopped fresh coriander or parsley

1 Soften the apricots in warm water. Cut the fish fillet in half, drizzle with lemon juice, cover and let sit.

2 Meanwhile, peel and finely dice the shallots. Drain the apricots and slice into strips.

3 Pat the fish dry with a paper towel, season with salt and pepper, and dust with the flour. Heat the oil in a nonstick skillet and sauté the shallots and the fish on both sides until brown. Remove the fish and keep warm.

4 Add the apricots to the shallots in the pan and briefly shake back and forth. Pour in ½ cup (125 mL) water and the cider vinegar; reduce slightly on high heat. Stir in the honey. Briefly reheat the fish in the sauce, sprinkle with coriander or parsley, and serve.

Fish Kebabs with Zucchin and Pepper, top
Perch Fillet with Dried Apricots, bottom

Pollock with Palm Hearts

Fat	●●●	25 min.
Cholesterol	41 mg	
Fiber	●	

Per serving: approx. 389 calories
43 g protein · 14 g fat · 43 g carbohydrates

MAKES 2 SERVINGS
1 pollock fillet (about 8 oz/250 g)
1 tbsp (15 mL) freshly squeezed lemon juice
5 oz (150 g) snow peas (about 2 cups/500 mL)
1 can (12 oz/425 mL/400 g) palm hearts (7 oz/250 mL/
    220 g, drained)
Salt and freshly ground white pepper
Ground coriander seeds
1 tbsp (15 mL) flour
1 tbsp (15 mL) canola oil
2 tsp (10 mL) granulated sugar
2 tbsp (30 mL) fish sauce
2 tbsp (30 mL) soy milk
Pepper cress

1 Drizzle the fillet with lemon juice, cover and let sit for 10 minutes. Meanwhile, slice the snow peas on an angle to form strips ½ inch (1 cm) long. Drain the palm hearts in a sieve and cut into pieces ½ inch (1 cm) thick.

2 Pat the pollock dry with a paper towel, season with salt, pepper and coriander, and dust with flour on both sides.

3 Heat the oil in a nonstick skillet. Sauté the pollock on medium heat on both sides until golden. Remove and keep warm. In the same pan, cook the snow peas for 3 minutes, stirring constantly, until tender-crisp. Stir in the palm hearts and heat through.

4 Stir in the sugar and let the mixture brown slightly. Stir in the fish sauce and soy milk and cook until hot and slightly thick. Arrange the vegetables on two plates. Cut the pollock in half and lay it on top of the vegetables. Sprinkle with cress as desired and serve.

!! **TIPS** Rice or baguette go well with this dish.

!! **VARIATION** Instead of palm hearts, try asparagus, bamboo shoots, lotus root or black salsify.

Pollock with Soy Sprouts

Fat	●●●	25 min.
Cholesterol	50 mg	
Fiber	●	

Per serving: approx. 288 calories
33 g protein · 11 g fat · 14 g carbohydrates

MAKES 2 SERVINGS
1 pollock fillet (about 8 to 10 oz/ 250 to 300 g)
1 tbsp (15 mL) freshly squeezed lemon juice
1 medium onion
2 oranges (1 preferably organic)
7 oz (200 g) soy sprouts (about 2 cups/500 mL)
Salt and freshly ground black pepper
2 tbsp (30 mL) vegetable oil
2 tbsp (30 mL) Asian fish sauce
1 tsp (5 mL) cornstarch

1 Cut the fillet in half, drizzle with lemon juice, cover and let sit for 10 minutes.

2 Meanwhile, peel and finely slice the onion into rings. Take 1 tsp (5 mL) of zest off the untreated orange in long strips, then squeeze the juice of both oranges. Wash and coarsely chop soy sprouts.

3 Pat the fish fillets dry with a paper towel and season with salt and pepper. Heat the oil in a non-stick skillet. Sauté the onion rings and the fish on both sides for 5 minutes, until golden. Remove the fish and keep warm. Continue to sauté the onion rings until lightly browned. Pour in the orange juice.

4 Heat the soy sprouts in the sauce. Season with fish sauce, salt and pepper. Mix the cornstarch with a little water and stir into the sauce. Arrange on two plates, lay the fish fillets on top and sprinkle with the orange zest.

 TIP Rice goes well with this dish.

FISH

Pollock with Palm Hearts, top
Pollock with Soy Sprouts, bottom

Cod Fillet with Tomatoes and Herbs

Fat	●●	15 min.
Cholesterol	63 mg	(+ 30 min. baking)
Fiber	●●	

Per serving: approx. 203 calories
24 g protein · 9 g fat · 7 g carbohydrates

PREHEAT OVEN TO 350°F (180°C)
OVENPROOF DISH, BRUSHED WITH 1 TSP (5 ML) OIL

MAKES 2 SERVINGS
8 oz (250 g) cod fillet, fresh or frozen
1 tsp (5 mL) freshly squeezed lemon juice
1 medium onion
2 cloves garlic
1 tbsp (15 mL) olive oil, divided
8 oz (250 g) diced tomatoes
1 tbsp (15 mL) chopped fresh parsley
½ tsp (2 mL) dried oregano
½ tsp (2 mL) dried rosemary
Salt
Pinch granulated sugar

1 Thaw frozen fish for 10 minutes. Wash the fillet and pat dry with a paper towel. Drizzle with lemon juice and let sit.

2 Peel and finely dice onion and garlic. Heat 2 tsp (10 mL) olive oil in a saucepan and cook the onion on low heat until translucent. Add the garlic and cook briefly. Mix in the tomatoes and heat through. Stir in the parsley, oregano, rosemary, salt and sugar.

3 Arrange the fillets in the prepared dish, cover with the sauce and bake in the preheated oven for 25 to 30 minutes.

TIP Boiled potatoes or French bread and a tossed salad go well with this dish.

Cod Steaks with Tarragon Carrots

Fat	●●	30 min.
Cholesterol	86 mg	
Fiber	–	

Per serving: approx. 234 calories
31 g protein · 7 g fat · 11 g carbohydrates

MAKES 2 SERVINGS
2 cod steaks (about 4 oz/125 g each)
3 tbsp (45 mL) freshly squeezed lemon juice, divided
Salt and freshly ground white pepper
3 or 4 medium carrots (about 10 oz/300 g)
1 tbsp (15 mL) oil
⅓ cup + 2 tbsp (100 mL) vegetable stock
3 whole juniper berries
4 tbsp (60 mL) coarsely chopped fresh tarragon
2 tsp (10 mL) cornstarch
2 tbsp (30 mL) soy milk

1 Drizzle the cod steaks with lemon juice and season with salt and pepper.

2 Peel and slice the carrots on an angle into thin rounds. Heat the oil in a nonstick skillet and cook the carrots on medium heat for 5 minutes. Pour in enough vegetable stock to cover. Crush the juniper berries and add to the carrots along with the tarragon.

3 Lay the cod steaks on top. Cover and cook on low heat for 8 to 10 minutes, until the carrots are done.

4 Remove the fish and arrange on two warm plates. Mix the cornstarch with a little water, stir into the carrots and bring to a boil again. Season with the remaining lemon juice, salt and pepper, and stir in the soy milk. Arrange around the cod steaks.

TIP Rice or mashed potatoes go well with this dish.

Cod Fillet with Tomatoes and Herbs, top
Cod Steaks with Tarragon Carrots, bottom

Fish Casserole with Apples and Peppers

Fat	●●	25 min.
Cholesterol	88 mg	(+ 40 min. baking)
Fiber	●●	

Per serving: approx. 234 calories
27 g protein · 8 g fat · 13 g carbohydrates

PREHEAT THE OVEN TO 350°F (180°C)
OVAL OVENPOOF DISH

MAKES 3 TO 4 SERVINGS
1 perch fillet or 1 package frozen pollock fillets (about
    14 oz/ 400 g)
Juice from ½ lemon
1 medium onion
2 red bell peppers
1 tbsp (15 mL) olive oil
2 tart apples
Salt and freshly ground pepper
3 tbsp (45 mL) chopped fresh dill, divided
⅔ cup (150 mL/150 g) sour cream

1 Cut the perch fillet in half or in thirds, drizzle with lemon juice, cover and let sit briefly.

2 Meanwhile, peel and finely slice the onion into rings. Halve, clean and cut the peppers into strips.

3 Heat the oil in a nonstick skillet. Cook the onion rings on medium heat for 5 minutes, until golden. Add the pepper strips and cook for 2 to 3 minutes, stirring constantly. Layer half in the dish.

4 Peel, core and cut the apple into small wedges. Combine with the remaining peppers and onions. Pat the fish dry with a paper towel, season with salt and pepper, and arrange in the dish. Cover with the peppers, apple and onions.

5 Mix 2 tbsp (30 mL) dill with the sour cream and pour over. Cover the casserole with aluminum foil (shiny side down) and bake for 20 minutes, then uncover and bake for another 20 minutes, until done. Garnish with the remaining dill and serve.

 TIP Boiled potatoes or tender-crisp snow peas go well with this dish.

Clay Pot Pollock Risotto

Fat	●●●	15 min.
Cholesterol	60 mg	(+ 45 min. baking)
Fiber	●●●	

Per serving: approx. 524 calories
40 g protein · 13 g fat · 59 g carbohydrates

CLAY ROASTING POT AND LID, SOAKED IN COLD WATER AT LEAST
20 MINUTES

MAKES 2 SERVINGS
10 oz (300 g) pollock fillet(s)
1 tbsp (15 mL) freshly squeezed lemon juice
⅔ cup (150 mL/150 g) brown rice
1 medium onion
1 tbsp (15 mL) olive oil
2 cups (500 mL) vegetable stock
3 vine-ripened tomatoes
2 oz (30 g) freshly grated Grana Padano or
    Parmesan cheese
Salt and freshly ground pepper

1 Drizzle the pollock with lemon juice, cover and let sit. Wash and drain rice. Peel and finely dice onion.

2 Heat the oil in a nonstick skillet. On low heat, cook the onion until translucent. Add the rice and stir until translucent. Transfer to the clay roasting pot and pour in the vegetable stock. Cover with the lid and place on the bottom rack of a cold oven. Turn the oven on to 275°F (140°C) and let the rice cook for 30 minutes, until all the liquid has been absorbed.

3 Slice the tomatoes into rounds. Stir the cheese into the rice and set aside half. Season the fish with salt and pepper and arrange on top of the rice in the pot. Cover with the reserved rice and garnish with the tomato slices. Cook, uncovered, for another 15 minutes, until the tomatoes are lightly browned. Serve the risotto in the clay pot.

Fich Casserole with Apples and Peppers, top
Clay Pot Pollock Risotto, bottom

Fish with Tomato Sauce

Fat	+	25 min.
Cholesterol	90 mg	
Fiber	–	

Per serving: approx. 256 calories
28 g protein · 15 g fat · 4 g carbohydrates

MAKES 2 SERVINGS
2 hake, cod or ocean perch fillets (about 5 oz/150 g each)
1 tbsp (15 mL) freshly squeezed lemon juice
2 vine-ripened tomatoes
4 green (spring) onions
2 cremini mushrooms
4 black olives
2 tbsp (30 mL) olive oil, divided
1 tbsp (15 mL) tomato paste
2 tsp (10 mL) capers
Dash balsamic vinegar
Salt and freshly ground black pepper

1 Drizzle the fillets with lemon juice, cover and let sit for 10 minutes.

2 Meanwhile, cut an X in the bottom of the tomatoes, blanch in boiling water for 1 minute, peel and dice. Trim the root ends, halve the green onions lengthwise and mince. Clean and finely dice mushrooms. Pit the olives and slice into thin strips.

3 Heat 1 tbsp (15 mL) oil in a small saucepan. On medium heat, sauté the green onions and mushrooms briefly. Stir in the tomato paste and briefly sauté. Add the tomatoes and pour in 1/3 cup + 2 tbsp (100 mL) water. Bring to a boil and cook on medium heat until thick. Stir in the capers. Season with vinegar, salt and pepper, and keep warm.

4 Pat the fish dry with a paper towel, and season with salt and pepper. Heat the remaining oil in a nonstick skillet. On medium heat, sauté the fish on both sides for 4 to 5 minutes, until golden. Arrange on top of the tomato sauce and serve.

Fish with Peppers and Vegetables

Fat	●●	35 min.
Cholesterol	75 mg	(+ 25 min. baking)
Fiber	●●●	

Per serving: approx. 264 calories
25 g protein · 9 g fat · 10 g carbohydrates

PREHEAT OVEN TO 325°F (160°C)
OVENPROOF DISH

MAKES 2 SERVINGS
8 oz (250 g) hake, cod or ocean perch fillets
1/4 tsp (1 mL) chili powder
1 tsp (5 mL) dried thyme, divided
1 medium onion
1 clove garlic
2 green bell peppers
1 red bell pepper
1 tbsp (15 mL) olive oil
Salt
1 dried red chili
2/3 cup (150 mL) dry white wine

1 Wash the fillets, pat dry with a paper towel and sprinkle with chili powder and 1/2 tsp (2 mL) thyme. Peel and finely chop onion and garlic. Halve and clean peppers. Coarsely chop 1 green pepper and purée. Cut the remaining peppers into bite-sized pieces.

2 Heat the oil in a skillet. On medium heat, sauté the fish on both sides for 3 minutes. Season with salt, transfer to a casserole dish and bake in the preheated oven for 25 minutes.

3 Place the onion, garlic and pepper pieces in the same skillet and cook for 5 minutes, stirring constantly. Crush and stir in the chili. Pour in the wine and 1/4 cup (50 mL) water. Season with the remaining 1/2 tsp (2 mL) thyme and salt; cook for 5 minutes, until almost all the liquid has evaporated. Stir in the puréed pepper and cook another minute.

4 Take the fish out of the oven and arrange on two warm plates with the peppers and vegetables.

 TIP Mashed potatoes go well with this dish.

Fish with Tomato Sauce, top
Fish with Peppers and Vegetables, bottom

Steamed Ocean Perch with Summer Vegetables

Fat	●●●	35 min.
Cholesterol	48 mg	
Fiber	●●●	

Per serving: approx. 267 calories
28 g protein · 11 g fat · 14 g carbohydrates

MAKES 2 SERVINGS
8 oz (250 g) ocean perch, red snapper or orange roughy
 fillet(s)
1 tbsp (15 mL) freshly squeezed lemon juice
1 cup (250 mL/100 g) green beans
Salt
1 red bell pepper
1 yellow bell pepper
2 cloves garlic
1 small white onion
2 vine-ripened tomatoes
1 tbsp (15 mL) olive oil
⅓ cup + 2 tbsp (100 mL) vegetable stock
Freshly ground white pepper
1 tbsp (15 mL) white balsamic vinegar
2 tbsp (30 mL) chopped fresh basil

1 If you have a large fish fillet, cut it in half. Drizzle with lemon juice, cover and let sit for 10 minutes.

2 Meanwhile, trim and halve the beans; blanch for 5 minutes in boiling salted water. Drain and plunge immediately into ice water so they keep their color.

3 Halve and clean peppers and slice into strips. Peel and coarsely dice garlic and onion. Cut an X in the bottom of the tomatoes, blanch for 1 minute, peel and slice into strips.

4 Heat the oil in a nonstick skillet. On low heat, cook the onion and garlic until translucent. Stir in the pepper strips, beans and tomatoes, and cook briefly. Pour in the vegetable stock.

5 Pat the fish fillets dry with a paper towel, season with salt and pepper, and lay them on top of the vegetables. Cover and cook on low heat for 7 minutes, until the fish flakes easily. Arrange the fish on two warm plates. Season the vegetables with the vinegar, salt and pepper, arrange next to the fish and garnish with basil.

Sea Breem (Porgy) in a Soy-Curry Marinade

Fat	●●●	25 min.
Cholesterol	130 mg	(+ 1 to 2 hrs marinating)
Fiber	●	

Per serving: approx. 364 calories
36 g protein · 12 g fat · 26 g carbohydrates

OVENPROOF DISH

MAKES 2 SERVINGS
1 shallot
2 tbsp (30 mL) soy sauce
2 tbsp (30 mL) sherry
1 tbsp (15 mL) granulated sugar
½ tsp (2 mL) sambal oelek (Indonesian chilli sauce)
½ tsp (2 mL) Madras curry powder
2 small dressed sea breem (porgy), trout or mackerel
4 slices fresh or canned pineapple
½ tsp (2 mL) cornstarch

1 Peel and finely dice the shallots. Combine with the soy sauce, sherry, sugar, sambal oelek and curry powder.

2 Score both sides of the fish on an angle, 1 inch (2.5 cm) apart, and place in a bowl or dish. Pour in the soy mixture, cover and refrigerate for 1 to 2 hours.

3 Preheat the oven to 325°F (160°C). Slightly drain the fish, reserving the marinade. Place the fish in the ovenproof dish and bake in the preheated oven for 12 minutes, until the dorsal fin comes away easily.

4 Meanwhile, in a small saucepan, bring the reserved marinade and ½ cup (125 mL) water to a boil. Heat the pineapple slices and arrange on two plates. Whisk the cornstarch in a little cold water, stir into the sauce and bring to a boil. Pour the sauce over the pineapple slices. Carefully lift the fish out of the dish and arrange with the pineapple slices.

 TIP Rice goes well with this dish.

Steamed Ocean Perch with Summer Vegetables, top
Sea Breem (Porgy) in a Soy-Curry Marinade, bottom

Meat and Poultry

Stir-Fried Beef with Soy Sprouts

Fat	+		25 min.
Cholesterol	70 mg		
Fiber	●		

Per serving: approx. 289 calories
28 g protein · 15 g fat · 10 g carbohydrates

MAKES 2 SERVINGS
7 oz (200 g) lean, tender beef, such as striploin/New York
    steak or sirloin
1¼ cups (300 mL/125 g) slender green beans
2 medium carrots
1 cup (250 mL/100 g) soybean sprouts
¼-inch (0.5 cm) piece fresh ginger
2 tbsp (30 mL) canola oil, divided
2 tbsp (30 mL) Asian fish sauce or soy sauce

1 Trim any sinews and fat, and cut the beef into thin strips. Cut the beans into 1 inch (2.5 cm) pieces. Peel and julienne the carrots about as large as the bean pieces. Wash, drain and coarsely chop sprouts. Peel and finely dice ginger.

2 In a wok or a large nonstick skillet, heat 1 tbsp (15 mL) oil. Stir in the ginger, beans and carrots. On medium heat, stir-fry for 5 minutes, until tender-crisp. Remove and set aside.

3 Heat the remaining oil in the same wok or skillet. On high heat, sear the meat on all sides. Stir in the soy sprouts and vegetables and stir-fry another 1 to 2 minutes. Pour in the fish sauce or soy sauce and bring to a boil. Serve immediately on two warm plates.

VARIATION This dish also goes well with tofu. Use 1 carrot and 3½ oz (100 g) firm smoked or extra-firm flavored tofu, cut into strips. When the meat is half done, add the tofu with the soy bean sprouts and vegetables.

Clay Pot Lamb Fillet with Chard

Fat	●●		1 hr.
Cholesterol	70 mg		
Fiber	●●		

Per serving: approx. 202 calories
26 g protein · 9 g fat · 3 g carbohydrates

CLAY ROASTING POT AND LID, SOAKED IN COLD WATER FOR AT LEAST 20 MIN.

MAKES 2 SERVINGS
1¼ lb (600 g) Swiss chard
Salt
1 small onion
2 cloves garlic
1 tbsp (15 mL) olive oil
Freshly ground pepper
7-oz (200 g) boneless lamb fillet or tenderloin
1 tbsp (15 mL) Dijon mustard

1 Remove the heavy stalks of 8 large leaves of chard. Place in boiling salted water, pour immediately into a sieve and drain well. Cut the remaining stems and leaves into strips.

2 Peel and finely slice the onion into rings. Peel the garlic and crush in a garlic press. Heat the oil in a nonstick skillet. On medium heat, cook the onion and garlic for 2 to 3 minutes. Add the chard strips and cook for 3 minutes. Lightly season the vegetables with salt and pepper and transfer to the clay pot.

3 Lay the blanched chard leaves out, slightly over-lapping, to form a large square (or two squares, depending on the cut of meat). Trim any sinews and fat from the lamb and season with salt and pepper. Spread mustard on all sides and place in the center of the chard leaves. Fold the leaves over the meat and place on top of the mixture in the clay pot.

4 Place the clay roasting pot on the bottom rack of a cold oven. Turn the oven to 400°F (200°C) and cook for 35 minutes.

5 Remove the meat and carve into 4 pieces on an angle. Serve the vegetables and meat on two warm plates.

TIP The clay roasting pot allows fat-free cooking. If you don't have one, you can also prepare lamb with chard in a roasting pan with a tight seal or a roasting bag. Before placing in an oven pre-heated to 375°F (190°C), add about ½ cup (125 mL) vegetable stock so the vegetables won't dry out.

Stir-Fried Beef with Soy Sprouts, top
Clay Pot Lamb Fillet with Chard, bottom

Roasted Lamb with Green Beans

Fat	●●		55 min.
Cholesterol	70 mg		
Fiber	●		

Per serving: approx. 222 calories
24 g protein · 9 g fat · 8 g carbohydrates

PREHEAT OVEN TO 350°F (180°C)
OVENPROOF SKILLET OR ROASTING PAN

MAKES 2 SERVINGS
2 boneless lamb fillets, tenderloin or pieces of shoulder
    meat (about 3½ oz/100 g each)
2 cloves garlic
¼ tsp (2 mL) dried rosemary
¼ tsp (2 mL) dried oregano
Freshly ground black pepper
1 tbsp (15 mL) olive oil
2 tbsp (10 mL) Asian chili sauce, such as sambal oelek
1 tbsp (10 mL) soy sauce
1 tsp (5 mL) wine vinegar
2 medium tomatoes
¼ cup (50 mL) red wine or water
2 cups (500 mL/250 g) green beans
Salt
¼ tsp (2 mL) dried savory

1 Trim the meat of excess fat. Finely chop 1 clove of garlic for marinade; crush the other in a garlic press. Season the meat with the crushed garlic, rosemary, oregano and pepper.

2 Mix the olive oil, chili sauce, soy sauce, vinegar and garlic in a small bowl. Brush some of this mixture all over the meat and place in the skillet or pan. Cut the tomatoes into eighths and add to the meat. Roast in the preheated oven for 45 minutes, occasionally brushing the meat with the olive oil mixture and pouring in 1 to 2 tbsp (15 to 30 mL) red wine or water as necessary.

3 Meanwhile, wash and trim beans. Bring salted water to a boil. On medium heat, cook the beans with the savory for 8 minutes, until tender-crisp, and drain well.

4 Arrange the meat, beans, tomatoes and sauce on two warm plates.

!! **TIP** Serve with boiled potatoes or French bread.

Castilian Casserole with Lamb and Root Vegetables

Fat	+		90 min.
Cholesterol	70 mg		(+ overnight marinating)
Fiber	●●		

Per serving: approx. 388 calories
22 g protein · 18 g fat · 24 g carbohydrates

MAKES 2 SERVINGS

7 oz (200 g) boned leg of lamb
1 medium onion
2 or 3 cloves garlic
3 small carrots (about 8 oz/250 g)
½ cup (125 mL) dry white wine
1 tbsp (15 mL) white wine vinegar
Salt
1 bay leaf
1 tsp (5 mL) dried mixed herbs, such as thyme, rosemary,
    oregano, sage
3 whole juniper berries
5 black peppercorns
8 oz (250 g) potatoes
2 tbsp (30 mL/30 g) low-fat yogurt, divided

1 Cut the meat into 1 inch (2.5 cm) cubes and place in a saucepan. Peel and finely chop onion and garlic. Peel the carrots and cut into small pieces.

2 Mix the onion, garlic and carrots with the wine, vinegar, salt, bay leaf, herbs, juniper berries and peppercorns. Rub the meat with this mixture, cover and marinate in the refrigerator for several hours or overnight, turning occasionally.

3 Bring the meat and marinade to a boil. Cover and braise on low heat for 40 minutes, adding water as needed.

4 Meanwhile, peel and finely dice the potatoes. Parboil in boiling salted water for 8 minutes, then drain. Add to the meat and continue cooking for a further 20 minutes.

5 Arrange the casserole on two warm plates, garnish each with 1 tbsp (15 mL) yogurt and serve.

Roasted Lamb with Green Beans, top
Castilian Casserole with Lamb and Root Vegetables,
bottom

Pork with Soy Sprouts and Snow Peas

Fat	●●●		40 min.
Cholesterol	70 mg		
Fiber	●		

Per serving: approx. 262 calories
34 g protein · 12 g fat · 11 g carbohydrates

MAKES 2 SERVINGS
2 oz (50 g) snow peas (about ½ cup/125mL)
7 oz (200 g) soybean sprouts (about 2 cups/500mL)
Salt
½ bunch green (spring) onions
½ red bell pepper (about ½ cup/125mL/100g)
1 small piece ginger
7 oz (200 g) pork fillet or tenderloin
3 tbsp (45 mL) soy sauce
¼ cup (50 mL) vegetable stock
1 tsp (5 mL) dark (toasted) sesame oil
1 tsp (5 mL) Asian chili sauce
¼ tsp (5 mL) sambal oelek (Indonesian chili sauce)
1 tbsp (15 mL) peanut or canola oil

1 Trim the ends of the snow peas, if needed. Rinse the sprouts in a sieve or drain canned sprouts. Bring salted water to a boil. Blanch the snow peas and sprouts for 3 minutes, plunge in ice water and drain. Slice the green onions into fine rings. Halve, clean and coarsely dice the red pepper. Peel and finely chop the ginger. Cut the meat into strips.

2 Mix the soy sauce, vegetable stock, sesame oil, chili sauce and sambal oelek in a small bowl and set aside.

3 Heat the oil in a wok or a large nonstick skillet and briefly sauté the ginger. Add the meat and sear well on high heat for 2 to 3 minutes, turning often. Move the meat up the side of the wok. Gradually stir the diced pepper, snow peas and sprouts into the center of the wok and stir-fry for 1 minute, then push up the side of the wok. Combine the meat and vegetables, pour in the sauce, cover and cook for another 3 minutes.

‼ TIP Fold in cooked and drained Asian whole wheat noodles, and you have a full meal. A serving of 2 oz (50 g) uncooked whole wheat noodles yields 5 oz (150 g) of cooked noodles and has 175 calories.

‼ TIP Rice goes well with this dish.

Pork with Cellophane Noodles and Peanuts

Fat	●●●		45 min.
Cholesterol	70 mg		
Fiber	●		

Per serving: approx. 343 calories
31 g protein · 12 g fat · 27 g carbohydrates

MAKES 2 SERVINGS
3 tbsp (45 mL) soy sauce, divided
1 tbsp (15 mL) rice wine or semi-dry sherry
7 oz (200 g) lean pork, such as a cutlet or boned chop
1 medium carrot (about 3½ oz/100 g)
1 small leek (about 3½ oz/100 g)
1 large rib celery (about 3½ oz/100 g)
2 cloves garlic
¼ cup (50 mL) vegetable stock
1 tbsp (15 mL) Asian fish sauce
1 tsp (5 mL) wine vinegar
½ tsp (2 mL) cornstarch
Pinch sugar
2 oz (50 g) cellophane (bean thread or glass) noodles
1 dried red chili
1 tbsp (15 mL) peanut or canola oil
2 tbsp (30 mL/20 g) roasted peanuts

1 To make the marinade, combine 2 tbsp (30 mL) soy sauce and rice wine or sherry. Cut the meat into cubes and let sit in the marinade.

2 Peel the carrots. Slice the leek lengthwise and wash thoroughly. Julienne the carrots, celery and leek. Peel and finely chop garlic. To prepare the sauce, combine the vegetable stock, the remaining 1 tbsp (15 mL) soy sauce, fish sauce, vinegar, cornstarch and sugar.

3 Bring a pot of water to a boil. Cook the cellophane noodles for 3 minutes and drain (or prepare the noodles according to package instructions). Remove the seeds of the chili, if desired (it will keep down the heat), and crush.

4 Heat the oil in a wok or a large nonstick saucepan and stir in the chili. Remove the meat from the marinade and sear on high heat for 2 to 3 minutes, turning frequently. Move the meat up the side of the wok. Add the carrot and celery and stir-fry for 3 minutes. Add the garlic and briefly stir-fry. Stir in the leek and the remaining marinade and sauce; cover and cook for 4 to 5 minutes, until done. Using scissors, cut the cellophane noodles into small pieces, fold in and heat through. Sprinkle with peanuts and serve.

Pork with Soy Sprouts and Snow (Mange-Tout) Peas, top
Pork with Cellophane Noodles and Peanuts, bottom

Roasted Chicken Legs

Fat	++		20 min.
Cholesterol	128 mg		(+ 35 min. baking)
Fiber	●●		

Per serving: approx. 350 calories
31 g protein · 22 g fat · 5 g carbohydrates

PREHEAT OVEN TO 350°F (180°C) AND REMOVE A RACK
ROASTING BAG

MAKES 2 SERVINGS
2 chicken legs (each about 7 oz/200 g each, bone in)
Salt
½ tsp (2 mL) sweet paprika
1 tbsp (15 mL) canola oil
1 tbsp (15 mL) semi-dry sherry
1 small onion
1 small leek (about 3½ oz/100 g)
½ red bell pepper (about 3½ oz/100 g)
⅔ cup (150 mL/150 g) broccoli (about ⅓ medium bunch)
2 tbsp (30 mL) chopped fresh parsley

1 Trim the skin and underlying fat off the chicken legs. Rub with salt and paprika. Heat the oil in a skillet and brown the legs on high heat. Remove the legs and pour the sherry and 1 tbsp (15 mL) water into the pan, scraping up any bits.

2 Peel and quarter the onion. Slice the leek lengthwise, wash thoroughly and cut into 1½-inch (4 cm) pieces. Quarter and clean the pepper, and cut into 1 inch (2.5 cm) pieces. Divide the broccoli into medium florets; peel and julienne stem.

3 Place the chicken legs, pan juices and vegetables in the roasting bag; seal with the accompanying clip about 2 inches (5 cm) from the contents. Using a fork, poke the top of the bag once. Place the roasting bag on the cold oven rack and slide into the middle of the preheated oven. Bake for 35 minutes.

4 Remove the roasting bag and open carefully. Arrange the chicken and vegetables on two plates, sprinkle with parsley and serve.

!! **TIP** Rice or boiled potatoes go well with this dish.

South American Chicken Legs

Fat	+		1 hr. 40 min.
Cholesterol	128 mg		
Fiber	●		

Per serving: approx. 388 calories
31 g protein · 23 g fat · 13 g carbohydrates

PREHEAT OVEN TO 350°F (180°C)
OVENPROOF DISH OR ROASTING PAN

MAKES 2 SERVINGS
2 chicken legs (each about 7 oz/200 g, bone in)
1 clove garlic
¼ tsp (1 mL) salt
¼ tsp (1 mL) freshly ground black pepper
2 tbsp (30 mL) chopped fresh parsley
1 tsp (2 mL) liquid honey

FOR THE SAUCE
1 medium onion
1 garlic clove
1 green bell pepper
4 green olives
½ cup (125 mL) tomato juice
3 tbsp (45 mL) ketchup
3 tbsp (45 mL/20 g) slivered almonds
½ tsp (2 mL) ground cloves
1 tsp (5 mL) ground coriander seeds
Salt
Pinch freshly ground black pepper
Pinch cayenne pepper
1 tbsp (15 mL) medium-dry sherry

1 Trim the skin and underlying fat off the chicken legs. Peel and crush garlic and mix with salt, pepper and parsley. Rub into the chicken legs.

2 For the sauce, peel and finely chop onion and garlic. Halve, clean and finely dice pepper. Pit and slice olives.

3 In a small saucepan, heat the tomato juice and ketchup. Stir in the onion, garlic, bell pepper, almonds and olives. Bring to a boil and season well with cloves, coriander, salt, black pepper and cayenne.

4 Place the chicken legs in the dish, pour in the sauce and bake in the preheated oven for 40 minutes, basting frequently. Dilute the sauce with tomato juice as needed. Spread honey over the chicken legs and bake for a further 5 minutes, until done. Stir the sherry into the sauce and serve with the chicken legs.

Roasted Chicken Legs, top
South American Chicken Legs, bottom

Stir-Fried Chicken with Peanuts

Fat	+++	30 min.
Cholesterol	90 mg	
Fiber	●	

Per serving: approx. 504 calories
59 g protein · 22 g fat · 30 g carbohydrates

MAKES 2 SERVINGS
½ cup (125mL/100 g) scented Thai (jasmine) or
   basmati rice
2 chicken breasts (about 10 oz/300 g)
1 tbsp (15 mL) yellow curry paste
2 lemon or lime leaves or 1 stalk lemon grass
4 oz (125 g) snow peas (about 1½ cups, 375 mL)
3½ oz (100 g) mung bean sprouts (about 1 cup/250mL)
⅓ cup (75mL/50 g) peanuts
1 cup (250 mL) water
Salt
1 tbsp (15 mL) peanut oil
1 tsp (5 mL) granulated sugar
2 tbsp (30 mL) Asian fish sauce or soy sauce

1 Wash the rice and soak in cold water. Meanwhile, trim the fat and sinew from the chicken breasts and cut the meat into small strips. Mix with the curry paste, cover and let sit for 10 minutes.

2 Cut the lemon or lime leaves or lemon grass into paper-thin strips. Trim the snow peas. Coarsely chop snow peas and bean sprouts. Finely chop peanuts.

3 Bring the rice to a boil in the water. Add salt to taste, cover and cook on low heat for 10 minutes.

4 On high heat, heat the oil in a wok and stir-fry the chicken. Remove and set aside. On medium heat, stir-fry the lemon leaves, snow peas and sprouts. Stir in the sugar and fish sauce or soy sauce.

5 Put the chicken back in the wok, stir in the peanuts, heat through and cook briefly on low heat. Serve on the rice.

Turkey Breast with Leek and Cashews

Fat	●●●	25 min.
Cholesterol	60 mg	
Fiber	●	

Per serving: approx. 254 calories
29 g protein · 10 g fat · 8 g carbohydrates

MAKES 2 SERVINGS
3 tbsp (45 mL) soy sauce
2 to 3 tbsp (30 to 45 mL) rice wine
7 oz (200 g) turkey breast
1 medium leek (about 7 oz/200 g)
10 cashews
1 tbsp (15 mL) canola or sunflower oil
Salt

1 Mix the soy sauce and rice wine in a small bowl. Cut the turkey breast into strips. Combine with the marinade and let sit for 15 minutes.

2 Slice the leek lengthwise, wash thoroughly and julienne. Coarsely chop the cashews or leave whole. On low heat, toast the cashews in a dry skillet until golden. Remove and set aside.

3 Heat the oil in a skillet or wok. Reserving the marinade, remove the turkey meat, drain well and stir-fry on high heat for 5 minutes. Add the leek and reserved marinade, cover and braise on low heat for 5 minutes. Season to taste with more soy sauce or salt. Garnish with cashews and serve.

 TIP Rice and a leafy salad complete this dish nicely.

Stir-Fried Chicken with Peanuts, top
Turkey Breast with Leek and Cashews, bottom

Chicken Cutlets with Mango Chutney

Fat	●●●	30 min.
Cholesterol	90 mg	
Fiber	●	

Per serving: approx. 406 calories
35 g protein · 12 g fat · 33 g carbohydrates

MAKES 2 SERVINGS
1 ripe mango
1 shallot
2 tbsp (30 mL) canola oil, divided
¾ cup + 2 tbsp (200 mL) apple juice
2 tbsp (30 mL) cider vinegar
1 tsp (5 mL) liquid honey
1 to 2 tsp (5 to 10 mL) saffron
2 chicken breasts (about 5 oz/150 g each)
Salt and freshly ground black pepper
1 tbsp (15 mL) flour

1 Peel the mango and slice off the sides; remove pit. Julienne or dice flesh of the mango. Peel and finely dice the shallot.

2 To prepare the chutney, heat 1 tbsp (15 mL) oil in a nonstick skillet. On low heat, cook the shallot until translucent. Add the mango and cook for 1 minute, stirring constantly. Stir in the apple juice, vinegar, honey and saffron. Boil on medium heat for 10 minutes, until almost all the liquid has evaporated.

3 Meanwhile, trim any fat and sinew from the chicken breasts and shape into cutlets. Season with salt and pepper and coat lightly with flour.

4 Heat the remaining 1 tbsp (30 mL) oil in a nonstick skillet and sauté the cutlets on medium heat for 3 minutes a side, until golden. Add the mango chutney and heat through for 1 to 2 minutes on low heat.

!! **TIP** Serve with rice, such as flavorful perfumed Thai (jasmine) rice, or crusty baguette, as desired.

!! **VARIATIONS** Instead of mango, try apricot chutney. Cut 10 oz (300 g) fresh apricots in half, remove pits and cut into small wedges (you should have about 1 cup/250 mL). Then follow the instructions in step 2. You can make this dish spicier by stirring in 1 tbsp (15 mL) finely diced hot red or green pepper with the honey.

Chicken Cutlets on Chestnuts and Chicory

Fat	+	30 min.
Cholesterol	90 mg	
Fiber	●●●	

Per serving: approx. 711 calories
43 g protein · 16 g fat · 95 g carbohydrates

MAKES 2 SERVINGS
2 chicken breasts (about 5 oz/150 g each)
Salt and freshly ground white pepper
7 oz (200 g) chicory or endive (about 2 cups/500mL)
1 tart apple
1 tbsp (15 mL) freshly squeezed lemon juice
2 tbsp (30 mL) olive or canola oil
1 (20.5 oz /600 mL) can chestnuts (14 oz/425 g drained weight)
2 tbsp (30 mL) chopped fresh parsley or coriander

1 Trim any fat and sinews from the chicken breasts and carefully flatten with a meat tenderizer. Season with salt and pepper.

2 Clean and halve the chicory, trim the stalk and cut the leaves into strips. Peel the apple, grate into strips and drizzle immediately with lemon juice.

3 Heat the oil in a large nonstick skillet. On medium heat, sauté the cutlets for 6 minutes a side, until golden. Remove and wrap in aluminum foil to keep warm.

4 Transfer the chicory and apple to the same pan and cook for 2 minutes, stirring constantly, until tender-crisp. Add the chestnuts and their juice and heat through.

5 Arrange the vegetables on two warm plates. Place the cutlets on top, sprinkle with the parsley or coriander and serve.

Chicken Cutlets with Mango Chutney, top
Chicken Cutlets on Chicory and Chestnuts, bottom

Spicy Turkey Loaf

Fat	●	30 min.
Cholesterol	60 mg	(+ 1 hr. baking)
Fiber	–	

Per serving: approx. 198 calories
26 g protein · 5 g fat · 13 g carbohydrates

MAKES 3 TO 4 SERVINGS

2 slices whole-grain toast
1 medium onion
2 cloves garlic
1 tbsp (15 mL) vegetable oil
14 oz (400 g) turkey breast
1 medium carrot
1 tsp (5 mL) salt
1 tsp (5 mL) freshly ground pepper
1 tsp (5 mL) dried marjoram
3 tbsp (45 mL) fine dry bread crumbs
1/2 cup (125 mL) vegetable stock
1 tsp (5 mL) Dijon mustard
1 tbsp (15 mL) soy milk

1 Soak the toast in water. Peel and mince the onion. Peel the garlic and crush in a garlic press. Heat the oil in a nonstick skillet. On low heat, cook the onion and garlic until golden.

2 Trim any fat and sinew from the turkey breast, dice and grind finely in a meat grinder or food processor. Squeeze out the toast slices and grind in the meat grinder or mince well with a food processor or hand-held blender.

3 Peel and coarsely grate carrot. Thoroughly mix the ground turkey, onion, garlic, carrot, salt, pepper and marjoram. Form into a long loaf. Pour the bread crumbs onto a plate and coat the roll in the breadcrumbs.

4 Transfer the loaf to a roasting bag. Firmly seal at each end and poke the top a few times with a fork. Place the loaf in a cold oven, turn the oven on to 300°F (150°C) and roast for 1 hour.

5 Pour the vegetable stock into a small saucepan. Stir in the mustard and soy milk and bring to a boil. Slice the loaf on an angle, arrange on a plate and surround with the sauce.

!! **TIPS** Boiled potatoes go well with this dish. Any leftover loaf will make wonderful sandwiches, or try serving it cold with a leafy salad.

Turkey Strips with Spaetzle

Fat	+	30 min.
Cholesterol	94 mg	
Fiber	●●●	

Per serving: approx. 604 calories
51 g protein · 16 g fat · 67 g carbohydrates

MAKES 2 SERVINGS

¾ cup + 2 tbsp (200 mL) skim, 1% or 2% milk
Salt
1 tbsp (15 mL) oat bran
2 tbsp (30 mL) mixed fresh herbs, such as rosemary,
   thyme, basil, marjoram, oregano
1½ cups (375 mL/200 g) whole wheat flour
14 oz (300 g) turkey breast
1 bunch green (spring) onions
2 tbsp (30 mL) vegetable oil
Freshly ground black pepper
Hot pepper sauce

1 To prepare the spaetzle, combine the milk, salt, oat bran and herbs. Gradually stir in the flour until it forms a thick dough. Let the dough rest for 10 minutes to set up—it should then be firm enough to make small spaetzles.

2 Bring plenty of salted water to a boil. Transfer the dough to a spaetzle grater or cutting board and scrape small amounts into the water, a serving or so at a time. Bring back to the boil. When the spaetzle float to the top, remove with a slotted spoon, rinse in hot water and transfer to a bowl.

3 Cut the turkey breast into strips. Coarsely slice the green onions into rings. Heat the oil in a nonstick skillet. On high heat, brown the turkey and onions. Gently stir in the spaetzle and sauté until they are dry. Season with salt, pepper and a dash of hot pepper sauce.

!! **TOMATOES WITH BUTTERMILK DRESSING** A simple salad goes well with this dish. For the dressing, combine salt, pepper, ground coriander seeds, a dash of hot pepper sauce, ½ cup (125 mL) buttermilk, and 2 tbsp (30 mL) fresh or 1 tbsp (15 mL) dried Italian herbs. This will dress 10 to 14 oz (300 to 400 g) of tomatoes.

Spicy Turkey Loaf, top
Turkey Strips with Spaetzle, bottom

Turkey Breast on Pineapple Lentils

Fat	●●●	25 min.
Cholesterol	91 mg	
Fiber	●●●	

Per serving: approx. 478 calories
50 g protein · 13 g fat · 39 g carbohydrates

MAKES 2 SERVINGS
2 shallots
2 tbsp (30 mL) olive oil
¾ cup + 2 tbsp (200 mL) vegetable stock
½ cup (125 mL/100 g) red lentils
2 turkey cutlets (about 5 oz/150 g each)
Salt and freshly ground black pepper
Curry powder
¼ fresh pineapple
1 red bell pepper

1 Peel and finely dice the shallots. Heat 1 tbsp (15 mL) oil in a nonstick skillet. On low heat, cook the shallots until translucent. Pour in the vegetable stock, add the lentils and simmer 15 to 20 minutes, until the lentils are tender and the liquid absorbed.

2 Meanwhile, carefully flatten the turkey with a meat tenderizer or mallet, cut each cutlet in half and season with salt, pepper and curry powder to taste. Peel, clean and core pineapple; slice into fine pieces. Halve, clean and cut red pepper into thin strips. Add the pineapple to the lentils and heat through.

3 Heat the remaining 1 tbsp (15 mL) oil in a non-stick skillet. On medium heat, sauté the turkey pieces for 4 minutes a side, until golden. Remove and keep warm. Add the pepper strips to the same skillet, cook briefly and pour in a little water, scraping up any bits from the bottom.

4 Arrange the lentils on two plates with the cutlets on top and garnish with the pepper strips.

TIP If you prefer spicy foods, add 1 to 2 drops of sambal oelek, or to taste, to each serving of lentils. But be careful—sambal oelek is hot stuff.

Turkey Stroganoff

Fat	●●	20 min.
Cholesterol	63 mg	
Fiber	–	

Per serving: approx. 182 calories
25 g protein · 8 g fat · 1 g carbohydrates

MAKES 2 SERVINGS
14 oz (300 g) turkey cutlet
3½ oz (100 g) mushrooms
3½ oz (100 g) gherkins
2 tbsp (30 mL) vegetable oil
2 tbsp (30 mL) sour cream
Salt and freshly ground black pepper
1 tbsp (15 mL) freshly squeezed lemon juice
2 tbsp (30 mL) chopped fresh parsley

1 Trim any fat and sinew off the turkey cutlet and cut into small strips. Wash, clean and finely slice mushrooms. Finely slice gherkins lengthwise.

2 Heat 1 tbsp (15 mL) oil in a nonstick skillet. On high heat, sear the turkey for 3 to 5 minutes. Remove and wrap in aluminum foil to keep warm.

3 Heat the remaining 1 tbsp (15 mL) oil until very hot. On medium heat, sauté the mushrooms, stirring constantly so they won't soak up much liquid. Add the gherkins and heat through.

4 Remove from the stove, stir in the sour cream and season with salt, pepper and lemon juice. Add in the turkey and any juices that have accumulated and let sit for 1 to 2 minutes. Arrange on plates, sprinkle with parsley and serve.

TIP Broad egg noodles, rice or boiled potatoes go well with this dish.

Turkey Breast on Pineapple Lentils, top
Turkey Stroganoff, bottom

Rabbit with Fennel and Mushrooms

Fat	++		20 min.
Cholesterol	106 mg		(+ 40 min. baking)
Fiber	●●●		

Per serving: approx. 369 calories
36 g protein · 22 g fat · 5 g carbohydrates

PREHEAT OVEN TO 350°F (180ºC)
OVAL OVENPROOF DISH

MAKES 2 SERVINGS
1 bulb fennel (about 10 oz/300 g)
2 rabbit legs
Salt and freshly ground black pepper
½ cup (125 mL) vegetable stock
1 tbsp (15 mL) olive oil
3½ oz (100 g) mushrooms
1 tbsp (15 mL) vegetable oil
2 tbsp (30 mL) plain soy milk
2 tbsp (30 mL) chopped fresh parsley

1 Wash and trim fennel and remove the stalk in wedge-shaped pieces. Slice the fennel into half-moons and place in the ovenproof dish.

2 Trim any fat off the rabbit, season with salt and pepper and place on top of the fennel. Pour in the vegetable stock. Drizzle with olive oil and cover with aluminum foil (shiny side down). Bake in the pre-heated oven for 30 minutes. Remove the foil and roast another 10 minutes to brown the meat.

3 Clean the mushrooms. Heat the oil in a nonstick skillet on high heat. On medium heat, sauté the mushrooms, then cook gently while you mix in the soy milk. Garnish the rabbit and fennel with parsley and serve with the mushrooms.

Clay Pot Rabbit with Leeks and Apples

Fat	●●●	1 hr. 30 min.
Cholesterol	106 mg	
Fiber	●	

Per serving: approx. 269 calories
32 g protein · 12 g fat · 7 g carbohydrates

CLAY ROASTING POT AND LID, SOAKED IN WATER FOR AT
LEAST 20 MINUTES

MAKES 2 SERVINGS
1¼ lbs (600 g) rabbit
Salt and freshly ground pepper
Ground coriander seeds
2 small leeks
1 clove garlic
6 to 8 sprigs fresh thyme
1 tart red apple
½ cup (125 mL) vegetable stock

1 Divide whole rabbit into smaller pieces (breast, rump, legs, leaving legs whole). Rub with salt, pepper and coriander.

2 Cut the leek open lengthwise, wash thoroughly and slice into rings. Peel and finely dice garlic. Pluck the leaves from the thyme. Quarter and core apple; cut the quarters into rounds.

3 Combine the leek, garlic, thyme and apple in the prepared pot. Pour in the stock. Arranged the rabbit sections on top and cover with the lid. Place the pot on the bottom rack of a cold oven. Turn the oven on to 350°F (180ºC) and cook the rabbit for 1 hour and 15 minutes. Serve directly from the pot.

 TIP Boiled potatoes go well with this dish.

TIP A clay roasting pot doesn't tolerate temperature swings. It should always go into a cold oven or it's likely to crack.

MEAT AND POULTRY

Clay Pot Rabbit with Leeks and Apples, right

Pasta, Rice and Company

Pasta Salad with Tofu and Fennel

Fat	+		25 min.
Cholesterol	–		
Fiber	●●●		

Per serving: approx. 528 calories
23 g protein · 18 g fat · 70 g carbohydrates

MAKES 2 SERVINGS

1 tsp (5 mL) curry powder
5 oz (150 g) whole-grain pasta, such as elbows,
  spirals or noodles
3½ oz (100 g) firm smoked or extra-firm flavored tofu
1 small bulb fennel (about 8 oz/250 g)
½ small pineapple (about 8 oz/250 g cleaned)
1 tbsp (15 mL/10 g) walnuts
4 tbsp (60 mL) white balsamic vinegar
Herb salt and freshly ground black pepper
2 tbsp (30 mL) walnut oil

1 Bring a large pot of water to a boil. Season with salt and curry powder, add the pasta and cook on low heat according to package instructions until al dente.

2 Meanwhile, slice the tofu into slivers. Clean the fennel, removing outer leaves if necessary, cut in half and trim out the center stalk in wedge-shaped pieces. Slice the fennel bulb into strips. Chop the fennel greens and set aside. Peel, quarter and core the pineapple; finely slice into rounds. Coarsely chop the walnuts. Combine the tofu, fennel, pineapple and walnuts in a large bowl.

3 For the dressing, whisk the vinegar, herb salt, pepper and walnut oil. Toss with the tofu mixture.

4 Drain the pasta, plunge into ice water and fold in. Let the flavors combine for at least 30 minutes, garnish with the fennel greens and serve.

TIP Onion bread or freshly baked ciabatta go well with this dish.

Unripe Spelt Grain or Buckwheat Soup

Fat	●●		25 min.
Cholesterol	2 mg		
Fiber	●●●		

Per serving: approx. 209 calories
5 g protein · 8 g fat · 27 g carbohydrates

MAKES 2 SERVINGS

2 shallots
1 medium carrot
1 tbsp (15 mL) canola oil
¼ cup (50 mL /70 g) unripe spelt grain or buckwheat groats
  (see tip, below)
2 cups (500 mL) vegetable stock
3½ oz (100 g) mushrooms
1 tbsp (15 mL/10 g) coarsely chopped nuts, such as walnuts, hazelnuts or pine nuts
Salt and freshly ground black pepper
Freshly squeezed lemon juice

1 Peel and finely dice the shallots. Peel and coarsely dice carrot. Heat the oil in a nonstick skillet and cook the shallots on low heat until translucent. Add the carrots and cook briefly. Stir in the spelt grains or buckwheat groats and pour in the vegetable stock. Bring to a boil and simmer for 10 to 15 minutes on low, until the carrots are tender.

2 Meanwhile, clean and slice mushrooms. Toast the nuts in a dry nonstick skillet on low heat until golden.

3 Purée the soup with a blender or food processor and return to the pot. Stir in the mushroom slices and heat through. Season with salt, pepper and lemon juice, garnish with nuts and serve.

TIP You can thicken the soup with 2 tbsp (30 mL) plain soy milk or cream or sour cream for a creamier texture—but be careful not to let it boil again after this addition.

TIP If you can't find unripe spelt grains (a specialty of German cuisine, where it's toasted and eaten as Grünkern, "green seed"), you can also use coarsely ground buckwheat, oats or spelt.

Pasta Salad with Tofu and Fennel, top
Unripe Spelt Grain or Buckwheat Soup, bottom

Pasta with Tomatoes, Basil and Parmesan

Fat	●●●	25 min.
Cholesterol	8 mg	
Fiber	–	

Per serving: approx. 502 calories
20 g protein · 10 g fat · 81 g carbohydrates

MAKES 2 SERVINGS
14 oz (400 g) plum tomatoes
7 oz (200 g) linguine or fettuccini
1 medium onion
1 tbsp (15 mL) olive oil
1 small clove garlic
Salt and freshly ground pepper
6 to 8 sprigs fresh basil
1 oz (30 g) Parmesan cheese

1 Bring about 8 cups (2 L) salted water to a boil. Cut an X in the bottom of the tomatoes, blanch for 1 minute in the boiling water, peel, core and finely dice. Place the pasta in the boiling water and cook according to package instructions until al dente.

2 Peel and finely dice onion. On low heat, slightly heat the oil in a nonstick skillet large enough to hold the finished dish and cook the onion until translucent. Peel the garlic and crush in a garlic press. Add. Stir in the tomatoes and heat through.

3 Drain the pasta and mix well with the sauce. Season with salt and pepper. Tear or slice all but two of the basil leaves into wide strips; combine with the noodles. Arrange the pasta on a plate, grate the Parmesan overtop and garnish with the remaining basil.

TIP Freshly grated Parmesan is the perfect way to finish a simple pasta dish. Although 3½ oz (100 g) of Parmesan contains approximately 60 mg of cholesterol, it delivers no more than 9 mg in each serving of this dish. Parmesan is made from partially skimmed milk, so there's no need to avoid such a cheese altogether—and even a little delivers a whole lot of flavor.

TIP Plum tomatoes also deliver a lot of flavor. If you can't find them, use sun-ripened tomatoes of any type or good-quality canned plum tomatoes.

Leek and Noodle Stir-Fry with Cherry Tomatoes

Fat	+	25 min.
Cholesterol	8 mg	
Fiber	●	

Per serving: approx. 537 calories
20 g protein · 15 g fat · 80 g carbohydrates

MAKES 2 SERVINGS
7 oz (200 g) broad noodles, such as tagliatelle or egg-free (or whites-only) noodles
1 large leek
2 tbsp (30 mL) olive oil
Salt and freshly ground black pepper
1 tsp (5 mL) dried thyme
10 to 12 cherry tomatoes (about 3½ oz/100 g)
1 small clove garlic
2 oz (30 g) Parmesan cheese

1 Bring approximately 8 cups (2 L) of salted water to a boil. Add the noodles and cook according to package instructions until al dente.

2 Meanwhile, slice the leek lengthwise and wash thoroughly; cut lengthwise into strips the width of the noodles. Wash and quarter the cherry tomatoes.

3 Slightly heat the olive oil in a nonstick skillet. Cook the leek briefly, seasoning well with salt, pepper and thyme. Peel the garlic and crush in a garlic press. Add. On low heat, cook the leek, stirring constantly, for 5 minutes, until tender and coloring slightly but not browned.

4 Drain the noodles well and carefully mix with the leek. Stir in the tomatoes and briefly heat everything through. Grate the Parmesan. Arrange the noodles on two plates, sprinkle with Parmesan and serve.

Pasta with Tomatoes, Basil and Parmesan, top
Leek and Noodle Stir-Fry with Cherry Tomatoes, bottom

Spaghetti with Spicy Greens and Pine Nuts

Fat   ++   25 min.
Cholesterol   26 mg
Fiber   –

Per serving: approx. 628 calories
20 g protein · 22 g fat · 82 g carbohydrates

MAKES 2 SERVINGS

½ to 1 bunch (about 4 oz/125 g) mixed spicy greens, such as watercress, sorrel, dandelion, arugula (rocket) and radicchio
1 small red onion
1 clove garlic
⅓ cup + 2 tbsp (100mL/100 g) ricotta
⅓ cup (75 mL) vegetable stock
⅓ cup (75 mL) dry white wine
7 oz (200 g) spaghetti
3 tbsp (45 mL) pine nuts
1 tbsp (15 mL) olive oil
Salt and freshly ground black pepper
1 tbsp (15 mL) freshly squeezed lemon juice

1 Wash the greens, remove any tough stems and chop coarsely. Peel the onion and cut into small wedges. Peel the garlic. Whisk the ricotta with the stock and wine.

2 In a large pot, bring 8 to 12 cups (2 to 3 L) salted water to a boil. Add the spaghetti and cook according to package instructions until al dente.

3 Meanwhile, coarsely chop the pine nuts and toast on low heat in a dry nonstick skillet until golden. Remove and set aside.

4 Slightly heat the olive oil in the same skillet. On low heat, cook the onion wedges until translucent. Peel and crush in the garlic press and add. Add the greens and cook for 3 to 4 minutes. Pour in the ricotta-stock mixture and season with salt, pepper and lemon juice.

5 Drain the spaghetti well. Arrange with the sauce on two plates, sprinkle with pine nuts and serve.

TIP Spicy greens are available at markets. You can also get wild greens for free if you know where to look. Or use watercress, dandelion greens or rapini.

Spaghetti with Zucchini and Cheese Sauce

Fat   +   30 min.
Cholesterol   14 mg
Fiber   –

Per serving: approx. 597 calories
22 g protein · 19 g fat · 83 g carbohydrates

MAKES 2 SERVINGS

1 red onion
1 large zucchini
2 to 3 sprigs fresh sage or 1 tsp (5 mL) dried sage
7 oz (200 g) spaghetti
3 tbsp (45 mL) pine nuts
1 tbsp (15 mL) olive oil
1 small clove garlic
⅓ cup + 2 tbsp (100mL/100 g) low-fat cream cheese
¼ cup (50 mL) vegetable stock
Salt and freshly ground black pepper

1 Peel and finely dice the onion. Trim the ends and coarsely grate the zucchini. Pluck the leaves of the sage. Set aside a few leaves; cut the remainder into fine strips.

2 In a large pot, bring approximately 12 to 16 cups (3 to 4 L) salted water to a boil. Add the spaghetti and cook according to package instructions until al dente.

3 On medium heat, toast the pine nuts in a large dry skillet until golden. Remove and set aside. Heat the oil in the same skillet. On low heat, cook the onion until translucent. Peel the garlic, press in a garlic press and add. Stir in the sage strips, then the grated zucchini. Mix in the cream cheese and stock. Season the sauce with salt and pepper.

4 Drain the spaghetti thoroughly. Arrange on two plates and top with the sauce. Garnish with the pine nuts and reserved sage leaves and serve immediately.

PASTA, RICE AND COMPANY

Spaghetti with Spicy Greens and Pine Nuts, top
Spaghetti with Zucchini and Cheese Sauce, bottom

Fried Rice Noodles with Carrots and Leek

Fat	+	
Cholesterol	–	
Fiber	●	30 min.

Per serving: approx. 386 calories
13 g protein · 17 g fat · 49 g carbohydrates

MAKES 2 SERVINGS
3½ oz (100 g) broad rice noodles
1 green or red chili
3 tbsp (45 mL) cashews
½ inch (1 cm) piece fresh ginger
1 small clove garlic
2 medium carrots
1 large leek
2 tbsp (30 mL) oil
2 tsp (10 mL) garam masala
3 tbsp (45 mL) soy sauce

1 Place the rice noodles in a bowl, cover with hot water and let sit for 10 minutes.

2 Slice the chili lengthwise, remove seeds, if desired (it will cut down the heat), and cut into strips. Coarsely chop the cashews. Peel and finely chop ginger and garlic.

3 Peel the carrots and cut into 2 inch (5 cm) strips. Slice the leek open lengthwise and wash thoroughly. Cut the tender parts of the stalk and leaves into 2-inch (5 cm) pieces and slice the pieces lengthwise into strips.

4 Heat the oil in a nonstick skillet and toast the cashews on medium heat until golden. Add the ginger and garlic and brown lightly. Drain the rice noodles and transfer to the skillet along with the chili, carrots and leek. Mix well and season with garam masala and soy sauce. Stir-fry on medium heat for 2 to 3 minutes.

TIPS Instead of the mild Indian flavor the garam masala will give, you can season the stir-fry with curry or Chinese five-spice powder. And instead of fresh chilies, you can use sambal oelek or dried pepper flakes for a bit of a kick. But don't overdo it—you can always add more.

Farfalle with Turkey and Fennel

Fat	●●	
Cholesterol	76 mg	
Fiber	●●	30 min.

Per serving: approx. 584 calories
45 g protein · 8 g fat · 82 g carbohydrates

MAKES 2 SERVINGS
1 small bulb fennel
1 medium onion
8 oz (250 g) turkey breast
7 oz (200 g) farfalle (bowtie-shaped pasta)
1 tbsp (15 mL) olive oil
Salt and freshly ground black pepper
Ground coriander seeds
2 tsp (10 mL) stone-ground whole wheat flour
⅔ cup (150 mL) vegetable stock
1 tbsp (15 mL) freshly squeezed lemon juice
1 tbsp (15 mL) chopped fresh parsley

1 Trim and slice the fennel bulb into fine strips. Chop the tender fennel greens and set aside. Peel and finely dice the onion. Slice the turkey breast into fine strips.

2 In a saucepan, bring approximately 8 cups (2 L) salted water to a boil. Add the farfalle and cook according to package instructions until al dente.

3 Meanwhile, heat the olive oil in a nonstick skillet. Lightly brown the turkey on all sides for 2 to 3 minutes, until golden. Season with salt, pepper and coriander, remove from the skillet and set aside.

4 In the same skillet, cook the diced onion on low heat until translucent. Stir in the fennel. Dust with flour and cook lightly. Stir in the vegetable stock and simmer for 5 to 10 minutes.

5 Add back the turkey and continue to cook. Adjust the seasoning with more salt, pepper, coriander and lemon juice. Thoroughly drain the noodles and arrange on two plates with the turkey and fennel. Sprinkle with the fennel greens and parsley and serve.

Fried Rice Noodles with Carrots and Leek, top
Farfalle with Turkey and Fennel, bottom

Curried Rice with Coconut Vegetables

Fat	●●	20 min.
Cholesterol	1 mg	
Fiber	●●●	

Per serving: approx. 338 calories
16 g protein · 9 g fat · 53 g carbohydrates

MAKES 2 SERVINGS
1 medium onion
2 tsp (10 mL) soy oil
1 tbsp (15 mL) curry powder
½ cup (125 mL/100 g) basmati rice
1 cup (250 mL) vegetable stock
1 small Chinese (napa) cabbage (about 10 oz/300 g)
2 carrots
½ cup (125 mL) snow peas (about 2 oz/50 g)
1 cup (250 mL) mung bean sprouts (about 3½ oz/100 g)
1¼ cups (300 mL) coconut milk
Freshly ground black pepper
3 to 4 tbsp (45 to 50 mL) soy sauce

1 Peel and finely dice the onion. Heat the oil in a small saucepan. On low heat, cook the onion until translucent. Sprinkle with curry powder and brown lightly, stirring constantly.

2 Stir in the rice and cook until translucent. Pour in the stock. Cover and cook on low heat for 20 minutes, adding water as needed.

3 Trim the base and cut the cabbage into 1 inch (2.5 cm) strips. Peel and cut the carrots into very thin rounds. Trim and cut the snow peas in half or in thirds on an angle. Wash and drain sprouts.

4 Bring the coconut milk to a boil. On low heat, simmer the carrots and snow peas for 5 minutes. Add the Chinese cabbage and sprouts and cook for another 5 minutes. Turn up the heat to evaporate some of the liquid and cook until done to your taste. Season with pepper and soy sauce. Arrange the vegetables and curried rice on two plates and serve.

TIP You can make this dish more quickly by replacing the fresh vegetables with 10 to 14 oz (300 to 400 g) of frozen Asian or Chinese mixed vegetables.

Dried Mushroom Risotto

Fat	++	40 min.
Cholesterol	9 mg	
Fiber	●●●	

Per serving: approx. 536 calories
16 g protein · 28 g fat · 55 g carbohydrates

MAKES 2 SERVINGS
1 oz (25 g) dried porcini or dried mushroom of choice
1 bunch green (spring) onions
¼ cup (50 mL/40 g) pine nuts
2 tbsp (30 mL) olive oil
½ cup (125 mL/125 g) Arborio rice
½ cup (125 mL) vegetable stock
¼ cup (50 mL) dry white wine
Salt and freshly ground black pepper
1 oz (30 g) Parmesan

1 Place the mushrooms in a deep container, cover with 1 cup (250 mL) hot water and let sit for 5 to 10 minutes. Trim the root ends and finely slice the green onions into rings, setting aside the white and green parts.

2 On low heat, toast the pine nuts in a dry nonstick skillet. Remove and set aside.

3 Heat the olive oil in the same skillet. Add the white onion rings and cook until translucent. Add the rice and combine with the onions until the rice is translucent. Pour in the stock and wine and bring to a boil. Simmer on low heat until the rice has absorbed the liquid.

4 Add the mushrooms and soaking water to the rice and cook on low heat until all the liquid has been absorbed. Add the green onion pieces and cook another 3 to 4 minutes, adding water as needed. The rice should be creamy but still have some bite. Season with salt and pepper.

5 Grate the Parmesan. Arrange the risotto on two plates, sprinkle with pine nuts and Parmesan and serve.

Curried Rice with Coconut Vegetables, top
Dried Mushroom Risotto, bottom

Nasi Goreng

Fat ●●●
Cholesterol 80 mg
Fiber –

30 min.

Per serving: approx. 267 calories
25 g protein · 11 g fat · 15 g carbohydrates

MAKES 2 SERVINGS
½ cup (125 mL/100 g) Thai scented (jasmine) or
  basmati rice
1 medium leek
1 large red chili
1 clove garlic
5 oz (150 g) chicken breast
2 oz (50 g) peeled shrimp
2 tbsp (30 mL) soy oil
3 tbsp (45 mL) light soy sauce
Freshly ground pepper

1 Bring 2 cups (250 mL) water to a boil. Add the rice to the water and bring back to a boil. Cover and cook on low heat for no more than 15 minutes.

2 Meanwhile, slice the leek lengthwise, wash thoroughly and finely slice half into rounds. Peel and finely dice garlic. Slice the chili lengthwise, remove seeds, if desired, and cut into thin strips.

3 Cut the chicken into very thin strips. Rinse the shrimp with cold water and drain.

4 Heat the oil in a wok. Add the leek, garlic and chili and stir-fry for 1 minute. Move the vegetables to the side. Place the chicken in the center of the wok and stir-fry on medium heat. Add the shrimp and continue to stir-fry.

5 Stir in the rice and sauté, turning frequently. Season well with soy sauce and pepper.

TIP This tasty rice dish originates in Java and is a classic of Indonesian cuisine. Traditionally, the dish is finished with fine strips of omelet on top. Because the omelet is high in cholesterol, it's omitted here—but the whole dish is just as delicious.

Barley with Dried or Wild Mushrooms

Fat ●●●
Cholesterol –
Fiber ●●

40 min.
(+ 4 hr. soaking)

Per serving: approx. 443 calories
13 g protein · 12 g fat · 72 g carbohydrates

MAKES 2 SERVINGS
1 cup (250 mL/200 g) barley
1 oz (25 g) dried porcini or other dried mushrooms, or 7 oz
  (200 g) fresh woodland mushrooms, such as morels or
  chanterelles
4 green (spring) onions
2 cloves garlic
2 tbsp (30 mL) olive oil
Salt and freshly ground black pepper
½ tsp (2 mL) dried marjoram

1 Rinse the barley under cold running water. Pour 2 cups (500 mL) water into a medium saucepan, add the barley and soak for at least 4 hours or overnight. At the same time, soak the dried mushrooms, if using, in cold water in a small saucepan.

2 Bring the barley and dried mushrooms to a boil in their soaking water. Cook the barley on low heat for 8 to 15 minutes, until all the water has been absorbed. Cook the dried mushrooms on low heat for 10 minutes.

3 Meanwhile, trim the root ends and finely slice the green onions into rings. Peel the garlic. Drain the mushrooms (reserve the water for another use, such as stock) and coarsely chop the fresh mushrooms. Heat the oil in a nonstick skillet. On low heat, cook the mushrooms for 1 to 2 minutes. Mince the garlic in a garlic press, add and cook until fragrant. Stir in the barley. Season well with salt, pepper and marjoram and serve.

TIP A crisp leafy salad or gherkins go well with this hearty meal. Or serve it with a tomato sauce.

TIP You can use both fresh and dried mushrooms—sauté at the same time as the green onions.

Nasi Goreng, top
Barley with Dried or Wild Mushrooms, bottom

Polenta with Tomato-Sage Sauce

Fat	●●		40 min.
Cholesterol	3 mg		(+ 30 min. cooling)
Fiber	●		

Per serving: approx. 325 calories
8 g protein · 8 g fat · 54 g carbohydrates

9-INCH (23 CM) SQUARE PAN, GREASED WITH OLIVE OIL

MAKES 2 SERVINGS
2 cups (500 mL) vegetable stock
¾ cup (175 mL/125 g) finely ground cornmeal
Salt and freshly ground pepper
1 medium onion
3 to 4 sprigs fresh sage
1 tsp (5 mL) olive oil
1 clove garlic
1 can (14oz/398 mL) chopped tomatoes

1 In a medium saucepan, bring the stock to a boil. Add the cornmeal in a slow, steady stream, stirring constantly; cook, uncovered, on low heat for 15 minutes. Stir occasionally. Season with salt and pepper. Spread evenly in the prepared pan and let cool.

2 Peel and finely dice the onion. Pluck the sage leaves and set aside a few for the garnish; chop the rest. Heat the oil in a saucepan. On low heat, cook the onion until translucent. Peel the garlic, crush in a garlic press and add. Stir in the chopped sage and tomatoes, and season with salt and pepper. Simmer, uncovered, on medium heat for 10 minutes.

3 Turn the polenta out of the pan and slice. You can serve slices as is or grill or fry lightly till golden on both sides. Taste and adjust the seasoning of the sauce as required. Arrange the sauce and polenta on two plates, garnish with the reserved sage and serve.

TIP Polenta (or cornmeal) is especially enjoyed in Italy, Austria and Switzerland. Since the whole dried kernels are ground, their healthy parts are preserved.

Orecchiette with Tuna Sauce

Fat	●●		35 min.
Cholesterol	34 mg		
Fiber	●		

Per serving: approx. 373 calories
24 g protein · 7 g fat · 52 g carbohydrates

MAKES 2 SERVINGS
1 small onion
1 small bulb fennel (about 5 oz/150 g)
4 oz (125 g) orecchietti (ear-shaped pasta)
1 can (19 oz/540 mL) diced tomatoes or 1 lb (500 g) fresh tomatoes
1 tbsp (15 mL) olive oil
1 tbsp (15 mL) capers
1 can (6 oz/170 g) tuna packed in water
Dried oregano
Salt and freshly ground black pepper

1 Peel and finely chop onion. Clean and cut fennel in half, remove and discard the hard center stalk and slice the fennel bulb into thin strips. Chop the tender fennel greens and set aside. Dice the tomatoes, if fresh.

2 Bring 2 cups (500 mL) salted water to a boil. Add the pasta and cook according to package instructions until al dente.

3 Heat the oil in a nonstick skillet. On low heat, cook the onion until translucent. Add the fennel strips and cook 1 to 2 minutes. Add the tomatoes and capers, cover and cook for 10 minutes. Add the tuna and its water, breaking up with a fork, and heat through. Season well with oregano, salt and pepper.

4 Drain the pasta and arrange on two plates with the sauce.

Polenta with Tomato-Sage Sauce, top
Orecchiette with Tuna Sauce, bottom

Fried Rice with Peppers and Mushrooms

Fat	●●		25 min.
Cholesterol	45 mg		
Fiber	●●		

Per serving: approx. 418 calories
28 g protein · 8 g fat · 59 g carbohydrates

MAKES 2 SERVINGS
⅔ cup (150 mL/150 g) long-grain rice
1 medium onion
5 oz (150 g) turkey breast
1 red bell pepper
½ yellow bell pepper
8 oz (250 g) mushrooms
1 tbsp (15 mL) canola oil
2 tsp (10 mL) hot paprika
Salt and freshly ground black pepper

1 Rinse the rice. Bring 1⅓ cups (325 mL) salted water to a boil. Add the rice, cover and cook on low heat for 20 minutes.

2 Peel and finely dice the onion. Cut the turkey cutlet into thin strips. Clean and cut the peppers into small diamonds or cubes. Clean and finely slice the mushrooms.

3 Heat the oil in a deep nonstick skillet. On medium heat, brown the onion and turkey. Add the peppers and stir-fry for 2 minutes. Stir in the mushrooms and sauté briefly.

4 Stir in the paprika and mix well. Stir in the rice and cook on low heat for 1 minute. Season with salt and pepper and serve.

TIP You can leave out the turkey or replace it with sliced smoked or flavored tofu—then the dish will contain absolutely no cholesterol.

Thai Curry with Toasted Pistachios

Fat	++		30 min.
Cholesterol	–		
Fiber	●●●		

Per serving: approx. 279 calories
8 g protein · 21 g fat · 16 g carbohydrates

MAKES 2 SERVINGS
3 oz (80 g) green pistachios
1 clove garlic
½-inch (1 cm) piece fresh ginger
1 Japanese eggplant
1 red bell pepper
1 yellow bell pepper
2 tbsp (30 mL) soy oil
1 can (14 oz/400 mL) coconut milk
1 to 2 tbsp (15 to 30 mL) red Thai curry paste, divided
Salt
½ bunch green (spring) onions

1 Shell the pistachios. Toast in a dry skillet until they start to give off a scent, remove and set aside.

2 Peel and finely chop garlic and ginger. Trim the ends and cut eggplant into bite-sized pieces. Halve, clean and chop peppers.

3 Heat the oil in a saucepan or skillet. On low heat, cook the garlic and ginger until translucent. Stir in the eggplant and peppers and lightly sauté. Pour in the coconut milk. Season with some of the curry paste and salt and bring to a boil. Simmer on low heat for 8 minutes.

4 Meanwhile, trim the root ends and finely slice the green onions into rings; add along with the toasted pistachios. Bring back to a boil and season again with curry paste and salt.

TIP Basmati rice goes well with this dish. If you have any leftovers—or want to prepare only half—serve as a side dish. This curry goes well with grilled mackerel or other fish.

TIP Pistachios from California are a good choice. The nuts are processed within 24 hours to prevent the poisonous and carcinogenic aflatoxin fungi from forming.

Fried Rice with Peppers and Mushrooms, top
Thai Curry with Toasted Pistachios, bottom

Sweets and Desserts

Whole Wheat Crêpes Filled with Cheese

Fat	●	30 min.
Cholesterol	156 mg	(+ 15 to 20 min. baking)
Fiber	–	

Per serving: approx. 368 calories
24 g protein · 10 g fat · 46 g carbohydrates

11 INCH (28 CM) OVAL OVENPROOF DISH

MAKES 2 SERVINGS
¾ cup + 2 tbsp (200 mL) skim, 1% or 2% milk, divided
1 tbsp (15 mL) granulated sugar
1 egg
Pinch salt
⅔ cup (150 mL/80 g) whole wheat flour
2 to 4 tsp (10 to 20 mL) canola oil

FOR THE FILLING
1 tsp (5 mL) grated lemon jest
Juice of ½ lemon
¾ cup + 2 tbsp (200 mL/200 g) low-fat quark, puréed
    cottage cheese or strained yogurt
2 tbsp (30 mL) raisins
1 tbsp (15 mL) sliced almonds
1 to 2 tbsp (15 to 30 mL) granulated sugar

1 Combine 2 tbsp (30 mL) milk and the 1 tbsp (15 mL) sugar and set aside. Whisk the remaining milk, egg and salt; gradually whisk in the flour. Let rest for 10 minutes. Preheat the oven to 350°F (180°C).

2 Meanwhile, stir the lemon zest, juice and quark until smooth. Stir in the raisins, almonds and sugar.

3 In a small nonstick skillet, heat 1 tsp (5 mL) oil for each crêpe. Divide batter to make 2 to 4 crêpes and cook 3 to 4 minutes a side, until golden. Spread 2 tbsp (30 mL) filling on each, roll and place in the ovenproof dish. Spread the reserved milk mixture overtop. Bake in the preheated oven for 15 to 20 minutes, until crispy.

!! **VARIATIONS** The crêpe batter will make 2 large main-dish or 4 dessert crêpes. You can also mix 2 tbsp (30 mL) apricot jam or fresh seasonal fruit with the quark as desired.

Tofu Slices with Sesame Seeds and Orange Sauce

Fat	+	20 min.
Cholesterol	–	
Fiber	●	

Per serving: approx. 289 calories
13 g protein · 18 g fat · 21 g carbohydrates

MAKES 2 SERVINGS
4 oz (125 g) firm tofu
2 tbsp (30 mL) good-quality honey, such as honeydew
    (Black Forest honey)
3 tbsp (45 mL) sesame seeds
1 tbsp (15 mL) olive or canola oil
1 orange
½ tsp (2 mL) ground cardamom
Confectioners' (icing) sugar

1 Cut the tofu into ¼ inch (0.5 cm) slices. Slowly warm the honey. Place the sesame seeds on a plate. Dip the tofu slices in the honey and then coat with the sesame seeds.

2 Heat the oil in a nonstick skillet. On low heat, fry the tofu for 2 to 3 minutes a side, until golden.

3 Squeeze the orange juice and stir into the remaining warm honey. Stir in the cardamom. Divide the sauce between two plates and arrange the tofu slices on top. Dust with confectioners' sugar.

!! **TIP** You can serve the tofu slices warm or at room temperature, with a runny sauce. Or chill the sauce in the refrigerator until it sets and serve on the side.

!! **FYI** Agar-agar is a vegetable jelling agent available in health food or organic food stores. Be careful when serving it to children—it contains a lot of iodine. Adults should never use more than 1 tbsp (15 mL) per day, and half that for children.

SWEETS AND DESSERTS

Tofu Slices with Sesame Seeds and Orange Sauce, top
Whole Wheat Crêpes with Cheese Filling, bottom

Spiced Millet with Plums

Fat	●●●	30 min.
Cholesterol	4 mg	(+ 30 min. baking)
Fiber	●●	

Per serving: approx. 488 calories
20 g protein · 12 g fat · 71 g carbohydrates

10 INCH (25 CM) CASSEROLE DISH, LIGHTLY GREASED

MAKES 2 SERVINGS
½ cup (125 mL/100 g) millet
Pinch salt
1 cup (250 mL) water
¼-inch (0.5 cm) piece fresh ginger
¼ tsp (1 mL) grated lemon zest
Juice of ½ lemon
⅔ cup (150 mL/150 g) creamy low-fat quark, puréed
   cottage cheese or strained yogurt
1 tbsp (15 mL) honey
2 tbsp (30 mL) ground hazelnuts
14 oz (400 g) plums
2 tbsp (30 mL) granulated sugar
⅔ cup (150 mL/150 g) low-fat kefir

1 Bring the millet and salt to a boil in the water. Cover and cook on low heat for 15 to 20 minutes, until all the liquid is absorbed. Preheat the oven to 350°F (180°C).

2 Peel and finely grate or mince ginger. Combine the millet with the ginger, lemon zest and juice, quark, honey and hazelnuts.

3 Scrape the millet into the prepared dish and smooth the top. Cut the plums in half, remove pits and slice into thin wedges. Distribute over the millet and sprinkle with sugar. Bake in the preheated oven for 30 minutes, or until plums are tender. Serve with the kefir on the side.

!! **VARIATION** Use the same amount of cherries or a mixture of berries.

Sweet Pasta Stir-Fry with Blackberries

Fat	●●●	30 min.
Cholesterol	–	
Fiber	–	

Per serving: approx. 436 calories
12 g protein · 11 g fat · 72 g carbohydrates

MAKES 2 SERVINGS
5 oz (150 g) small pasta
1 tbsp (15 mL) diet margarine
2 tbsp (30 mL) slivered almonds
1 tbsp (15 mL) granulated sugar
¼ tsp (2 mL) vanilla
3½ oz (100 g) blackberries
Lemon balm
Confectioners' (icing) sugar

1 Cook the noodles in lightly salted water according to package instructions until al dente. Drain well.

2 Slightly heat the margarine in a nonstick skillet. Toast the almonds until golden. Sprinkle with sugar and brown slightly, then stir in the pasta and vanilla.

3 Carefully wash, sort and drain blackberries. Add to the noodles and carefully heat on low heat. Don't stir too often or the noodles will turn purple.

4 Divide between two plates, dust with confectioners' sugar and garnish with lemon balm.

!! **TIP** If you want to cook the noodles ahead of time, you should not only rinse them under cold running water but also cool them completely so they don't continue to cook on their own and get soft.

!! **VARIATION** This sweet pasta stir-fry can be made with other fruit, such as blueberries, raspberries or a colorful combination of berries.

SWEETS AND DESSERTS

176

Spiced Millet with Plums, top
Sweet Pasta Stir-Fry with Blackberries, bottom

Buttermilk Mousse in a Phyllo Basket

Fat	+	20 min.
Cholesterol	4 mg	(+ 1 hr.
Fiber	–	chilling)

Per serving: approx. 418 calories
10 g protein · 16 g fat · 60 g carbohydrates

PREHEAT OVEN TO 300°F (150°C)
4 TART MOLDS OR 1 MUFFIN TIN

MAKES 2 SERVINGS
1 sheet phyllo or strudel pastry
2 sheets or ½ (¼ oz/7g) package or
1½ tsp (7 mL) unflavored gelatin
¾ cup + 2 tbsp (200mL/200 g)
buttermilk
1 tbsp (15 mL) freshly squeezed
lemon juice
2 tbsp (30 mL) granulated sugar
1 tsp (5 mL) vanilla sugar
1 tsp (5 mL) liquid honey
2 tbsp (30 mL) soy milk
4 strawberries
Confectioners' (icing) sugar

1 Cut the phyllo into eight 4-inch (10 cm) squares. Lay two squares on top of each other to form a star. Line tart molds or muffin tins and bake for 5 minutes, until golden. Remove and let cool.

2 Soak the gelatin sheets in cold water or sprinkle powdered gelatin over ¼ cup (50 mL) water (and reduce the buttermilk by this amount). Mix the buttermilk with the lemon juice, sugar, vanilla sugar and honey. Dissolve the gelatin on low heat, mix with 2 tbsp (30 mL) buttermilk mixture and immediately stir into the rest of the mixture. Fold in the soy milk and chill for 1 hour.

3 To serve, scoop the mousse into the pastry baskets. Garnish with strawberries and dust with confectioners' sugar.

 **TIP** Instead of strawberries, use any fruit that's in season.

Poppy Seed Mousse with Fruit Sauce

Fat	●	20 min.
Cholesterol	2 mg	(+ 1 hr.
Fiber	●	chilling)

Per serving: approx. 146 calories
9 g protein · 5 g fat · 14 g carbohydrates

MAKES 2 SERVINGS
2 sheets or ½ (¼ oz/7g) package or
1½ tsp (7 mL) unflavored gelatin
¼ vanilla bean
½ cup (125 mL) skim, 1% or 2% milk
2 tbsp (30 mL) poppy seeds
2 tbsp (30 mL) skim, 1% or 2% milk
1 tbsp (15 mL) liquid honey
¼ cup (50 mL/50 g) creamy low-fat
quark, puréed cottage cheese or
strained yogurt
5 oz (150 g) mixed fresh or frozen
berries
1 to 2 tbsp (15 to 30 mL) pear nectar
Confectioners' (icing) sugar

1 Soak the gelatin sheets in cold water or sprinkle powdered gelatin over ¼ cup (50 mL) of the milk. Slice the vanilla bean, scrape out the seeds and add to the ½ cup (125 mL) or remaining ¼ cup (50 mL) milk. Stir in the poppy seeds, bring to a boil, cover and cook on low heat for 10 minutes. Cool slightly.

2 Dissolve the gelatin on low heat, mix with the 2 tbsp (30 mL) milk and stir immediately into the poppy seed milk. Mix in the honey and quark. Refrigerate to set for at least 1 hour.

3 Set aside a few berries and purée the rest with the pear nectar. Divide the fruit sauce between two bowls. With two spoons, shape small ovals from the poppy seed mousse and place on top of the sauce. Garnish with the remaining fruit, dust with confectioners' sugar and serve.

 **TIP** The mousse will be firmer if you grind the poppy seeds first.

Buttermilk Ice with Berry Sauce

Fat	–	15 min.
Cholesterol	4 mg	(+ 2 to 3 hr.
Fiber	●●	freezing)

Per serving: approx. 101 calories
7 g protein · 1 g fat · 15 g carbohydrates

MAKES 2 SERVINGS
¾ cup + 2 tbsp (200 mL/200 g)
buttermilk
½ tsp (2 mL) vanilla
2 tbsp (30 mL) frozen apple juice
concentrate
1 egg white
7 oz (200 g) mixed frozen berries
1 tbsp (15 mL) confectioners' (icing)
sugar
Fresh mint

1 Stir the buttermilk, vanilla and apple juice concentrate until smooth. Beat the egg white until stiff peaks form; fold into the mixture.

2 Transfer to a freezer-proof bowl, cover and freeze 2 to 3 hours. Whisk occasionally to prevent crystals from forming.

3 Meanwhile, thaw the berries (a microwave is useful for this). Set aside a few berries, purée the rest and strain through a fine sieve, if desired, to remove any seeds. Stir in the confectioners' sugar and chill.

4 Before serving, let the buttermilk ice stand briefly at room temperature, then mix with a hand-held blender or mixer until creamy. Scoop the ice onto the berry sauce and garnish with the whole berries and mint.

Buttermilk Mousse in a Phyllo Basket, top
Poppy Seed Mousse with Fruit Sauce, bottom left
Buttermilk Ice with Berry Sauce, bottom right

Cocoa-Pistachio Mini-Muffins

Fat	–	40 min.
Cholesterol	12 mg	(+ 12 min. baking)
Fiber	–	

Per serving: approx. 17 calories
1 g protein · 0 g fat · 2 g carbohydrates

PREHEAT OVEN TO 350°F (180°C)
BAKING SHEET, LINED WITH 55 SMALL PAPER CANDY CUPS

MAKES 55 MINI-MUFFINS
1 level tbsp (15 mL) unsweetened cocoa powder
Pinch ground cardamom
3 oz (75 g) pistachios
2 tbsp (30 mL) flour
Pinch baking powder
1 tbsp (15 mL) diet margarine
1 heaping tbsp (15 mL) candied lemon peel
2 eggs
Pinch salt
3 tbsp (45 mL/50 g) granulated sugar, divided

1 Mix the cocoa and cardamom. Shell the pistachios, rub in a dishtowel to remove skins and salt; grind until fine. Mix the flour and baking powder. In a small saucepan or microwave-safe dish, melt the margarine. Finely chop the candied lemon peel.

3 Separate the eggs. Beat the whites with 1 tbsp (15 mL) cold water and salt until very stiff, slowly adding all the sugar except for 2 tsp (10 mL). Beat the egg yolks, 1 tbsp (15 mL) warm water and the remaining 2 tsp (10 mL) sugar until frothy.

4 Fold the beaten whites into the yolks. Sprinkle with the cocoa, pistachios and lemon peel. Carefully whisk in the margarine.

5 Use 2 tsp (10 mL) dough to fill each paper candy cup about ⅔ full. Bake in the preheated oven for 10 to 12 minutes. Cool on a wire rack.

!! **FYI** Health in a nutshell—pistachios have the lowest fat content of all nuts, are rich in folic acid and contain more calcium than whole milk.

Raspberry Yogurt Sorbet with Pistachios

Fat	●●	20 min.
Cholesterol	–	(+ 1 hr. freezing)
Fiber	●●●	

Per serving: approx. 211 calories
8 g protein · 7 g fat · 30 g carbohydrates

2 DESSERT BOWLS OR GLASSES, CHILLED

MAKES 2 SERVINGS
2 oz (50 g) green pistachios
1 tsp (5 mL) orange zest
10 oz (300 g) fresh or frozen raspberries
3 tbsp (45 mL/25 g) confectioners' (icing) sugar
1 tsp (5 mL) raspberry syrup
1 tsp (5 mL) freshly squeezed lemon juice
¾ cup (175 mL/175 g) plain skim milk yogurt

1 Shell the pistachios, blanch briefly in boiling water and drain. Coarsely chop and toast in a dry skillet until they start to give off a scent, remove and set aside. Stir in the orange zest.

2 Freeze fresh raspberries, if using, on a baking sheet for about 3 hours. Use a blender or food processor to purée frozen berries with sugar, raspberry syrup, lemon juice and yogurt.

3 Immediately scoop the puréed mixture into the prepared bowls and sprinkle with the pistachios and orange zest.

!! **FYI** Increasing the proportion of monounsaturated fats in your appropriate total fat intake can have a positive effect on your health. These kinds of fats are found in such foods as pistachios, avocados and olive oil. Pistachios are particularly good as a snack. A serving of approximately 1 oz (30 g), or roughly 47 nuts, is rich in vitamins, trace elements—especially vitamin B_6, thiamine, magnesium, potassium, phosphorous and copper—and fiber. What's more, pistachios contain few saturated fats and no cholesterol.

SWEETS AND DESSERTS

Cocoa-Pistachio Mini-Muffins, top
Raspberry Yogurt Sorbet with Pistachios, bottom

Mango and Kiwi with Coconut Sauce

Fat	●●	20 min.
Cholesterol	–	(+ 20 min.
Fiber	●●	chilling)

Per serving: approx. 244 calories
2 g protein · 9 g fat · 37 g carbohydrates

MAKES 2 SERVINGS

4 tbsp (60 mL) shredded coconut
1 tbsp (15 mL) sugar
½ cup (125 mL) unsweetened apple
   juice
1 tsp (5 mL) vegetable binder, such
   as cornstarch
1 tbsp (15 mL) plain skim milk yogurt
1 large ripe mango
1 kiwi
1 tbsp (15 mL) freshly squeezed lime
   or lemon juice

1 In a dry nonstick skillet, toast the coconut on low heat until golden. Remove about 1 tbsp (15 mL) and set aside. Sprinkle the sugar over the remaining coconut and cook until pale gold. Carefully pour in the apple juice. Bring to a boil on high heat, then remove from the stove. Pour the sauce through a fine sieve, thoroughly squeezing the coconut. Whisk the strained coconut mixture with the binder and yogurt until smooth and let cool.

2 Peel and dice mango. Peel and slice or dice kiwi. Mix the fruit with the lemon or lime juice.

3 Arrange the fruit salad with the coconut sauce in dessert bowls and sprinkle with the reserved coconut.

Berry Jell with Vanilla Sauce

Fat	–	10 min.
Cholesterol	7 mg	
Fiber	●●	

Per serving: approx. 233 calories
3 g protein · 3 g fat · 41 g carbohydrates

MAKES 2 SERVINGS

10 oz (300 g) fresh or frozen mixed
   berries
1 tsp (5 mL) cornstarch
1 tsp (5 mL) liquid sweetener or 4
   tbsp (60 mL/60 g) granulated
   sugar
2 tbsp (30 mL) rum or ½ tsp (2 mL)
   rum extract

FOR THE VANILLA SAUCE

4 tbsp (60 mL) condensed milk (4%)
½ tsp (2 mL) vanilla

1 Wash fresh berries, if using. Transfer, still wet, to a saucepan and bring to a boil on medium heat, stirring constantly. Or slowly thaw frozen berries on low heat, then bring to a boil.

2 Dissolve the cornstarch in a little cold water, stir into the berries and boil for 1 minute, stirring constantly. Stir in the sweetener or sugar and rum or rum extract. Pour into two dessert bowls or glasses, let cool and refrigerate until ready to serve.

3 To make the sauce, combine the condensed milk and vanilla. Pour 2 tbsp (30 mL) sauce over each portion and serve.

!! **TIP** Double or triple the recipe and make more servings of this jell at the same time—they'll keep for several days in the refrigerator.

!! **TIP** When using raw eggs, make sure they're fresh. Or look for pasteurized eggs, whites or yolks in your supermarket.

Wine Jell with Yogurt Sauce

Fat	–	20 min.
Cholesterol	–	(+ 2 hr. chilling)
Fiber	–	

Per serving: approx. 192 calories
7 g protein · 1 g fat · 24 g carbohydrates

MAKES 2 SERVINGS

3 sheets or ¾ (¼ oz/7g) package or
   2 tsp (10 mL) unflavored gelatin
¾ cup (175 mL) red or black grapes
   (about 3½ oz/100 g)
1 cup (250 mL) dry white wine
1 tbsp (15 mL) confectioners' (icing)
   sugar
1 egg white
1 tsp (5 mL) vanilla sugar
⅓ cup + 2 tbsp (100 mL/100 g) plain
   skim milk yogurt

1 Soak the gelatin sheets in cold water for 5 to 10 minutes or sprinkle the powdered gelatin over ¼ cup (50mL) of the wine to soften. Wash the grapes, cut in half and remove any pits.

2 In a small saucepan, heat ½ cup (125 mL) wine and stir in the confectioners' sugar. Remove the saucepan from the stove, wring out the gelatin sheets (or add the softened gelatin) and dissolve in the hot wine, then add the remaining wine.

3 Set aside a few grapes for garnishing and place the rest in dessert bowls or glasses. Pour in the wine mixture and refrigerate until set.

4 To make the sauce, beat the egg white. Slowly add the vanilla sugar and beat until stiff. Fold the whipped egg white into the yogurt. Spoon over the jell and garnish with the reserved grapes.

Mango and Kiwi with Coconut Sauce, top
Berry Jell with Vanilla Sauce, bottom left
Wine Jell with Yogurt Sauce, bottom right

Silken Tofu and Banana Smoothie

Fat	–	5 min.
Cholesterol	–	
Fiber	–	

Per serving: approx. 129 calories
3 g protein · 1 g fat · 27 g carbohydrates

MAKES 2 SERVINGS
1 small banana
5 oz (150 g) silken tofu
Pinch salt
1 tbsp (15 mL) freshly squeezed lemon juice
Pinch ground cinnamon
1 tsp (5 mL) vanilla sugar
½ tsp liquid sweetener or 2 tbsp (30 mL/30 g)
   granulated sugar

1 Peel and coarsely chop the banana. Using a blender or food processor, purée the tofu with the banana, salt, lemon juice, cinnamon and vanilla sugar until smooth. Sweeten to taste with liquid sweetener or granulated sugar, refrigerate and serve chilled.

!! **TIPS** Depending on your tastebuds and seasonal offerings, you can use 3½ oz (100 g) of any fruit to purée with the tofu. And instead of tofu, you can use low-fat yogurt, creamy low-fat quark, puréed cottage cheese, low-fat sour cream or buttermilk.

!! **FYI** Tofu is available in various forms in Asian grocery stores, health food stores and most supermarkets. Tofu contains good-quality protein, has few calories and is cholesterol free. Silken tofu is a special type that's not pressed. After the thickening process, the tofu is strained. Its consistency is similar to that of stirred quark—perfect for smoothies with fruit.

Mocha Mousse

Fat	–	15 min.
Cholesterol	1 mg	(+ 1 to 2 hr. chilling)
Fiber	–	

Per serving: approx. 108 calories
14 g protein · 1 g fat · 12 g carbohydrates

MAKES 2 SERVINGS
1 heaping tsp (5 mL) instant espresso powder
2 sheets or ½ (¼ oz/7g) package or 1½ tsp (7 mL)
   unflavored gelatin
⅔ cup (150 mL/150 g) low-fat quark, puréed cottage cheese
   or strained yogurt
⅓ cup + 2 tbsp (10 mL/100 g) buttermilk
1 tsp (5 mL) liquid sweetener
1 tsp (5 mL) vanilla sugar
4 to 5 drops rum extract

1 Bring the coffee powder to a boil with 2 tbsp (30 mL) water and let cool. Soak the gelatin in plenty of cold water for 5 minutes or sprinkle the powdered gelatin over ¼ cup (50 mL) of the buttermilk to soften.

2 Whisk the quark with the (remaining) buttermilk and coffee. In a small saucepan, heat the wet (or softened) gelatin and dissolve, stirring constantly; immediately stir into the quark mixture. Stir in the sweetener, vanilla sugar and rum extract.

3 Rinse two small bowls with cold water, fill with the mousse and refrigerate for 1 to 2 hours, until firm.

!! **TIP** Turn the Mocha Mousse out onto dessert plates and garnish with fresh peaches, strawberries, kiwi or any fruit of your choice.

Silken Tofu and Banana Smoothie, top
Mocha Mousse, bottom

Sweet and Savory Baked Goods

Buttermilk Rolls

Fat	●●	20 min.
Cholesterol	1 mg	(+ 45 min. resting)
Fiber	●	(+ 20 min. baking)

Per serving (1 roll): approx. 214 calories
8 g protein · 9 g fat · 24 g carbohydrates

MAKES 6 ROLLS
1½ cups (375 mL/200 g) whole wheat flour
⅓ cup (75 mL/50 g) soy flour
½ tsp (5 mL) salt
½ cup (125 mL/125 g) buttermilk
1 tsp (5 mL) granulated sugar
1 package (¼ oz/7 g/2¼ tsp) active dry yeast
¼ cup (50 mL/50 g) diet margarine
Milk

1 In a large bowl, combine the whole wheat flour, soy flour and salt. Make a well in the center. Gently heat half the buttermilk to body temperature, stir in the sugar and yeast and dissolve. Pour the yeast mixture into the well, cover and let rise in a warm place for 15 minutes.

2 Using the kneading hook of a mixer, beat in the remaining buttermilk and pieces of the diet margarine. Knead with your hands until smooth. Cover and let rise for 15 minutes. Preheat the oven to 350°F (180°C). Line a baking sheet with parchment paper.

3 Divide the dough into 6 equal portions, shape each into a ball and place on the baking sheet. Cover and let rise for 15 minutes. With a sharp knife, score the top of each roll on an angle. Brush with milk and bake in the preheated oven for 20 minutes, until golden brown.

!! TIP These rolls are especially good served warm and spread with a low-fat cream cheese and fresh fruit. Or try the Cottage Cheese with Peppers and Curry (see recipe, page 46).

Apple-Nut Cinnamon Buns

Fat	●	30 min.
Cholesterol	–	(+ 20 min. baking)
Fiber	–	

Per serving (1 bun): approx. 93 calories
3 g protein · 4 g fat · 11 g carbohydrates

PREHEAT OVEN TO 350°F (180°C)
BAKING SHEET, LINED WITH PARCHMENT

MAKES 15 BUNS
FOR THE DOUGH
⅓ cup (75 mL/150 g) whole-grain spelt flour
1½ tsp (7 mL) baking powder
⅓ cup + 2 tbsp (100 mL/100 g) low-fat quark, puréed cottage cheese or strained yogurt
2 tbsp (30 mL/25 g) granulated sugar
3 tbsp (45 mL) olive oil
2 to 3 tbsp (30 to 45 mL) skim, 1% or 2% milk

FOR THE FILLING
1 tbsp (15 mL/15 g) diet margarine
2 tart apples
2½ tbsp (37 mL/25 g) pecans or walnuts
1 tsp (5 mL) ground cinnamon

1 Sift the flour into a bowl. Add the baking powder, quark, sugar and oil. Using the kneading hook on a mixer, knead together, adding enough milk to produce a smooth dough.

2 Briefly knead the dough by hand on a floured work surface and roll out to 16- by 12-inch (40 by 30 cm) rectangle.

3 To make the filling, melt the margarine and spread over the dough. Peel and finely grate apples and distribute evenly over the dough. Chop the nuts and sprinkle over the dough along with the cinnamon. Beginning with the long side, carefully roll the dough into a firm roll.

4 Using a sharp knife, cut slices approximately ¾ inch (1.5 cm) thick and place on the prepared baking sheet. Bake in the preheated oven for 15 minutes, until golden brown.

!! TIPS If you want to serve the buns for dessert, you can add a yogurt sauce consisting of ⅔ cup (150mL/150 g) low-fat yogurt, a pinch of vanilla sugar and a little granulated or brown sugar. The pecans can also be replaced by any other nut.

Buttermilk Rolls, top
Apple-Nut Cinnamon Buns, bottom

Mini Millet Rounds Topped with Tomatoes

Fat	–	30 min.
Cholesterol	1 mg	(+ 30 min. baking)
Fiber	–	

Per serving (1 round): approx. 35 calories
2 g protein · 1 g fat · 5 g carbohydrates

BAKING SHEET, LINED WITH PARCHMENT PAPER

MAKES 20 ROUNDS
1 cup (250 mL) vegetable stock
½ tsp (5 mL) salt
½ cup (125 mL/125 g) millet
½ cup (125 mL/125 g) low-fat quark, puréed cottage cheese
    or strained yogurt
1 tsp (5 mL) hot paprika
3 or 4 small tomatoes
2 tbsp (30 mL) chopped fresh basil
1 oz (30 g) finely grated Grana Padano or Parmesan cheese

1 Bring the stock, salt and millet to a boil. Cover and cook on low heat for 20 minutes, until all the liquid has been absorbed. Preheat the oven to 325°F (160°C).

2 Stir the quark and paprika until smooth and combine with the millet. Spoon 1 or 2 tsp (4 to 10 mL) onto the prepared baking sheet and press flat to form 1½-inch (4 cm) circles.

3 Slice the tomatoes into thin rounds and arrange on top of the circles. Sprinkle with basil and cheese. Bake for 30 minutes, until the cheese is melted and browned.

!! VARIATIONS Instead of tomatoes and basil, you can use rings of bell peppers and marjoram. And instead of Grana Padano, a hard Italian cheese, you can use Parmesan.

Mini Focaccias

Fat	●●	40 min.
Cholesterol	–	(+ 1 hr. resting)
Fiber	–	(+ 8 min. baking)

Per serving (1 focaccia): approx. 180 calories
4 g protein · 8 g fat · 22 g carbohydrates

2 BAKING SHEETS, BRUSHED WITH OIL

MAKES 8 FOCACCIAS
1 package (¼ oz/7 g/2¼ tsp) active dry yeast
1 tsp (5 mL) granulated sugar
⅔ cup (150 mL) lukewarm water, divided
2 cups (500 mL/250 g) whole wheat flour, divided
6 tbsp (90 mL) olive oil, divided
Salt
4 tsp (20 mL) dried thyme or pizza herbs
1 clove garlic

1 Dissolve the yeast and sugar in ⅓ cup (75 mL) of the lukewarm water and stir until smooth. Stir in 3 tbsp (45 mL) flour, cover and let rise for 15 minutes in a warm place.

2 Transfer to a medium mixing bowl and stir in the remaining flour, 3 tbsp (45 mL) oil, a pinch of salt and the remaining ⅓ cup (75 mL) water. Using the kneading hook on a mixer, knead the dough until smooth. Cover and let rise at room temperature for 45 minutes.

3 Divide the dough into 8 portions. On a floured work surface, roll out to form 4 inch (10 cm) rounds and place on the prepared baking sheets. Cover and let rise for 15 minutes. Preheat the oven to 425°F (220°C).

4 Combine the remaining oil with the salt and thyme or the pizza herbs. Peel, crush and stir in the garlic. Brush this mixture sparingly over the focaccias and bake for 8 minutes.

!! TIP For more flavor, spread a thin layer of tomato paste over the focaccias before seasoning.

Mini Millet Rounds Topped with Tomatoes, top
Mini Focaccias, bottom

Onion Crisps

Fat	●	15 min.
Cholesterol	4 mg	(+ 30 min. chilling)
Fiber	●●●	(+ 25 min. baking)

Per serving (1 crisps): approx. 140 calories
7 g protein · 6 g fat · 14 g carbohydrates

BAKING SHEET, BRUSHED WITH OIL

MAKE 16 CRISPS
FOR THE BASE
2 cups (500 mL/250 g) whole wheat flour
½ tsp (2 mL) salt
¾ cup + 2 tbsp (200 mL/200 g) low-fat quark, puréed
   cottage cheese or strained yogurt
4 tbsp (60 mL) olive oil

FOR THE FILLING
1¼ lb (600 g) onions
1 tbsp (15 mL) olive oil
Salt and freshly ground pepper
Hot paprika
2 tsp (10 mL) dried thyme
2 tbsp (30 mL) whole wheat flour
½ cup (125 mL) skim, 1% or 2% milk
½ cup (125 mL) vegetable stock
3½ oz (100 g) grated low-fat cheese (15% bf)

1 To make the base, combine the flour, salt, quark, oil and 5 to 6 tbsp (75 to 90 mL) water. On a work surface, knead until smooth. Cover and chill for 30 minutes.

2 Meanwhile, peel, halve and finely slice the onions. Heat the oil in a large skillet, stir in the onions and cook on medium heat for 20 minutes, until light golden brown. Season with salt, pepper, paprika and thyme.

3 Sprinkle the flour over the onions and, stirring constantly, gradually add the milk and the stock. Simmer on low heat for 5 minutes, then remove from the stove.

4 Preheat the oven to 350°F (180°C). On a lightly floured work surface, knead the dough one more time. Roll out to cover the prepared baking sheet in a thin layer; form an edge all around the outside. Distribute the onion mixture evenly and sprinkle with cheese. Bake for 25 minutes. Cut into 16 pieces.

!! **TIP** Buying low-fat cheese already grated is convenient, and it keeps for several weeks in the refrigerator.

Leek-Apple Quiche

Fat	●	30 min.
Cholesterol	30 mg	(+ 30 min. chilling)
Fiber	–	(+ 30 min. baking)

Per serving (1 wedge): approx. 122 calories
6 g protein · 5 g fat · 14 g carbohydrates

10 INCH (25 CM) QUICHE PAN

MAKES 1 QUICHE (TO SERVE 12)
FOR THE CRUST
1½ cups (375 mL/175 g) whole wheat flour
½ tsp (2 mL) salt
½ cup (125 mL/125 g) low-fat quark, puréed cottage cheese
   or strained yogurt
2 tbsp (30 mL) canola oil

FOR THE FILLING
1½ lb (700 g) leeks
1 tbsp (15 mL) canola oil
Salt and freshly ground pepper
1 tart apple
4 sprigs fresh tarragon or 1 tsp (5 mL) dried tarragon
¾ cup + 2 tbsp (200 mL/200 g) skim milk yogurt
1 egg
⅓ cup + 2 tbsp (100mL/100 g) skim, 1% or 2% milk
1 tbsp (15 mL) cornstarch
3 tbsp (45 mL) sunflower seeds

1 To make the crust, combine the flour, salt, quark, oil and 3 tbsp (45 mL) water. Kead well, cover and chill for 30 minutes.

2 Meanwhile, slice the leek lengthwise and wash thoroughly; finely slice into rings. Slightly heat the oil in a skillet. Sauté the leek briefly and season with salt and pepper; cook on medium heat for another 5 to 10 minutes.

3 Preheat the oven to 350°F (180°C). On a floured surface, roll the dough into a circle and transfer to the quiche pan.

4 Peel, quarter, and core the apple. Slice the quarters thinly. Immediately combine with the leek. Chop the tarragon leaves and whisk with the yogurt, egg, milk and cornstarch. Fold into the leek-apple mixture, season with salt and pepper, and distribute over the crust. Sprinkle with sunflower seeds. Bake in the preheated oven for 20 minutes. Cut into 12 wedges.

Onion Crisps, top
Leek-Apple Quiche, bottom

Mini Calzones

Fat	●●	30 min.
Cholesterol	–	(+ 20 min. resting)
Fiber	–	(+ 15 to 20 min. baking)

Per serving (1 calzone): approx. 199 calories
10 g protein · 8 g fat · 23 g carbohydrates

BAKING SHEET, LINED WITH PARCHMENT PAPER

MAKES 8 MINI CALZONES

FOR THE CRUST
2 cups (500 mL/250 g) whole wheat flour
⅔ cup (150 mL/150 g) low-fat quark, puréed cottage cheese
    or strained yogurt
1 tsp (5 mL) salt
½ tsp (2 mL) dried thyme
3 tbsp (45 mL) olive oil

FOR THE FILLING
1 medium onion
1 tsp (5 mL) olive oil
1 clove garlic
2 tsp (10 mL) dried thyme
2 small firm tomatoes
1 small green bell pepper
4 oz (125 g) mozzarella
Salt and freshly ground pepper
Olive oil
Dried thyme

1 Using the kneading hook on a mixer, knead the flour, quark, salt, thyme and olive oil with 4 to 6 tbsp (60 to 90 mL) water. Cover and let rest for at least 30 minutes.

2 Meanwhile, peel and finely dice onion. Slightly heat the oil. On low heat, cook the onions until translucent. Peel and crush garlic and add to the onions, season with thyme and remove from the stove. Cut an X in the bottom of the tomatoes, blanch for 1 minute in boiling water, peel, squeeze out the seeds and dice finely. Halve, clean and finely dice pepper. Finely dice or grate mozzarella. Combine the filling ingredients; season with salt and pepper. Preheat the oven to 400°F (200°C).

3 Knead the dough again and divide into 8 equal portions. Shape each into a round ball and, on a floured work surface, roll out to a 6 inch (15 cm) circle. Spoon 1 to 2 tbsp (15 to 30 mL) filling into the center of each circle, fold in half and press the edges together. Lifting carefully, use your fingers to create a decorative edge and pull the dough over the filling so the edge is at the top and the pocket is boat-shaped. Place on the prepared baking sheet, brush with oil and sprinkle with thyme. Bake for 15 to 20 minutes, until golden.

Picnic Pockets

Fat	●●	30 min.
Cholesterol	–	(+ 30 min. resting)
Fiber	●●	(+ 15 min. baking)

Per serving (1 pocket): approx. 319 calories
11 g protein · 8 g fat · 52 g carbohydrates

BAKING SHEET, LINED WITH PARCHMENT PAPER

MAKES 8 POCKETS

FOR THE CRUST
½ cups (375 mL/200 g) whole wheat flour
½ tsp (2 mL) salt
⅔ cup (150 mL/150 g) low-fat quark, puréed cottage cheese
    or strained yogurt
3 tbsp (35 mL) canola oil

FOR THE FILLING
2 bunches green (spring) onions
½ red bell pepper
1½ cups (375 mL/375 g) fresh, frozen or canned corn
Cayenne pepper
Salt
1 tbsp (15 mL) milk
2 tbsp (30 mL) sesame seeds

1 Using the kneading hook on a mixer, knead the flour, salt, quark and oil with 3 to 4 tbsp (45 to 60 mL) water. Cover and chill for at least 30 minutes.

2 Meanwhile, trim the root ends and finely slice the green onions into rings. Clean and finely dice pepper. Combine the green onions, pepper and corn; season with cayenne and salt. Preheat the oven to 400°F (200°C).

3 On a lightly floured surface, knead the dough again. Divide into 8 portions and roll out to a 6 inch (15 cm) circle. Distribute the filling over each and fold the lower edge over the upper. Using your fingers, press the edges together to form a decorative edge so the pockets are well sealed. Place on the prepared baking sheet, brush with milk and sprinkle with sesame seeds. Bake for 15 minutes, until golden.

Mini Calzones, top
Picnic Pockets, bottom

Savory Pinwheels

Fat	●●	50 min.
Cholesterol	8 mg	(+ 4 hr. chilling)
Fiber	●●	(+ 30 min. baking)

Per serving (1 pinwheel): approx. 392 calories
13 g protein · 24 g fat · 30 g carbohydrates

BAKING SHEET, LINED WITH PARCHMENT PAPER

MAKES 4 PINWHEELS
FOR THE PASTRY
¾ cup (175 mL/150 g) whole wheat flour
⅔ cup (150mL/150 g) low-fat quark, puréed cottage cheese
   or strained yogurt
½ cup (125 mL/100 g) diet margarine
Pinch salt

FOR THE FILLING
1 yellow bell pepper
1 large tomato
2 green (spring) onions
3 oz (75 g) sheep's milk cheese (20% mf)
Salt and freshly ground pepper
Milk

1 Using the kneading hook on a mixer, knead the flour, quark, diet margarine and a pinch of salt. Cover and refrigerate for 4 hours.

2 Halve, clean and slice the pepper into fine strips. Slice the tomato into rounds. Trim the root ends and slice the green onions into rings. Finely dice the sheep's milk cheese. Carefully mix the pepper, tomatoes, green onions and cheese; season with salt and pepper. Preheat the oven to 350°F (180°C).

3 Knead the dough again. On a lightly floured work surface, roll out to a 12 inch (30 cm) square about ½ inch (1 cm) thick. Cut into 4 smaller squares. Place the squares on the baking sheet and make a cut from each corner and on each side about halfway to the center. Spoon one-quarter of the filling into the center of each pastry. Fold every second section (the corner points) into the center to form a pinwheel and pinch the points in the center together. Brush with milk and bake for 30 minutes, until golden.

Sesame Rings

Fat	●●	20 min.
Cholesterol	–	(+ 70 min. resting)
Fiber	●●	(+ 25 to 30 min. baking)

Per serving (1 ring): approx. 296 calories
9 g protein · 11 g fat · 41 g carbohydrates

2 BAKING SHEETS. GREASED

MAKES 8 RINGS
3½ cups (875 mL/450 g) whole wheat flour
2 packages (each ¼ oz/7 g/2¼ tsp) active dry yeast
1 tsp (5 mL) sugar
1 tsp (5 mL) salt
¼ cup (50 mL/50 g) soft diet margarine
Vegetable oil
½ cup (125 mL/80 g) sesame seeds
Milk

1 With your hands, fluff the flour in a large mixing bowl and make a well in the center. Dissolve the yeast and sugar in ½ cup (125 mL) lukewarm water and pour into the well. Combine with some of the flour, cover and let rest for 10 minutes in a warm place.

2 Sprinkle salt on the dry flour, add diet margarine in pieces and stir as you add ½ cup (125 mL) water. Using the kneading hook of a mixer, knead the dough for 4 to 5 minutes. Put some oil on your hands and thoroughly knead again, cover and let rise for 1 hour in a warm place. Preheat the oven to 400°F (200°C).

3 Knead the dough again, form into a ball and divide into 8 equal portions. Roll each out to a rope about 12 or 14 inches (30 to 35 cm) long and form rings, firmly pressing the ends together. Place on the prepared baking sheets. Brush with milk and sprinkle with sesame seeds. Let the rings rise another 10 minutes, then bake for 25 to 30 minutes, until golden.

Savory Pinwheels, top
Sesame Rings, bottom

Egg-Free Filled Apple Cake

Fat	+	40 min.
Cholesterol	4 mg	(+ 15 min. resting)
Fiber	●●●	(+ 30 min. baking)

Per serving: approx. 304 calories
7 g protein · 15 g fat · 37 g carbohydrates

8-INCH (20 CM) SPRINGFORM PAN

MAKES 8 SERVINGS
FOR THE CAKE
½ cup (125 mL/100 g) diet margarine
1½ cup (375 mL/200 g) whole wheat flour
⅓ cup (75 mL/50 g) soy flour
1½ tsp (7 mL) baking powder
2 tbsp (30 mL/30 g) sugar
Pinch salt
⅓ cup + 2 tbsp (100 mL/100 g) skim, 1% or 2% milk

FOR THE FILLING
2 lb (1 kg) tart apples, such as Granny Smith, Mutsu or
   Cox's Orange Pippin
1 tsp (5 mL) lemon zest
Juice of ½ lemon
⅓ cup (75 mL/30 g) sliced almonds
3 tbsp (45 mL/40 g) sugar
Confectioners' (icing) sugar

1 For the cake, melt the margarine on low heat or in the microwave. In a medium bowl, combine the whole wheat flour, soy flour, baking powder and sugar. Stir in the margarine and milk. Using the kneading hook on a mixer, knead briefly. On a floured work surface, quickly knead again until smooth. Refrigerate for 15 minutes to rest. Preheat the oven to 350°F (180°C).

2 For the filling, peel and coarsely grate the apples. Combine with the lemon zest, lemon juice, almonds and sugar.

3 Roll out slightly more than half the dough to slightly larger than the pan and line the pan. Using your fingers, press to the top. Fill with the apple mixture. Roll out the remaining dough to an 8-inch (18 cm) circle and place on top of the filling. Firmly press together the edges and poke with a fork in a few places. Bake for 30 minutes, until the crust is golden and crisp. Dust with confectioners' sugar and cut into 8 pieces.

Rye Cake with Yellow Plum Topping

Fat	●	15 min.
Cholesterol	31 mg	(+ 30 min. resting)
Fiber	●●●	(+ 40 min. baking)

Per serving (1 piece): approx. 157 calories
4 g protein · 6 g fat · 21 g carbohydrates

10-INCH (25 CM) SPRINGFORM PAN, GREASED

MAKES 12 SERVINGS
1½ cups (375 mL/200 g) dark rye flour
⅓ cup (75 mL/50 g) soy flour
⅔ cup (150 mL/150 g) skim, 1% or 2% milk, divided
¼ cup (50 mL/50 g) granulated sugar, divided
1 package (¼ oz/7 g/2¼ tsp) active dry yeast
4 tbsp (60 mL/60 g) diet margarine
1 egg
Salt
1 tsp (5 mL) vanilla sugar
1 tsp (5 mL) lemon zest
1 lb (450 g) yellow plums
Confectioners' (icing) sugar

1 In a medium bowl, combine the rye flour and soy flour and make a well in the center. Heat the milk to about body temperature. Combine 4 tbsp (60 mL) milk with 1 tbsp (15 mL) sugar and stir in the yeast. Pour into the well and let rise for 15 minutes in a warm place.

2 Add the remaining milk and sugar, diet margarine in pieces, egg, salt, vanilla sugar and lemon zest. Knead with the kneading hook on a mixer. Cover and let rise 15 minutes.

3 Meanwhile, cut the plums in half, remove pits and cut into wedges. Preheat the oven to 350°F (180°C).

4 Transfer the dough to the prepared pan and spread evenly. Press in the plums. Bake for 20 minutes. Dust with confectioners' sugar and bake another 15 to 20 minutes, until the edges are golden. Cool on a wire rack. Before serving, dust again with confectioners' sugar and cut into 12 pieces.

Egg-Free Filled Apple Cake, top
Rye Cake Topped with Yellow Plum Topping, bottom

Orange-Rice Galette

Fat	●	1 hr.
Cholesterol	2 mg	(+ 3 hr. chilling)
Fiber	–	(+ 20 to 25 min. baking)

Per serving: approx. 171 calories
4 g protein · 5 g fat · 24 g carbohydrates

10-INCH (25 CM) SPRINGFORM PAN

MAKES 12 SERVINGS
FOR THE PASTRY
1 cup (250 mL/125 g) spelt flour
4 tbsp (60 mL/60 g) cold diet margarine
2 tbsp (30 mL) confectioners' (icing) sugar

FOR THE FILLING
2 cups (500 mL) skim, 1% or 2% milk
2 tsp (10 mL) vanilla sugar
2/3 cup (150 mL/130 g) long-grain rice
2 oranges
6 sheets or 1½ packages (each ¼ oz/7g) or 1½ tbsp
   (22 mL) unflavored gelatin
2 tbsp (30 mL/50 g) orange marmalade
3 tbsp (45 mL/50 g) candied orange peel
12 fresh mint leaves

1 Combine the flour, margarine and confectioners' sugar with 2 to 3 tbsp (30 to 45 mL) cold water and knead briefly. Wrap in plastic wrap and chill 30 minutes. Preheat the oven to 325°F (160°C).

2 Between 2 sheets of plastic wrap, roll out the dough to fit the pan and line the bottom. Using a fork, poke several holes in the dough and bake for 20 minutes. Cool on a wire rack.

3 Meanwhile, bring the milk to a boil. Sprinkle in the vanilla sugar and rice. Cook on low heat for 40 minutes. Turn off the heat and let sit to absorb all the liquid.

4 Grate the zest of the oranges. Peel and separate the orange into segments, reserving the juice. Soak the gelatin sheets in cold water for 5 minutes or sprinkle the powdered gelatin over ¼ cup (50 mL) of the orange juice. Dissolve in a warm double boiler or microwave oven. Combine with the reserved orange juice, orange zest and rice. Dice the orange segments and gently mix in.

5 Carefully transfer the pastry to a cake platter. Heat the marmalade and spread over pastry. Fasten a cake ring or the top of the springform pan around the pastry and fill with the rice. Cover and chill for at least 2 hours. Finely chop the candied orange peel. Garnish the cake with candied orange peel and mint; cut into 12 pieces.

SWEET AND SAVORY BAKED GOODS

French Apple Tart

Fat	●●	30 min.
Cholesterol	1 mg	(+ 1 hr. chilling)
Fiber	–	(+ 35 to 40 min. baking)

Per serving: approx. 173 calories
2 g protein · 7 g fat · 25 g carbohydrates

BAKING SHEET, LINED WITH PARCHMENT PAPER

MAKES 6 SERVINGS
FOR THE PASTRY
¾ + 2 tbsp cup (200 mL/100 g) all-purpose flour
4 tbsp (60 mL/50 g) cold diet margarine
2 tbsp (30 mL) confectioners' (icing) sugar

FOR THE FILLING
2 small tart apples
1 tbsp (15 mL) freshly squeezed lemon juice
3 tbsp (45 mL/20 g) sliced almonds
2 tsp (10 mL) granulated sugar
3 tbsp (45 mL/75 g) apple jelly

1 Mix the flour, margarine and confectioners' sugar with 1 to 2 tbsp (15 to 30 mL) cold water and knead briefly. Wrap in plastic wrap and chill for at least 1 hour.

2 Preheat the oven to 325°F (160°C). Roll out the dough between 2 sheets of plastic wrap to form a roughly 8-inch (20 cm) circle. Remove the upper sheet of plastic wrap and use the lower sheet to help carefully transfer the dough to the baking sheet. Remove the plastic wrap. Use the bottom of an 8-inch (20 cm) springform pan to cut a circle, then press to form a raised edge. Bake the pastry until golden. Using a fork, break any air blisters that may have formed.

3 Peel, quarter, core and slice the apples into thin wedges, drizzle with lemon juice and arrange decoratively on the pastry. Sprinkle the almonds and sugar on top and bake another 20 to 25 minutes. Heat the apple jelly and brush over the tart. Cut into 6 pieces and serve.

French Apple Tart, top
Orange-Rice Galette, bottom

Small Cheese Strudels with Apricots

Fat	–	40 min.
Cholesterol	26 mg	(+ 30 min. resting)
Fiber	–	(+ 35 min. baking)

Per serving: approx. 214 calories
13 g protein · 2 g fat · 35 g carbohydrates

BAKING SHEET, LINED WITH PARCHMENT PAPER

MAKES 12 SERVINGS
FOR THE PASTRY
2½ cups (625 mL/300 g) all-purpose flour
1 small egg
1 tbsp (15 mL) vinegar
1 tbsp (15 mL) oil
Pinch salt
½ cup (125 mL) lukewarm water

FOR THE FILLING
3 cups (750 mL/750 g) low-fat quark, puréed cottage
   cheese or strained yogurt
2 tbsp (30 mL/50 g) sultanas (golden raisins)
2 tsp (10 mL) vanilla sugar
⅓ cup (75 mL/75 g) granulated sugar
3 tbsp (45 mL) slivered almonds
5 to 6 fresh apricots
2 tbsp (30 mL) skim, 1% or 2% milk
1 tbsp (15 mL) confectioners' (icing) sugar

1 To prepare the pastry, knead together the flour, egg, vinegar, oil salt and water for 5 minutes, until smooth and elastic. Let the dough rest under a damp towel for at least 30 minutes.

2 For the filling, mix the quark, sultanas, vanilla sugar, sugar and almonds. Pit and finely dice apricots; mix carefully into the cheese mixture. Preheat the oven to 350°F (180°C).

3 Divide the dough into 3 portions. Roll out each on a lightly floured surface. Using your hands and a floured tea towel, pull to form a thin rectangle. Spread one-third of the filling over each rolled-out rectangle, leaving a ½-inch (2 cm) border. Fold the short sides over the filling, then start to roll, beginning with a long side.

4 Place the strudels side by side on the prepared baking sheet, seam side down. Make 4 shallow diagonal cuts on top of each strudel. Brush with milk and bake for 35 minutes. Dust with confectioners' sugar, slice along the cuts and serve.

Pear Tart

Fat	●	30 min.
Cholesterol	15 mg	(+ 30 min. baking)
Fiber	●	

Per serving: approx. 130 calories
4 g protein · 5 g fat · 18 g carbohydrates

PREHEAT OVEN TO 350°F (180°C)
RIMMED BAKING SHEET, OILED

MAKES 20 SERVINGS
FOR THE PASTRY
⅔ cup (150 mL/150 g) low-fat quark, puréed cottage cheese
   or strained yogurt
1 small egg
2 tbsp (30 mL/30 g) granulated sugar
Pinch salt
2 to 3 tbsp (30 to 45 mL) skim, 1% or 2% milk
2 tbsp (30 mL) oil
2¼ cups (550 mL/275 g) whole wheat flour
2 tsp (10 mL) baking powder

FOR THE FILLING
3 to 4 lbs (1.5 to 2 kg) firm, ripe pears
2 tsp (10 mL) vanilla sugar
3½ oz (100 g) sliced almonds

1 To prepare the pastry, mix the quark, egg, sugar, salt, milk and oil. Combine the flour and baking powder. Stir into the quark mixture and knead until smooth.

2 Roll out a thin layer of dough on a lightly floured surface and line the prepared baking sheet. Press edges to form a small rim on all sides.

3 Peel, quarter, core and cut the pears into wedges; distribute over the dough. Sprinkle with vanilla sugar and almonds. Bake in the preheated oven for 30 minutes. Serve fresh—preferably still warm.

!! **VARIATION** You can make this tart with other fruit, such as tart apples, plums or apricots. Don't use fruit that's too juicy or the pastry will get soggy.

Small Quark Strudels with Apricots, top
Pear Tart, bottom

Buckwheat Tart with Cheese Filling and Kiwis

Fat	●●	35 min.
Cholesterol	38 mg	(+ 40 min. baking)
Fiber	●●●	

Per serving: approx. 202 calories
6 g protein · 9 g fat · 23 g carbohydrates

10-INCH (25 CM) TART PAN, GREASED

MAKES 8 SERVINGS
FOR THE BASE
⅔ cup (150 mL/130 g) buckwheat groats
1 cup (250 mL) water
½ vanilla bean
1 tbsp (15 mL/30 g) ground hazelnuts (filberts)
2 tbsp (30 mL/20 g) raisins
¼ cup (50 mL/50 g) diet margarine
1 tbsp (15 mL) liquid honey
1 egg
⅓ cup (75 mL/40 g) whole wheat or spelt flour

FOR THE FILLING
⅔ cup (150 mL/150 g) creamy low-fat quark, puréed cottage cheese or strained yogurt
3 tbsp (45 mL) granulated sugar
3 kiwis
Confectioners' (icing) sugar

1 Rinse the buckwheat under cold water. Place in a saucepan with the water. Slice the vanilla bean lengthwise, scrape out the seeds and add along with the pod. Bring to a boil, cover and cook on low heat for 15 minutes, until all the liquid has been absorbed. Cool slightly. Preheat the oven to 325°F (160°C).

2 Mix the hazelnuts, raisins, margarine, honey, egg and buckwheat. Gradually stir in the flour until firm and spreadable and line the bottom of the prepared tart pan. Bake for 40 minutes, until crisp on the edges. Leave to cool.

3 To make the filling, mix the quark with the sugar and spread over the base. Peel the kiwis, slice into rounds and distribute over the filling. Dust with confectioners' sugar and cut into 8 pieces.

Quick Coffee Ring

Fat	●	30 min.
Cholesterol	34 mg	(+ 25 min. baking)
Fiber	–	

Per serving: approx. 168 calories
5 g protein · 6 g fat · 25 g carbohydrates

PREHEAT OVEN TO 400°F (200°C)
BAKING SHEET, LINED WITH PARCHMENT PAPER

MAKES 18 SERVINGS
3¼ cups (800 mL/400 g) stone-ground whole wheat flour
1 tbsp (15 mL) baking powder
Pinch salt
1 tsp (5 mL) ground cinnamon
½ cup (125 mL/100 g) granulated sugar
½ cup (125 mL/100 g) soft diet margarine
¼ cup (50 mL/50 g) low-fat quark, puréed cottage cheese or strained yogurt
2 small eggs
½ cup (125 mL/75 g) sultanas (golden raisins)
Confectioners' (icing) sugar

1 In a large bowl, mix the flour, baking powder, salt, cinnamon and sugar. Stir in the margarine until crumbly. Stir in the quark, eggs and sultanas; knead together.

2 Using your hands, knead the dough on a work surface. Form a 16-inch (40 cm) log, about the length of the prepared baking sheet. On the baking sheet, form a ring, press the ends together and shape evenly. Bake for 25 minutes, until golden. Dust with confectioners' sugar and serve.

!! TIP A sponge cake is usually made with a lot of fat and eggs and, as a result, isn't suitable for a cholesterol friendly diet. With this cake, you're learning a lean variation in which some of the fat and eggs are replaced by a low-fat ingredient.

Buckwheat Tart with Cheese Filling and Kiwis, top
Quick Coffee Ring, bottom

Cool Kefir and Raspberry Squares

Fat	●●●		30 min.
Cholesterol	36 mg		(+ 15 min. baking)
Fiber	●		(+ 3 hr. + 30 min. chilling)

Per serving: approx. 245 calories
7 g protein · 11 g fat · 27 g carbohydrates

7 BY 11 INCH (2 L) DISH, GREASED AND FLOURED

MAKES 10 SERVINGS
FOR THE BASE
⅓ cup + 2 tbsp (100mL/200 g) whole wheat flour
⅓ cup (75 mL/50 g) confectioners' (icing) sugar
1 small egg yolk
Pinch salt
¼ cup (50 mL/50 g) low-fat quark, puréed cottage cheese
   or strained yogurt
½ cup (125 mL/100 g) cold diet margarine

FOR THE FILLING
10 oz (300 g) frozen raspberries
8 sheets or 2 packages (each ¼ oz/7g) or 1½ tbsp (22 mL)
   unflavored gelatin
Zest and juice of 1 lemon
2 cups (500 mL/500 g) low-fat kefir
3 tbsp (45 mL) granulated sugar
1 small egg white
3 tbsp (45 mL) pistachios

1 Briefly knead together the flour, confectioners' sugar, egg yolk, quark and diet margarine. Cover and chill for at least 30 minutes. Preheat the oven to 350°F (180°C).

2 Roll out the dough between 2 sheets of plastic wrap cut to the size of the pan. Remove the upper sheet, lift the dough into the pan and remove the lower sheet. Press the dough into the corners, but don't create an edge. Using a fork, poke several holes. Bake for 15 minutes, until golden. Leave to cool.

3 For the filling, thaw the raspberries. Soak the gelatin in plenty of cold water for 5 minutes or sprinkle powdered gelatin over the juice of the lemon. Dissolve in warm water or lemon juice, heated. Stir in a little kefir, then combine the gelatin with the remaining kefir, lemon zest, lemon juice (if not already used) and sugar. Beat the egg white until stiff and fold in. Set aside a few raspberries for garnishing; fold the rest into the kefir.

4 Transfer to baked base and chill for at least 3 hours. Cut into 12 pieces, carefully lift out of the pan and garnish with raspberries and pistachios.

Mocha Cream Kisses

Fat	●		30 min.
Cholesterol	14 mg		(+ 90 min. baking)
Fiber	–		

Per serving: approx. 196 calories
8 g protein · 4 g fat · 32 g carbohydrates

PREHEAT OVEN TO 200°F (100°C)
BAKING SHEET, LINED WITH PARCHMENT PAPER

MAKES 8 SERVINGS
4 egg whites
1⅔ cups (400 mL/200 g) confectioners' (icing) sugar
1 tsp (5 mL) cornstarch or potato starch
3 sheets or ¾ (¼ oz/7g) package or 2 tsp (10 mL)
   unflavored gelatin
4 tbsp (60 mL) strong cold espresso
1¼ cups (300 mL/300 g) low-fat quark, puréed cottage
   cheese or strained yogurt
2 tbsp (30 mL) granulated sugar
¼ tsp (2 mL) vanilla
1 tbsp (15 mL) sifted unsweetened cocoa powder
⅓ cup + 2 tbsp (100 mL/100 g) whipping (35%) cream
Unsweetened cocoa powder and mocha coffee beans

1 Beat the egg whites until stiff peaks form, slowly adding the confectioners' sugar just toward the end (the beaten whites must be stiff enough to slice). Fold in the cornstarch.

2 Transfer to a pastry bag with a medium-sized flat tip and pipe 3-inch (7.5) circles onto the prepared baking sheet. Pipe small decorative tips along the edge. Turn off preheated oven and let dry in the oven for 90 minutes with the door partially open. Let cool.

3 Soak the gelatin in plenty of cold water or sprinkle powdered gelatin over the espresso and leave for 5 minutes. Wring out the sheets, if using, and heat the espresso until the gelatin is dissolved. Let it cool slightly, then mix with the quark, granulated sugar, vanilla and cocoa. Chill until the mixture begins to set. Beat the cream until stiff and fold in. Let rest for 15 minutes. Pipe into the center of each kiss. Garnish with cocoa and coffee beans.

Mocha Cream Kisses, top
Cool Kefir and Raspberry Squares, bottom

SWEET AND SAVORY BAKED GOODS

Poppy Seed Pockets

Fat	●	1 hr.
Cholesterol	1 mg	(+ 75 min. resting)
Fiber	●	(+ 15 min. baking)

Per serving (1 pocket): approx. 157 calories
8 g protein · 4 g fat · 22 g carbohydrates

BAKING SHEET, LINED WITH PARCHMENT PAPER

MAKES 12 POCKETS
FOR THE CRUST
1 package (¼ oz/7 g/2¼ tsp) active dry yeast
⅓ cup + 2 tbsp (100 mL/100 g) lukewarm milk
2 tbsp (30 mL) granulated sugar
2 cups (500 mL/250 g) spelt flour
⅓ cup + 2 tbsp (100 mL/100 g) low-fat quark, puréed
    cottage cheese or strained yogurt
Pinch salt

FOR THE FILLING
½ cup (125 mL/75 g) ground poppy seeds
⅓ cup + 2 tbsp (100 mL/100 g) milk
¾ cup + 2 tbsp (200 mL/200 g) low-fat quark, puréed
    cottage cheese or strained yogurt
3 tbsp (45 mL) granulated sugar or liquid honey
½ tsp (2 mL) vanilla
2 tsp (10 mL) vegetable binder, such as cornstarch
Milk
1 to 2 tbsp (15 to 30 mL) poppy seeds

1 Sprinkle the yeast over the warm milk and sugar. Cover and let rest for 10 minutes. Mix the flour, quark and salt, stir in the yeast and knead until smooth. Cover and let rest in a warm place for 50 minutes.

2 For the filling, mix the poppy seeds with the milk in a saucepan, bring to a boil and simmer on low heat for 2 minutes. Transfer to a bowl, let cool slightly and stir in the quark, sugar, vanilla and binder.

3 Thoroughly knead the dough on a floured surface and divide into 12 portions. Roll out each to an 8-inch (10 cm) circle. Place 1 tbsp (15 mL) filling in the center, fold over and press the edges together. Carefully lift and press to form a decorative edge, pulling upward so the seam is at the top of each pocket. Place on the prepared baking sheet, cover and let rest for 15 minutes. Preheat the oven to 350°F (180°C).

4 Brush the pockets with milk and sprinkle with poppy seeds. Bake for 15 minutes, until golden.

Cheese and Pistachio Pockets

Fat	–	45 min.
Cholesterol	1 mg	(+ 75 min. resting)
Fiber	●	(+ 15 min. baking)

Per serving (1 pocket): approx. 137 calories
8 g protein · 1 g fat · 24 g carbohydrates

MAKES 12 POCKETS
FOR THE CRUST
1 package (¼ oz/7 g/2¼ tsp) active dry yeast
⅓ cup + 2 tbsp (100 mL/100 g) lukewarm milk
2 tbsp (30 mL) granulated sugar
2 cups (500 mL/250 g) spelt flour
⅓ cup + 2 tbsp (100 mL/100 g) low-fat quark, puréed
    cottage cheese or strained yogurt
Pinch salt

FOR THE FILLING
1 cup (250 mL/250 g) low-fat quark, puréed cottage cheese
    or strained yogurt
2 tbsp (30 mL) granulated sugar
1 tsp (5 mL) lemon-flavored or vanilla sugar
¾ tbsp (12 mL) vegetable binder, such as cornstarch
2 tbsp (30 mL/50 g) sultanas (golden raisins)
25 whole pistachios
1 tbsp (15 mL) milk
1 tbsp ground pistachios

1 Sprinkle the yeast over the warm milk and sugar. Cover and let rest for 10 minutes. Mix the flour, quark and salt, stir in the yeast and knead until smooth. Cover and let rest in a warm place for 50 minutes.

2 For the filling, mix the quark, sugar, lemon sugar, binder, sultanas and pistachios.

3 Thoroughly knead the dough on a floured surface, shape into a log and divide into 12 portions. Roll out each to form an 8- to 9-inch (10 to 12 cm) circle. Spoon 1 tbsp (15 mL) filling into the center, fold over and press the edges together with a fork. Place on the prepared baking sheet, cover and let rest for 15 minutes. Preheat the oven to 350°F (180°C).

4 Brush the pockets with milk and sprinkle with ground pistachios. Bake for 15 minutes, until golden.

Poppy Seed Pockets, top
Cheese and Pistachio Pockets, bottom

Cherry Muffins

Fat		30 min.
Cholesterol	26 mg	(+ 20 min.
Fiber	–	baking)

Per serving (1 muffin): approx. 183 calories
4 g protein · 8 g fat · 25 g carbohydrates

PREHEAT OVEN TO 325°F (160°C)
12-CUP MUFFIN TIN, GREASED OR LINED
WITH PAPER CUPS

MAKES 12 MUFFINS
8 oz (240 g) canned or frozen sour
  cherries
1²⁄₃ cups (400 mL/200 g) whole
  wheat flour
2 tbsp (30 mL/60 g) ground
  hazelnuts
2½ tsp (12 mL) baking powder
½ tsp (2 mL) baking soda
1 egg
⅓ cup + 2 tbsp (100 mL/100 g)
  granulated sugar
⅓ cup (75 mL) sunflower or canola
  oil
1 cup (250 mL/225 g) buttermilk

1 Thoroughly drain the
  cherries.

2 Combine the flour with the
  hazelnuts, baking powder and
baking soda. In another bowl,
thoroughly mix the egg, sugar,
oil and buttermilk. Briefly stir in
the flour mixture, but don't
overwork batter. Halve and stir
in the cherries.

3 Fill each prepared muffin cup
  and bake in the preheated
oven for 20 minutes. Test for
doneness by inserting a cake
tester or toothpick. If it comes
out clean, they are done. If
still sticky, bake for another
2 minutes.

!! **TIP** If you don't have a
muffin tin, stack 2 paper
baking cups per muffin
on a baking sheet and fill with
the batter.

Walnut Discs

Fat		30 min.
Cholesterol	1 mg	(+ 15 min. resting)
Fiber		(+ 15 min. baking)

Per serving (1 disks): approx. 139 calories
5 g protein · 6 g fat · 16 g carbohydrates

BAKING SHEET, LINED WITH PARCHMENT
PAPER

MAKES 10 DISKS
1²⁄₃ cups (400 mL/200 g) whole
  wheat flour
⅓ cup (75 mL/50 g) soy flour
1 tbsp (15 mL) baking powder
1 tbsp (15 mL) sugar
Salt
¼ cup (50 mL/50 g) diet margarine
⅔ cup (150 mL/150 g) cold milk
2 tbsp (30 mL/40 g) chopped
  walnuts
Milk

1 In a medium mixing bowl,
  mix the whole wheat flour,
soy flour, baking powder, sugar
and a pinch of salt. Distribute
pieces of diet margarine on top
and lightly mix. Form a well in
the center and pour in the milk.
Using the kneading hook on a
mixer, knead until elastic. Finely
chop the walnuts and knead in.
Let rise for 15 minutes. Preheat
the oven to 325°F (160°C).

2 On a lightly floured surface,
  roll out the dough to a rope
about 2 inches (5 cm) in diameter. Cut into 10 rounds. Place the
rounds on the prepared baking
sheet and brush with a little
milk. Bake in the preheated oven
for 20 to 25 minutes. Cool on a
wire rack.

!! **TIP** Walnut discs are best
fresh with good jam—
but they're also a great
portable snack.

Vanilla Muffins

Fat		30 min.
Cholesterol	25 mg	(+ 20 min.
Fiber	–	baking)

Per serving (1 muffin): approx. 160 calories
3 g protein · 5 g fat · 37 g carbohydrates

PREHEAT OVEN TO 325°F (160°C)
12-CUP MUFFIN TIN, GREASED OR LINED
WITH PAPER CUPS

MAKES 12 MUFFINS
1 cups (500 mL/250 g) whole wheat
  flour
2 tsp (10 mL) baking powder
½ tsp (5 mL) baking soda
1 egg
⅔ cups (150 mL/140 g) sugar
1 tsp (5 mL) vanilla sugar
1 tsp (5 mL) vanilla seeds or extract
⅓ cup (75 mL) sunflower or canola
  oil
⅔ cup (150 mL/150 g) buttermilk

1 Mix the flour, baking powder
  and baking soda. In another
bowl, thoroughly combine the
egg, sugar, vanilla sugar, vanilla
seeds, oil and buttermilk. Briefly
stir into the flour but don't overwork muffin batter.

2 Spoon into the prepared
  muffin cups and bake in the
preheated oven for 20 minutes,
until golden. Test for doneness
by inserting a cake tester or
toothpick. If it comes out clean,
they are done. If still sticky, bake
for another 2 minutes.

Cherry Muffins, top
Walnut Discs, bottom left
Vanilla Muffins, bottom right

Strawberry Cream Pie

Fat	++	20 min.
Cholesterol	78 mg	(+ 3 hr. chilling)
Fiber	●	(+ 10 to 15 min. baking)

Per serving: approx. 329 calories
9 g protein · 26 g fat · 16 g carbohydrates

10-INCH (25 CM) SPRINGFORM PAN

MAKES 12 SERVINGS
FOR THE PASTRY
⅓ cup + 2 tbsp (100 mL/100 g) whole wheat flour
⅓ cup (75 mL/50 g) soy flour
¼ cup (50 mL/50 g) granulated sugar
Pinch salt
1 egg yolk
⅓ cup + 2 tbsp (100 mL/100 g) cold diet margarine

FOR THE FILLING
6 sheets or 1½ packages (each 1/4 oz/7g) or 1½ tbsp
   (22 mL) unflavored gelatin
10 oz (300 g) strawberries
1 cup (250 mL/250 g) low-fat quark, puréed cottage cheese
   or strained yogurt
1 cup (250 mL/250 g) buttermilk
3 tbsp (45 mL/ 40 g) granulated sugar
Zest and juice of 1 lemon

1 Mix the whole wheat flour, soy flour, sugar and salt. Form a well in the center and pour in the egg yolk. Distribute pieces of cold margarine on top and briefly knead until crumbly. Wrap in plastic wrap and chill for 1 hour.

2 Preheat the oven to 350°F (180°C). Roll the pastry out on a floured surface. Using the bottom of the springform pan, cut out a bottom and place it in the pan. Poke several times with a fork. Roll the dough you trimmed off to form a rope and press along the edge to form a rim. Bake for 10 to 15 minutes. Cool on a wire rack for 45 minutes.

3 For the filling, soak the gelatin sheets in cold water for 5 minutes or sprinkle powdered gelatin over ¼ cup (50 mL) of the buttermilk. Roughly quarter and purée the strawberries. Combine with the quark, remaining buttermilk, sugar, lemon zest and lemon juice. Wring out the gelatin sheets (skip this step for the powder gelatin) and dissolve the gelatin in a small saucepan or a microwave oven. Combine with a little of the strawberry mixture, then quickly stir into the rest. Chill for 20 minutes or until it starts to set.

4 Remove the pastry from the pan and place on a cake plate. Fasten a cake ring or the top of the springform pan around it. Fill with the strawberry cream and spread smooth. Chill for at least 2 hours. Cut 12 slices and serve.

Whole Wheat Waffles

Fat	–	75 min.
Cholesterol	1 mg	
Fiber	●●	

Per serving (1 waffle): approx. 139 calories
5 g protein · 1 g fat · 28 g carbohydrates

MAKES 12 WAFFLES
1 vanilla bean
2 cups (500 mL) milk
Pinch ground cinnamon
Pinch salt
⅓ cup (75 mL) liquid honey
3¼ cups (800 mL/400 g) whole wheat flour
Oil

1 Slice the vanilla bean lengthwise and scrape out the seeds. In a large saucepan, bring the milk and vanilla pod and seeds to a boil. Stir in the cinnamon, salt and honey until dissolved. Let cool slightly.

2 Remove the vanilla pod. Sift the flour over the cooled mixture and combine well.

3 Heat a waffle iron and grease with some oil. Ladle 1 to 2 tbsp (15 to 30 mL) batter into the iron and spread until smooth. Close the iron and bake for 2 to 3 minutes, until golden and crisp.

!! **TIP** Whole wheat waffles aren't as crisp as waffles made with white flour. Cutting the milk with an equal quantity of water will help them get crisper.

Strawberry Cream Pies, top
Whole Wheat Waffles, bottom

Berry Berry Cake

Fat	●●●		25 min.
Cholesterol	25 mg		(+ 30 to 35 min. baking)
Fiber	●●		

Per serving: approx. 213 calories
5 g protein · 10 g fat · 26 g carbohydrates

PREHEAT OVEN TO 350°F (180°C)
10 INCH (25 CM) SPRINGFORM PAN, GREASED

MAKES 12 SERVINGS
FOR THE CAKE
½ cup (125 mL/125 g) diet margarine
⅓ cup + 2 tbsp (100 mL/100 g) granulated sugar
Pinch salt
1 egg
1¼ cups (300 mL/150 g) spelt flour
⅓ cup (75 mL/50 g) soy flour
1 tsp (5 mL) baking powder
4 tbsp (60 mL) apple juice

FOR THE TOPPING
1½ lb (750 g) mixed berries, such as strawberries,
    raspberries, blackberries
2 tbsp (30 mL) granulated sugar
1 tbsp (15 mL) cornstarch
½ tsp (2 mL) vanilla or rum extract
⅓ cup (75 mL) apple or berry juice

1 Beat the margarine, sugar and salt until creamy. In another bowl, mix the spelt flour, soy flour and baking powder. Stir the flour mixture into the creamed margarine alternately with the apple juice and egg; mix well. Scrape into the prepared pan and bake for 30 to 35 minutes. Let the cake cool.

2 Clean and drain berries. Cut any large pieces in half. Cover the cake with the berries.

3 To make a glaze, mix the sugar and cornstarch in a small saucepan. Stir in the vanilla and apple juice and ⅓ cup (75 mL) water until smooth. Bring to a boil and cook until starting to thicken. Pour over the berries. Cut into 12 pieces and serve.

!! VARIATION With this type of fruit cake, you can let your imagination run wild and use any fruit, mixed or plain, depending on the season and your preferences.

Quince Pie

Fat	●●		40 min.
Cholesterol	2 mg		(+ 1 hr. baking)
Fiber	●●		

Per serving: approx. 182 calories
3 g protein · 8 g fat · 24 g carbohydrates

10 INCH (25 CM) PIE PLATE

MAKES 12 SERVINGS
FOR THE PASTRY
⅓ cup (75 mL/70 g) cold diet margarine
1 tbsp cold butter
1⅓ cups (325 mL/160 g) whole wheat flour
½ tsp (2 mL) salt

FOR THE FILLING
2 lb (1 kg) diced quinces or apples
½ cup (125 mL/120 g) granulated sugar
Zest and juice of 1 lemon
½ cup (125 mL/50 g) slivered almonds

1 Mix the diet margarine and butter until smooth. In a medium bowl, mix the flour, salt and half the margarine mixture and mix carefully with a fork. Stir in the remaining margarine mixture until slightly crumbly. Add 2 to 3 tbsp (30 to 45 mL) water, enough to shape the dough into a ball. Briefly mix until smooth (instead of kneading, press lightly or it will become too crumbly and toughen up when it's baked). Wrap in plastic wrap and chill for 1 hour.

2 On medium heat, cook the quinces in ¾ cup (175 mL) water for 20 to 30 minutes. Drain well, reserving the juice. Bring ½ cup (125 mL) of the juice to a boil with the sugar. Stir in the quinces, lemon zest, lemon juice and almonds. Preheat the oven to 300°F (150°C).

3 On a floured work surface, roll the pastry 1 inch (2.5 cm) thick and slightly larger than the pie plate. Line the plate with the dough, making sure the edge is a little thicker than the bottom. Fill with the quinces and bake for 1 hour, or until the center is firm. Cut into 12 pieces and serve.

Berry Berry Cake, top
Quince Pie, bottom

Chocolate Chunk Cake

Fat	●	20 min.
Cholesterol	–	(+ 45 min. baking)
Fiber	●	

Per serving: approx. 227 calories
7 g protein · 6 g fat · 36 g carbohydrates

PREHEAT OVEN TO 325°F (160°C)
9 BY 13 INCH (3 L) CAKE PAN OR TWO 9 BY 5 INCH (2 L) LOAF PANS,
GREASED AND SPRINKLED WITH BREAD CRUMBS

MAKES 14 SERVINGS
⅓ cup + 2 tbsp (100mL) sunflower oil
⅔ cup (150 mL/150 g) granulated sugar
Pinch salt
1¼ cups (300 mL/125 g) ground almonds
⅓ cup + 2 tbsp (100 mL) milk
⅔ cup (150 mL/150 g) low-fat quark, puréed cottage cheese
   or strained yogurt
1⅔ cups (400 mL/200 g) whole wheat flour
1 tbsp (15 mL) baking powder
2 tbsp (30 mL) unsweetened cocoa powder
1 to 2 tsp (5 to 10 mL) ground cinnamon
½ bar (14 oz/400 g) good-quality semi-sweet chocolate

1 Using the whisk attachment on a mixer, thoroughly combine the oil, sugar and salt for 3 minutes. Gradually beat in the almonds, milk and quark.

2 Combine the flour, baking powder, cocoa and cinnamon; stir into the batter. Coarsely chop and fold in the chocolate. Scrape into the prepared pan and bake for 45 minutes (about 30 minutes for the loaf pans). Cut into 14 pieces or slices and serve.

Coconut Bundt Cake

Fat	+	20 min.
Cholesterol	1 mg	(+ 70 min. baking)
Fiber	●	

Per serving: approx. 306 calories
5 g protein · 18 g fat · 32 g carbohydrates

PREHEAT OVEN TO 325°F (160°C)
10 INCH (3 L) BUNDT CAKE PAN, GREASED AND SPRINKLED WITH
BREAD CRUMBS

MAKES 16 SERVINGS
1¼ cups (300 mL) milk
2 cups (500 mL/150 g) shredded coconut
¾ cup + 2 tbsp (175 mL/200 g) diet margarine
⅔ cup (150 mL/140 g) sugar
2 tbsp (30 mL) soy flour
⅓ cup (75 mL) freshly squeezed orange juice or cold milk
3¼ cups (800 mL/400 g) whole wheat flour
⅓ cup (75 mL/50 g) cornstarch or potato starch
1 tbsp (15 mL) baking powder

1 Heat the milk slightly and steep the coconut in it for 5 minutes.

2 Using the whisk attachment on a mixer, beat the margarine and sugar for 3 minutes, until creamy. Mix in the soy flour, orange juice or cold milk, and stir until smooth. Stir in the coconut and milk. Combine the flour, cornstarch and baking powder; stir into the batter. Scrape into the prepared pan and bake for 60 to 70 minutes, until golden. Cut into 16 pieces and serve.

!! **TIP** This cake tastes especially good with a glaze and shredded coconut sprinkled over top. To make the glaze, combine 1¼ cups (300 mL/150 g) of confectioners' (icing) sugar with 3 tbsp (45 mL) of freshly squeezed orange juice or 1 to 2 tbsp (15 to 30 mL) freshly squeezed lemon juice and stir until smooth.

SWEET AND SAVORY BAKED GOODS

Chocolate Chunk Cake, top
Coconut Bundt Cake, bottom

Oat and Pistachio Rolls

Fat	●●●	30 min.
Cholesterol	–	(+ 1 hr. resting)
Fiber	●●●	(+ 25 min. baking)

Per serving (1 roll): approx. 317 calories
15 g protein · 10 g fat · 43 g carbohydrates

2 BAKING SHEETS, LINED WITH PARCHMENT

MAKES 12 ROLLS
10 oz (300 g) green pistachios, shelled, divided
2 cups (500 mL/200 g) quick-cooking rolled oats
1⅔ cups (400 mL/200 g) whole wheat flour
2¼ cups (550 mL/300 g) whole-grain rye flour
1 tsp (5 mL) salt
2 packages (each ¼ oz/7 g/2¼ tsp) active dry yeast
1 package ready-to-use sourdough starter (optional)
2 tbsp (30 mL) old-fashioned rolled oats

1 Coarsely chop the pistachios. In a large bowl, combine half the pistachios, the rolled oats, whole wheat flour, rye flour and salt. Make a well in the center and pour in the yeast. Add 4 tbsp (60 mL) lukewarm water and combine with a little flour from the edge. Cover and let rest for 5 minutes.

2 Add the sourdough starter, if using, and no more than 2 cups (500 mL) lukewarm water. Using the kneading hook on a mixer, knead the dough until smooth. Knead thoroughly for another 3 minutes. Cover and let rise in a warm place for 45 minutes, until doubled in size.

3 Gently knock down and knead for another 3 minutes. Divide the dough into 12 pieces, form 12 small rolls and place on the prepared baking sheets. Make small incisions across the top of each roll, brush with water and sprinkle with the remaining pistachios and old-fashioned rolled oats, pressing lightly onto each roll.

4 Preheat the oven to 400°F (200°C). Cover the rolls and let rise again for 15 minutes. Bake for 20 to 25 minutes. Cool on a wire rack.

!! **CHEESE DIP WITH CHIVES AND PISTACHIOS** Wash a bunch of chives and chop finely. Combine with 1¼ cups (300 mL/300 g) quark or low-fat cream cheese, 4 tbsp (60 mL) milk, and salt and pepper. Dust with paprika. Coarsely chop 2 oz (50 g) green pistachios, toast in a dry skillet until they start to give off a scent and sprinkle over the quark. Serve this dip with the rolls.

Apricot Cake

Fat	●	30 min.
Cholesterol	1 mg	(+ 30 min. baking)
Fiber	●●	

Per serving: approx. 251 calories
8 g protein · 6 g fat · 42 g carbohydrates

10 INCH (25 CM) SPRINGFORM PAN, GREASED

MAKES 12 SERVINGS
1½ lbs (800 g) ripe apricots or 1 large can apricots
4 tbsp (60 mL/60 g) diet margarine
½ cup (125 mL/120 g) granulated sugar
1¼ cup (300mL/ 300 g) low-fat quark, puréed cottage cheese or strained yogurt
2¾ cups (675 mL/350 g) spelt flour
⅓ cup (75 mL/50 g) cornstarch or potato starch
2 tbsp (30 mL) baking powder
¾ cup + 2 tbsp (200 mL) skim, 1% or 2% milk
3 tbsp (45 mL) chopped pistachios or almonds

1 Halve, pit and slice the apricots into wedges. Or drain canned apricots well, then slice finely.

2 Cream the margarine, sugar and quark. Combine the flour, cornstarch and baking powder, and stir in, alternating with the milk. Let the batter sit for 10 minutes, adding milk as required. Preheat the oven to 350°F (180°C).

3 Scrape the batter into the prepared pan and spread until smooth. Distribute the apricot wedges evenly overtop. Sprinkle with the chopped pistachios or almonds and bake for 30 minutes.

!! **TIP** This cake is quick and easy to make and is equally good with other fruit. Depending on the season, you can use rhubarb, cherries or pears, for example.

Oat and Pistachio Rolls, top
Apricot Cake, bottom

Glossary

Agar-agar
A vegetable thickener made from seaweed. An alternative to gelatin, agar-agar is mineral rich, neutral tasting and calorie-free. Available in health food and natural food stores in finely ground, pressed, stick or strip form. Follow the package instructions.

Asian chili sauce
A hot condiment made from chili peppers, sugar and vinegar, it's used as flavoring or as a table sauce. Available in Asian grocery stores.

Asian fish sauce
A salty, flavorful condiment with a spicy fish flavor and pungent aroma. Not to be confused with fish stock, it takes the place of soy sauce in a number of Asian cuisines. Available in Asian grocery stores.

Azuki beans
Small, dark red legumes with a sweet but pronounced flavor. Soaking time is approximately 1 hour and cooking time up to another 1 hour. They're rich in fiber, protein and carbohydrates.

Baking soda
A leavener that is one of the components of baking powder, baking soda can be used only in small quantities or the product will have a bitter aftertaste. Available in supermarkets.

Balsamic vinegar, red and white
A spicy, bittersweet vinegar made from the unfermented juice (must) of white Trebbiano grapes, though other types are used sometimes too. The authentic aceto balsamico tradizionale di Modena is dark brown and has a full-bodied flavor. Like good wine, the vinegar is aged over several years, stored in a series of barrels—oak, cherry, ash and, last, mulberry. This process makes it a delicacy and it carries a hefty price tag. Today, it's produced more quickly and less expensively and is available in almost every supermarket. White is milder than red.

Binder, vegetable
A product that helps to thicken or set liquids. The most common are agar-agar, gum arabic, tragacanth gum, xanthum gum, locust bean gum, guar gum and pectin. Starches such as cornstarch can also be used as binders.

Buckwheat and buckwheat flour
A member of the *Fagopyrum* family of herbs. Though it technically isn't a grain, it is used as such. Available in supermarkets, health food and natural food stores, the triangular seeds have a hearty, nutty flavor and can be cooked just like rice. Roasted groats are often called kasha and are even nuttier. Finely ground buckwheat flour is used in batters for pancakes, dumplings, etc., but the flour is gluten free, so it always has to be blended with another flour for baking. Baked goods made with buckwheat have a characteristic dry, nutty flavor.

Bulgur
Steamed, dried and crushed wheat with a delicate, nutty flavor. It can be cooked in water or steamed and served as a side dish and is especially popular in Middle Eastern cooking. Available in coarse, medium and fine grinds in supermarkets, health food stores, natural food stores and Middle Eastern markets.

Butternut squash
Small to medium-sized pear-shaped squash with a yellowy-orange flesh. This flavorful squash with few seeds can also be eaten raw.

Cellophane noodles
Made from mung bean flour, these thin noodles are white when raw but become clear when they're cooked and are sometimes called glass noodles. Available in Asian food stores and better supermarkets.

Chestnuts
Egg- or heart-shaped nuts with a distinct, creamy flavor and texture. After roasting or cooking, they become slightly sweet. Buy them fresh in the fall or canned or vacuum-packed all year round.

Chickpeas
Buff-colored, irregular legumes that can take a long time to cook. Soaking time is 8 to 12 hours, and cooking can take up to 2 hours—but they're readily available canned.

Coriander

A herb with green, parsley-like leaves. The dried seeds are used as a spice in both savory and sweet dishes, while the fresh herb has a pronounced flavor and is used primarily in Latin American, Indian and Asian cooking. Fresh coriander is often sold with the roots still attached and will keep for a few days in the refrigerator in a glass of water, the leaves loosely covered with a plastic bag. Parsley is less aromatic, but you can use it as a substitute. Available in natural food stores, Asian grocery stores and wherever herbs are sold.

Couscous

Couscous is made from durum wheat semolina pressed into small balls that don't clump because they've been steamed. Couscous is also the name for the national dish of North Africa. The quick-cooking variety has become popular for a wide range of uses. Available in supermarkets and Middle Eastern markets.

Cumin

A spice that releases its aroma and flavor best when it's toasted and freshly ground or pounded in a mortar. It's used primarily in Indian and Asian cooking. Available in supermarkets, health food and natural food stores, and Middle Eastern grocery stores.

Curry paste

A spicy paste used primarily in Thai cooking. Fans of Asian, exotic or simply spicy foods will enjoy the yellow (milder—it goes well with fish dishes), red (hot) and green (very hot) curry pastes. They enhance vegetable, fish and meat meals and can also be used in sauces. Available in Asian grocery stores.

Diet margarine

Produced from good-quality vegetable fats, diet margarine has no milk fat and few saturated fats, but it does have a high unsaturated fat content—almost 50% of the total fats. This is why diet margarine is highly recommended for a fat-reduced diet. In this case, "diet" means "good for your heart," not that this margarine is lower in fat or calories than conventional margarines.

Flax seeds

The flat, elongated, brown seeds of the flax plant. Rich in high-quality and omega-3 fats and linoleic and linolenic acids, they're also an end product of the extraction of linseed oil. They must be crushed or ground slightly for the body to assimilate the useful components.

Frozen concentrated apple juice and pear nectar

Sources of sweetness that are light in flavor but have considerably less sweetening power than sugar. Available in supermarkets, health food and natural food stores.

Garam masala

A blend of ground spices, such as coriander seeds, cumin, pepper, cardamom, cinnamon and cloves. Its composition varies, and so does the flavor. Available in health food and Indian grocery stores.

Hokkaido squash

One of the best of the edible gourds. This relatively small, bright orange squash gives dishes a particularly beautiful color and it is highly aromatic. Available in some natural food stores in summer.

Hazelnut butter or purée

Highly flavored paste made from ground hazelnuts. Puréed hazelnuts serve as a tasty spread on bread or waffles and can be used to enhance sweets, cakes and desserts. The oil that forms on the surface is a good-quality hazelnut oil and should be stirred back into the paste before using. Available in health food and natural food stores.

Maple syrup

Maple syrup comes from New England or Canada and is made from the sap of the sugar maple tree. The thick, caramel-like syrup has a fine flavor and is an interesting alternative to sugar. The classic presentation is on pancakes, but it's also useful for marinades, glazes and baking. You can buy the real thing in most supermarkets and health food and natural food stores.

Millet

The oldest grain harvested by humans. Millet is rich in protein and is considered a valuable staple because of its high iron content. Mild in flavor, the entire kernel can be prepared in a variety of ways, just like rice. It can also be used to prepare sweet dishes. Available in supermarkets, and health food and natural food stores.

Mung bean sprouts

The crisp, fresh, sweet sprouts of the mung bean. You can substitute soy sprouts. Sold canned or fresh by most greengrocers, supermarkets and Asian grocery stores.

Oils

An edible liquid fat extracted from fruit, nuts, grains or seeds. All vegetable oils should be stored in a cool place but not under 54°F (12°C), so not in the refrigerator. They should also be protected from light and used as soon as possible since they spoil quickly.

Peanut oil: A mild, light yellow oil with a slightly nutty flavor. Keeps well, and can also be heated to high temperatures, making it good for frying and deep-frying.

Olive oil: A fine edible oil with different nuances ranging from mild to spicy. Given that the quality of olive oil can vary greatly, buy only good-quality, cold-pressed oil designated "extra-virgin olive oil." This is made from pure olive oil from the first pressing.

Canola oil: A light yellow, tasteless oil. Canola oil has proved itself second only to olive oil. It delivers particularly high-quality fatty acids and goes well with all dishes that need to be cooked on high heat. Sunflower or vegetable oil can serve as alternatives.

Sesame oil (light and dark): A cold-pressed, high-quality oil made from unroasted (light) or roasted (dark) sesame seeds. It has an intensely nutty flavor and is used to add taste rather than for cooking. This expensive oil should be used sparingly, but it keeps a long time because it rarely goes rancid. Available in supermarkets, health food and natural food stores, and Asian grocery stores.

Soy oil: A light yellow, mild oil that can be heated to high temperatures.

Walnut oil: A dark yellow oil with a pronounced nutty flavor. It's used primarily to dress salads and to add flavor to spreads. Walnut oil that's already opened should be used within a few weeks as it quickly goes rancid and gets bitter. Available in supermarkets, health food and natural food stores.

Oat bran

Oat bran has a particularly high soluble fiber content, which helps lower cholesterol. Available in supermarkets and health food and natural food stores.

Phyllo dough

Paper-thin sheets of pastry dough approximately 12 by 20 inches (30 by 50 cm) in size. Phyllo is used for flaky pastries and pies. Available fresh or frozen in Greek grocery stores and many supermarkets.

Puy lentils

A small, dark, green-speckled lentil distinguished by its particularly fine taste. When cooked, the puy lentil retains its shape, which also distinguishes it from other types of lentils, which can overcook much more quickly. Available in health food and natural food stores. You can substitute other types of lentils.

Red lentils

Great for soups and purées. Red lentils have a relatively mild taste and a very short cooking time. Used primarily in Indian and Asian cooking. Available in health food and natural food stores and Asian and Indian grocery stores. Red lentils are best replaced by split yellow lentils (dal).

Rice noodles

Rice noodles come in a wide range of shapes, from the thinnest vermicelli to broad ribbons, and are lighter in color than durum wheat pasta. Available in supermarkets and Asian grocery stores.

Rolled oats

Rich in vitamin B. Can be used as a binder or seasoning for soups, sauces and salads, as well as for garnishing. Small amounts enhance spreads, cereal, grain and vegetable dishes. To preserve the vitamins, the flakes should be added once they've been cooked. Available in supermarkets and health food stores.

Saffron threads

A precious spice with a bitter, slightly pungent taste. Authentic saffron turns foods yellow. In Arab cooking, saffron is primarily used in sweets and hearty rice dishes, in North Africa in meat and poultry dishes. Saffron threads should be soaked in a little liquid from the recipe before using the saffron and the liquid. Available in health food stores.

Sambal oelek

A very hot, thick Indonesian condiment made from steamed chili peppers. Use sparingly in dips and in cooking or on the side as a condiment.

Silken tofu

A soft type of tofu that is not pressed but stirred only once after the soy bean has curdled. Therefore, the consistency resembles that of sour cream. Silken tofu is used in the preparation of creamy sauces, dressings and desserts or as a substitute for yogurt. Available in health food stores and Asian grocery stores.

Soy cream

Made from water, vegetable oil and soy beans, soy cream is a vegetable alternative to cream. Enhances soups and sauces, but is often sold as a coffee creamer. May be available in supermarkets and health food stores.

Soy flour

Extracted from hulled, partially roasted, ground soybeans. Soy flour works well for baked goods, pastries and confectionery. It has particular value in low-cholesterol cooking because of its high lecithin content, which means it can be used as a substitute for eggs. Available in health food and natural food stores.

Soy milk and soy drinks

Extracted from soybeans, soy milk is a low-fat and cholesterol-free alternative to cow's milk. When processed further with coagulants, it is used to make tofu. Available in health food and natural food stores, supermarkets and Asian grocery stores, but be sure it's not flavored and sweetened.

Soy sauce

An aromatic, spicy sauce made from fermented soybean extract. Depending on the type, it's partially fermented with rice or wheat. Lower-quality versions contain sugar, salt, flavoring, caramel (sugar coloring), etc. Dark Chinese soy sauce has a strong flavor; light Japanese soy sauce is sweeter and less salty. The largest selection can be found in Asian grocery stores, but soy sauce is also available in supermarkets.

Sprats

Small sardines that are mostly sold in cans. Most common are Kieler and smoked sprats, which can be found in the refrigerated section of fine grocery stores.

Texturized vegetable protein (TVP)

A protein-rich meat alternative made from fat-free soy flour. The crumbs, slices or cubes are high in fiber, and fat and cholesterol free. And since they are dried, they can be kept indefinitely. Before preparing, soak in water for at least half an hour (it will triple or quadruple in volume). Available in health food and natural food stores.

Tofu

Made from curdled and pressed soy milk, tofu is the most important source of protein in Asia. This cholesterol free, tasteless product is sold in various forms, including seasoned, marinated or smoked. It picks up flavor from marinades or the spices it's cooked with. Used to prepare sweet as well as spicy dishes, tofu can also be fried, grilled or stirred until creamy. Available in health food and natural food stores or Asian grocery stores.

Spelt flour

Made from an ancient cereal grain. It can be used like wheat flour, but its distinctiveness lies in its delicate, slightly spicy taste (and low gluten count). Available in supermarkets, health food and natural food stores.

Thai scented (Jasmine) rice

A long-grain rice that begins to release its delicate scent during cooking. Fluffy, not sticky, when cooked. To prepare, it's best to soak the rice in double its volume water

for approximately 15 minutes before cooking. Available in supermarkets, health food stores, natural food stores and Asian grocery stores.

Vinegar

An excellent condiment or preservative. Comes in many different kinds, such as

Tarragon vinegar: Goes best with fish, light sauces, potato and tomato salads, etc.

Lemon vinegar: White wine vinegar with a tangy, fresh lemony flavor.

White wine vinegar: Particularly fine, intense flavor. For this reason, white wine vinegar is used sparingly. It goes well with fish and poultry dishes.

Wheat germ

The germ of the wheat, sold in flakes. Like all grain germs, wheat germ is a good source of high-quality protein and is rich in linoleic acid, vitamin E and the B vitamins, and minerals such as calcium, magnesium, iron and zinc. Available in supermarkets and health food or natural food stores.

Wheat flour

The type of flour indicates the extent to which the grain has been ground. The coarser the grind, the more parts of the grain have been retained. The finest grind, cake and pastry flour, lacks most of the essential ingredients, while whole wheat flour (which is coarse) is rich in fiber and minerals. So it's healthy, but its suitability for baking is limited. Whole-grain flour needs a lot of water to bind it, so it has to soak for a while before the dough can be processed any further. Therefore, cake and pastry flour, which is commonly used in baking, can't be replaced by whole-grain flour on a 1:1 basis. Various types of flour are available in better supermarkets, health food and natural food stores, or directly from the mill.

Yellow lentils

Hulled lentils with a slightly sweet taste, available whole or split. The split lentils, called dal, are particularly popular in Indian cooking. Available in supermarkets, health food stores, natural food stores, and Asian and Indian grocery stores.

Unripe spelt grain, meal and flour

Unripe spelt grain is hulled, dried and roasted over an open fire. The kernels have a characteristic slightly smoky, nutty taste. In cooking, unripe spelt grain is used whole or coarsely ground or as a flour. The whole grain and coarsely ground grain can be cooked like rice and served as a side dish. It's also used in soups, casseroles, spreads and patties. Flour made from this grain is used to thicken soups and sauces, and in dumplings, pancakes, etc. They are hard to find outside Germany, but roasted buckwheat groats (kasha) and buckwheat flour can be used in much the same way.

Index

Foreword

Dr. Werner O. Richter is head of the Institutes for Lipometabolism and Hemorrheology, in Winden, near Munich, and a recognized expert in the area of nutrition and metabolic disorders. Since 1987, he has been a lecturer on metabolic diseases and healthy nutrition at the Ludwig Maximillian University, in Munich. He is also the leader of a study group called Nutritional Fats and Fats in the Diet at the German Society of Lipid Sciences, leader of a study group called Hyperlipoproteinemias at the Professional Association of Nutritional Physicians, editor of the journal *Lipid Report* and a board member of the Lipid-Liga e.V.

Recipe Authors

Angelika Ilies

Born in Hamburg and currently living near Frankfurt, Angelika Ilies began her career as a food writer immediately after finishing her studies in home economics and nutrition. She worked as a writer for a well-known publisher in London before returning to Germany, where she wrote a cooking column for the most widely read German food magazine. Since 1989, she has been succesfully pursuing a career as an independent author and food writer.

Doris Muliar

Born in Austria, Doris Muliar has been active in radio, television and publishing since 1985 and has written many books on health and fitness. In the past few years, she has concentrated her efforts on developing lighter and quicker recipes for low-fat diets. Doris Muliar lives and works in Cologne.

Edita Pospisil

This nutritional scientist and author has specialized in diet-dependent disorders and their prevention and treatment by dietary means. Translating the latest scientific thinking on diabetes, high blood pressure, lipometabolic disorders and excess weight into persuasive lay language lies at the heart of her work. Her experience and professional knowledge have been extremely helpful in developing and evaluating the recipes in this book.

Food Photography

Michael Brauner

After graduating from photography school in Berlin, Michael Brauner worked as an assistant to well-known photographers in France and Germany before striking out on his own in 1984. His unique, highly atmospheric style is highly prized in the worlds of advertising and publishing. In his studio in Karlsruhe, he captures the essence of the many recipes in numerous titles from Gräfe Und Unzer.

BIOGRAPHIES

239